GREAT SOULS:
The SEVEN RAYS at the SOUL LEVEL

Herbert Kitchener, Alice Bailey, A. P. Giannini, Leonardo da Vinci, Thomas Edison, Alfred Lord Tennyson, Marie Curie

by

KURT ABRAHAM

LAMPUS PRESS
19611 ANTIOCH ROAD
WHITE CITY, OREGON 97503

Copyright ©2002 by
Kurt Abraham

All rights reserved

First edition 2002

ISBN 0-9609002-7-6

Library of Congress
Catalogue Card Number

Manufactured in the United States of America

BOOKS BY KURT ABRAHAM

Psychological Types and the Seven Rays (1983)

Threefold Method for Understanding the Seven Rays and Other Essays in Esoteric Psychology (1984)

Introduction to the Seven Rays (1986)

The Seven Rays and Nations:
France and the United States Compared (1987)

The Moon Veils Vulcan and the Sun Veils Neptune (1989)

Balancing the Pairs of Opposites; The Seven Rays and Education, and Other Essays in Esoteric Psychology (1993)

Techniques of Soul Alignment; The Rays, the Subtle Bodies, and the Use of Keywords (1997)

Great Souls: The Seven Rays at the Soul Level:
Kitchener, Bailey, Giannini, Leonardo, Edison, Tennyson, Curie (2002)

ACKNOWLEDGEMENTS

For permission to use copyright material the author gratefully acknowledges the following:

The Lucis Trust for permission to quote from Alice Bailey's *Esoteric Psychology, Externalisation of the Hierarchy, Discipleship in the New Age, Letters on Occult Meditation, Treatise on Cosmic Fire,* and *The Unfinished Autobiography*

CONTENTS

Introduction...	1
Herbert Kitchener, First Ray Soul.......................	5
Alice A. Bailey, Second Ray Soul........................	31
A. P. Giannini, Third Ray Soul............................	57
Leonardo Da Vinci, Fourth Ray Soul...................	81
Thomas Alva Edison, Fifth Ray Soul...................	111
Alfred Lord Tennyson, Sixth Ray Soul.................	145
Marie Currie, Seventh Ray Soul	181
Further Reading and Study	217
Bibliography...	225
Index...	229

INTRODUCTION

According to the esoteric science of the seven rays (as outlined in the two volume book *Esoteric Psychology* by Alice Bailey), we know that:

1) *The soul can be on any one of the seven rays.* This however depends on the particular rays that are in manifestation at any given time. For example, the 4th ray of Harmony Through Conflict is not in manifestation at this time, but due to come in around 2025. This indicates that there are very few, if any, 4th ray souls in incarnation at the present time.

2) *The personality, as a sub-ray of the soul ray, can also be on any one of the seven rays.*

3) *The ray of the mental body is on either the 1st ray of Will and Power, the 4th ray of Harmony Through Conflict, or the 5th ray of Scientific Knowledge.* In the case of the "average" person or ordinary humanity this rule is infallible. In case of developed people, there are exceptions to this general rule.

The three fundamental modes of thought can be summarized briefly:

    a. *First ray*: The managerial-administrative-organizational mode of thought. This is a control or take-charge mode concerned with law, order, and responsibility.

    b. *Fourth ray*: The creative, often artistic, mode of thought that strives towards intuitive insight.

    c. *Fifth ray*: The scientific mode of thought is concern with exact knowledge generally acquired through detached observation and experiment. This mode of thought seeks to develop an objective type of knowledge.

4) *The rays of the astral or emotional body are ray 2, Love-Wisdom, and ray 6, Idealism and Devotion.* The plane of emotion is the 6th plane and is therefore conditioned primarily by the 6th ray of Idealism and Devotion. Eventually, however, the 2nd ray energy of the heart chakra would supercede the 6th ray energy of the solar plexus chakra. An inclusive and radiant love replaces an emotional-devotional idealistic striving.

5) *The rays of the physical body are either the 7th ray of Organization, or the 3rd ray of Intelligent Activity.*

It is very easy to assign in a speculative way this ray or that ray to the soul or to the personality of a person. This is a tendency that we want to avoid at all cost. For the sake of the integrity of the new-to-us esoteric science, it is most necessary to proceed with caution and clarity.

In the spirit of caution we have "examined" the lives and soul rays of seven well known historic figures. The soul rays of six of these well known people are given in the book *Esoteric Psychology*. The British general Herbert Kitchener is given as an example of a person with a 1st ray soul (ray of Will and Power) and a 7th ray personality (Organization and Ceremonial Magic). Leonardo da Vinci (along with Shakespeare) is given as an example of a 4th ray soul (ray of Harmony through Conflict). Thomas Edison is given as an example of a 5th ray soul (Scientific Knowledge). Alfred Lord Tennyson is given as an example of a 6th ray soul (the ray of Idealism and Devotion). Marie Curie is given as an example of a 7th ray soul (along with her husband Peter). The specific references in *Esoteric Psychology* are given at the beginning of each chapter.

We know that Alice Bailey herself had a 2nd ray soul and a 1st ray personality. This information is given in Mary Bailey's book *A Learning Experience.*

This leaves the 3rd ray soul. To the best of our knowledge, D.K. has given no example for a person with a 3rd ray soul. We attempt to make a case for A.P. Giannini as a person with a 3rd ray soul, the ray of Intelligent Activity. We let the reader decide whether we have made a reasonable case or not.

At the present time we have no direct means of objectively observing a particular ray energy as it "colors" a particular body. Nevertheless, through observation of behavior and through analysis of a person's own subjective experience, *a great deal of helpful psychological information can be gathered.* This is what we attempt to demonstrate in this book. This is not an attempt to prove anything. It is primarily a commentary upon one aspect of the great teaching that D.K. has given us.

In D.K.'s words:
"It is of major interest for us to know something about the energies

and forces which are producing the present international situation and presenting the complex problems with which the United Nations are confronted. In the last analysis, all history is the record of the effects of these energies or radiations (rays, in other words) as they play upon humanity in its many varying stages of evolutionary development. These stages extend all the way from those of primeval humanity to our modern civilisation; all that has happened is the result of these energies, pouring cyclically through nature and through that part of nature which we call the human kingdom."

Destiny of Nations 3.

"The study of the rays, and a true and deep comprehension of the inner significance of the teaching, . . . will throw much light upon the times and cycles in the unfolding panorama of history. In the last analysis, history is an account of the growth and development of man from the stage of the cave man, with his consciousness centred in his animal life, up to the present time wherein the human consciousness is steadily becoming more inclusive and mental, and so on and up to the stage of a perfected son of God. It is an account of the apprehension, by man, of the creative ideas which have molded the race and are establishing its destiny. It gives us a dramatic picture of the progress of those souls who are carried in or out of manifestation by the appearance or disappearance of a ray. We shall find, as we study, that words will greatly handicap our expression of the realities involved, and we must endeavour to penetrate beneath the surface meaning to the esoteric structure of truth. These rays are in constant movement and circulation, and demonstrate an activity which is progressive and cyclic and evidences increasing momentum. They are dominant at one time and quiescent at another, and according to the particular ray which is making its presence felt at any particular time, so will be the quality of the civilisation, the type of forms which will make their appearance in the kingdoms of nature, and the consequent stage of awareness (the state of consciousness) of the human beings who are carried into form life in that particular era."

Esoteric Psychology I, 3.

HERBERT KITCHENER
FIRST RAY SOUL

"The characteristic method of approaching the great Quest on this ray [the first ray of will and power] would be by sheer force of will. Such a man would, as it were, take the kingdom of heaven 'by violence.' We have seen that the born leader belongs to this ray, wholly or in part. It makes the able commander-in-chief, such as Napoleon or Kitchener. Napoleon was first and fourth rays, and Kitchener was first and seventh, the seventh ray giving him his remarkable power of organisation."   Esoteric Psychology I, 201.

So Fierce in War, So Gentle in Religion. It is most interesting to try to identify the true quality of soul as it plays out in the human drama. The work of many who truly contribute beneficial qualities to the community, nation, and race is often only recognized by posterity. Personalities frequently obstruct (even crucify) the work of advanced souls, for the two levels are generally moving in what seems to be opposite directions.

When Herbert Kitchener was posted in Palestine as a young soldier in the Royal Engineers, one of his assignments was to make maps of the area with the most precise accuracy. He immersed himself in Biblical archaeology and visited the holy sites of the Jews, Christians, and Muslims. "The Holy Sepulchre," he wrote to his sister Millie, "was naturally the first place I visited." He bemused on the old Crusaders and their fight against far greater forces. "What a glorious land this is when one can see it through the spectacles of imagination—those grand old knights, so fierce in war, so gentle in religion."

The old knights kindled his imagination, for there was something about them that resonated with the purpose and destiny of his own soul. What he admired in the "grand old knights", he would become. Those words would, indeed, come to describe Kitchener himself, with the addition of one more most important phrase: *So fierce in war, so gentle in religion, and so fair in peace.* As the legendary Merlin said to King Arthur, "Sometimes the only way to peace is with the sword." As a warrior and 1st ray soul, Kitchener understood the unavoidable function of war. But he also understood so well and so much better than his colleagues *how war could best be used to end war, and how a dignified peace of reconciliation assured a true and lasting peace.*

Herbert Kitchener, First Ray Soul, Seventh Ray Personality. Herbert Kitchener was born June 24, 1850. Major Henry Kitchener—Herbert's father—retired from the army, primarily for reasons of health, after serving in India. His wife Fanny (Anne Frances) was unable to endure the Indian climate. He sold his commission and bought a bankrupt farm in the South-West of Ireland. Born of wholly English parents, little Herbert spent the first 13 years of his life in Ireland.

Herbert's father was a strict disciplinarian—the household was run with military discipline and order. With a Cancer Sun, Herbert was a sensitive child who dearly loved his ailing mother. Since his father was training his sons for the army, Herbert learned early on in life to show no emotion. His mother was afraid that he would suffer from emotional repression.

Kitchener's Education. Rather than send him off for schooling in Dublin or London, his father preferred to have Herbert tutored at home. Mathematics and history were emphasized; there was a deficiency in the classics. He was not academically inclined in any way. He preferred to learn about cattle, horses, trees and crops, and other matters related to farm management in a practical, direct, hands-on manner.

When Herbert was thirteen, his father sold the farm and the family moved to Switzerland, again for health reasons—the doctors said that Fanny would never improve in the humid air of South-West Ireland.

Herbert and his two brothers went to a French school near Geneva. Here he learned to speak fluent French and passable German. His mother's health continued to decline; she died of consumption when Herbert was fourteen. This was probably a great sorrow to the sensitive side of Herbert—the side that he so very seldom revealed to anyone.

His military education was next on the horizon. His father wanted Herbert to choose the cavalry, but Herbert had his heart set on the Royal Engineers. We see here perhaps a possible little glimmer of the seventh ray influence, since skill in some of the scientific disciplines is often present in the 7th ray type. At seventeen years of age he was admitted to the Royal Military Academy (founded in London in 1741). The Royal Military Academy prepared youths for commissions in the Corps of Royal Engineers and in the Royal Regiment of Artillery.

At the Academy Herbert Kitchener blended in with the other youths. He was a "plodder" or slow learner. He was quiet and did not seek to stand out in any way. He learned surveying work, military bridging, how to lay and operate electric telegraph lines during a campaign, laying railway tracks, fortifications, as well as many other related skills. Also, at this time, he studied Hebrew with a friend, in order to increase his understanding of the Old Testament. Kitchener had an aptitude for learning languages and this would serve him well throughout his military career. He was commissioned second lieutenant in the Royal Engineers in 1871.

One of his first postings was in Palestine. His work was to do a precise survey of all military installations and equipment in the region. A French archaeologist commented that Kitchener had an astonishing "ardour for work" and that he had a "marked proficiency" as an archaeologist. He took a keen interest in the historically rich area. He also expanded his language skills by learning Arabic.

The Spiritual-Religious Side of Kitchener. Within the Church of England at the time there was the High Church and the Low Church. The Low Church was closer to Protestantism. The High Church adhered closer to the Catholic elements in the spiritual heritage. Kitchener loved the ritual of the High Church—the lights, the incense, the vestments, the Eucharist. He kept the religious festivals and fasted at the appropriate times. The 7th ray energy at the personality level most likely inclined him in this direction.

At twenty-eight he joined The Guild of the Holy Standard—a brotherhood founded by Major Malet of the Horse Guards. Major Malet, a clergyman's son, was concerned about soldiers' abandonment of their religious practices as soon as they entered the military. The Brothers of the Holy Standard pledged to be "sober, upright and chaste; to be regular in their private prayers; to receive the Holy Communion at least three times a year, to be reverent during services, to avoid immoral books, to pray for other people, help chaplains, and promote the religious and social welfare of soldiers and their families." Kitchener was a lifelong member of the Brotherhood.

At the age of thirty-three Kitchener became a Freemason. Freemasonry was alive and well among the military. It provided a strong moral code and sounded a very strong 7th ray note in its symbolism and ceremony. Its clear hierarchical order would also appeal to the 1st ray type.

Character Traits Emerging.. Kitchener quickly became known as a person who was "physically hard with great powers of endurance" and also a person who was thorough and who mastered all the details. These two qualities—powers of endurance and an eye for detail in an organizational setting—are often (though certainly not always) indicators of the first and seventh rays. He also became known as a person of tact with considerable diplomatic skills.

He was very reserved when first meeting people; many observers call attention to a certain shyness in Kitchener. He had a sensitive, caring heart, but this was revealed only on very rare occasions.

A very important quality that emerged early in his career had to do with a certain sensitivity to the native or local people. He complained in letters to friends that the English came with their English ideas and they had something like a "scorn for native habits." When he was posted in Cyprus, he observed that the English, since they were out-of-touch with the people, made "absurd laws" that then had to be countermanded, which resulted in "chaos."

This very important quality of being sensitive to the people enabled him, along with other qualities, to become a truly great general and administrator. His sun was in the sign of Cancer, and Cancer deals with mass consciousness, as opposed to individual consciousness exemplified in regal Leo (the sun sign of Napoleon). Watery Cancer is well-equipped to sense the pulse of the people. Yet as a person with a 1st ray soul, his emotions were well under control. One might say that Kitchener used the sensitive feeling nature *to read* the populace, the situation, and those around him, while at the same time he did not allow his own personal feelings to be displayed in any adverse way.

While doing surveying, land registering, and excavating work in Cyprus, Kitchener helped to found the Cyprus Museum and was its first secretary.

Major in the Egyptian Army and the Desert Experience. In 1883 Kitchener became *bimbashi* (equivalent to a major) in the Egyptian Army. He was selected because of his language ability (he spoke fluent Turkish and Arabic—skills developed when stationed in Cyprus) and also because of his "cool head and hard constitution." The Egyptian Army, created by the British, consisted of Egyptian soldiers and British officers.

Being in charge of a unit of soldiers, we see the stern, hard side of Kitchener developing—his reputation as being a taskmaster spread rapidly. He continued to have warm feelings for the people (the *fellahin*, the peasants), which he did not display in any obvious manner. The other British officers disliked him at first because he worked harder than they did.

While on leave, he accepted an invitation from the Palestine Exploration Fund to participate in the work of surveying the Sinai Desert. In the meantime there was an uprising in the Sudan: A 35 year old middle-rank Egyptian official and ex-slave-trader proclaimed himself el-Mahdi (the Coming One). He and his followers slaughtered an expedition of the Egyptian Army. A message got through to Kitchener, recalling him from leave.

Dressed like a native and with four Arabs, four camels, and a horse, he crossed the Sinai Desert in four days. They rode ten hours a day and covered 200 miles. Some of the natives say that the devil lives in the desert and makes the camels lose their way. Others say that the rhythm of the desert gait becomes a walk into eternity. During such a rhythmic "walk", one comes to hold a conversation with the voice of silence. Kitchener became part of the desert experience—both physically and spiritually. He learned to see that communion with the "desert" was something that lived deeply in the heart and soul of the Arab people.

The Sudan—The Effort to Rescue General Gordon at Khartoum.
The Sudan became the center of Kitchener's life for the next 16 years (ages 33 to 49). General Charles "China" Gordon (a 50 year old major-general of engineers) had been sent to Khartoum for the purpose of effecting an evacuation of the Egyptian garrisons and selecting a Sudanese successor. The diplomatic mission soon turned into a military one. Gordon was under siege by the Madhi forces for 320 days. Gladstone and his Cabinet were painfully undecided whether to send reinforcements or to say that Gordon had broken orders and should therefore be left to his fate. Due to Gordon's immense popularity with the British people, Gladstone and Cabinet eventually decided to send reinforcements. Not to do so would have brought major political repercussions.

Gordon was Kitchener's hero. On his return to Egypt, Kitchener was able to make a study of the friendly Abadeh tribe, one of the tribes in the Sudan. He recommended that an Abadeh Field Force be formed for future operations—a recommendation that was well received both by the commanding officer of the British Army in Cairo (Consul General) and also by the Prime Minister's Cabinet in London.

The Abadeh Field Force developed well, and Kitchener had 1400 men under his command. As he rode about in the desert inspecting his men and the lines of communication, one could hardly distinguish him from an Arab. He was heavily bearded, tanned skin, and he wore a turban and an Arab robe. Accompanying him was a group of 20 handpicked men who had taken an oath on the Koran that Kitchener's friends were their friends, and his enemies were their enemies. As he and his men rode on camels, Kitchener blended perfectly into the desert and into the native mind and soul. He could be fully in the moment as he rhythmically undulated in the desert, because this was exactly where he wanted to be. He liked being in charge of his own native force. He loved the military and he was achieving in what he loved. And with his Cancer Water, he was able to identify with the people, the Arabs; he was able to blend with them, to look like them, to speak their language, and even to think like them. He could share with them the unspoken mystic bond with the sun, wind, and sand.

His main duty at this time was to establish a line of communication to Gordon in Khartoum—no easy task, yet a vital one. The telegraph line had been cut. Undercover messengers were organized to keep some line of communication open. Kitchener persuaded the leader of the strategic city of Dongola to side with the British. Kitchener saw to the fortifying of another strategic city, Debbeh, laying in stores for the British Army—Gordon's relief force—which was soon to arrive. Messages from Gordon included Gordon's recommendation that Kitchener should be appointed governor-general of the Sudan, as he was the "best man." As the British reinforcements arrived in Cairo and advanced up the Nile, there were confusions and delays. Kitchener at one point recommended a short cut across the desert, but the British general chose the slower surer route along the Nile. Finally they did arrive in Khartoum, but it was too late. General Charles "China" Gordon had been killed one day earlier. Gordon had been Kitchener's hero. With Gordon gone Kitchener felt that the heart and soul of the expedition into the Sudan was also gone.

Governor General of Eastern Sudan. The British controlled Eastern Sudan. This strip of land had strategic importance since it bordered the Red Sea which led to the Gulf of Suez. In 1886 at the young age of thirty-six Kitchener was appointed governor general of this coastal region. Its headquarters was at Suakin.

Once again he avoided any colonial tendency to separate from the indigenous population in an aloof, superior manner. On the contrary, he reached out to the local sheiks, getting to know each one personally. The Arabs in the Sudan were not all supporters of the Mahdi (now under the leadership of Khalifa Abdullahi). The Khalifa supported his large army of "rebellion" or "liberation" (depending on one's political perspective) by extracting his necessities from an already impoverished people. Many of the local sheiks considered Mahdism a false creed, originating from a false Messiah, and they were not at all pleased with the general disorder in the land. Slowly but steadily Kitchener gained the respect and the confidence of the local sheiks. Once again he was able to add many friendly tribesmen to his predominantly Egyptian army.

Kitchener was wounded in a raid on a Mahdi camp. The purpose of the raid was to strike a blow, push the Madhi back, and free some of their captured Black Sudanese slaves. When Kitchener took a bullet in the jaw and throat, the local tribesmen failed to follow through on the necessary charge. The raid failed. Kitchener was taken to a hospital in Cairo for care and recuperation. When he returned to Suakin, he received "a most cordial reception from the people who all turned out when I landed and illuminated the town in the evening" (letter written to his sister Millie).

Kitchener was proving himself in many ways. Adding to his abilities as an engineer (surveying, telegraph lines, laying railway tracks, fortifications), as a linguist (French, German, Hebrew, Turkish, Arabic), an organizer, and a military commander, one could now add an administrator and governor. Inextricably interwoven with these skills was his personal character, his high moral tone (sobriety, uprightness, and chastity), his ability to handle men and measures, his capacity to work hard and long, and his ability to lead and command. The service that he performed was for the British crown, to be sure, but quite evidently it was much more than that.

Adjutant General of the Egyptian Army. His service at Suakin earned him a promotion to Adjutant General of the Egyptian Army in 1888 (38 years old). This position brought him to Cairo. Kitchener's single minded purpose at this time was to recapture the Sudan. The Sudan under the dervishes was being horribly mismanaged. Millions of people were dying from disease and starvation, from executions and rebellions. In London the question of whether or not to recapture the Sudan was primarily one of money. Prime Minister Salisbury—a conservative with a long history of expertise in foreign affairs—was sympathetic to the cause. It appeared to be a matter of opportunity and timing. In the meantime the British troops in Egypt sat idle. Colonel Hunter, soon to become Kitchener's "sword arm", complained that "for years we haven't had a wet sword among us."

In 1896 the opportunity came. The Italians in Eritrea were concerned that the Mahdist in the Sudan might attack their stronghold in Kassala (a town on the border of the Sudan and Ethiopia). The Italians wanted the British to divert the Mahdists, and the British—to everyone's excitement in Egypt—complied. The British began their campaign in the Sudan by capturing Dongola.

Reconquest of the Sudan; the Organizational Problems. Due to the many problems of terrain and climate in Egypt and the Sudan, the transportation of men, armaments, and supplies became the primary challenge. Getting a well equipped army to Khartoum was the problem. Once there, the war was decided in a single day. In solving the problems of logistics, we find Kitchener's seventh ray organizational skills serving well his first ray will.

He reconditioned and reconstructed the railway that had been built during the expedition to rescue Gordon. Soldiers, convicts, and locals were used to collect fragments of the railroad that had been torn out and used for other purposes. Kitchener was well known for being able to accomplish much with very little money—a practice that pleased the Prime Minister but often did not please the soldiers. Among the men he developed the reputation of being something of a slave driver. He was also thought of as being stern and hard, someone to fear. Everyone who truly got to know him well, however, almost always remarked how untrue this reputation was. He had a brusque exterior but underneath it all he "has a heart as tender as his will was strong." Another person who knew him well said that "he was a much kinder man than he ever dared admit." (Pollock 314.) Kitchener had learned the lesson that feelings can cloud judgment and a display of anger is a loss of power. Kitchener was sensitive and compassionate, but he was almost afraid to show these feelings. Sensitivity could be used to help understand a situation, but it could not be openly displayed or allowed to gain the upper hand.

Perhaps one of the reasons he demanded much of others is that he worked so hard himself. Needing only four hours of sleep, he was the last one to retire for the day and the first one up in the morning. His office, contrary to what one would expect, was a mess, but one could say that it was an organized mess, for Kitchener knew exactly where to find a list or a report. He also had an "extraordinary memory and grasp of detail." This enabled him to require fewer advisers and rely primarily on himself. He carried within his mind a detailed grasp of the whole situation. Thus everything could move forward in a smooth organized fashion. There was no unconsidered detail that suddenly emerged to hold up the whole expedition. He had learned well from observing the mistakes of others in the day-late Gordon expedition.

In the handling of men and measures Kitchener was often criticized as being somewhat of a cynic. This was probably due to the fact that he doubted the opinion of others. He saw that *opinions were primarily framed out of self-interest, and it is self-interest that obscures a true assessment.* There were few who were detached enough to see the given situation as it truly was. In matters of war one had to penetrate those obscuring factors in order to avoid costly mistakes.

Kitchener had to have an iron will in order to avoid the pressuring influence of self-interest. Needless to say, this approach will generally win more enemies than friends. If one is able to assess the situation correctly, the proof will be in the accomplishment.

Kitchener had a keen eye for recognizing ability, genius, and specialized expertise. One such person was Lieutenant Percy Girouard, a French Canadian who was a genius at building and repairing railways. Another vitally important person was General Archibald Hunter, a Scotsman who "gloried in battle", who was a good tactician, and who had a good deal of experience fighting the dervishes. Another was Reginald Wingate, the Chief Intelligence Officer who kept a very helpful network of spies.

As the campaign unfolded with some skirmishes on the way to Khartoum, another important quality was observed in Kitchener. He did everything he could to win the battle but he was not a mean man. He had a respect for all warriors. He never looked at them as being less than human. Kitchener was always respectful and merciful towards prisoners. At the battle of Firket 400 dervishes had been killed and many taken prisoner. Rudolf Slatin, an intelligence officer, wrote to the Queen that the prisoners were treated well and the wounded were cared for. The prisoners "were astonished at the clemency and the mercy" since many of them had murdered innocent people (*Letters of Queen Victoria*, third series, vol. 3).

After taking Dongola, he developed a plan to build a 230 mile railway across the Nubian desert, reducing the distance to Khartoum by hundreds of miles and avoiding three difficult Nile cataracts. The experts said it was impossible. The French Canadian Percy Girouard and a group of young, enthusiastic engineers, along with an 8000 man labor force (Egyptian troops and convicts) accomplished the "impossible." They gave credit to Kitchener: "He took the risk and the responsibility. He organized the preparations, was the mastermind and the driving force. He would listen to advise, sometimes acted on, sometimes rejected" (Pollock 108).

During one point of the advance and on a side issue, a sheik refused to break camp and proceed towards Berber. The sheik complained of inauspicious signs. Kitchener told him in a forceful way: "All days are made by God and must be equally lucky. You are going in a good cause and will leave tomorrow." Kitchener's forcefulness and assurance appeased and motivated Sheik Ibrahim Farah. Berber was captured within three days.

If the British were to take Khartoum, they would need gunboats to bombard the fortress. A single gunboat had the fighting power of a battalion of infantry. Getting the gunboats up the Nile was another logistic challenge for Kitchener and his engineers. One cataract was nine miles long with an accent of 60 feet. Winston Churchill, who served in the 21st Lancers and also as a journalist for the *Morning Post*, described the cataract as "a rugged stairway formed by successive ledges of black granite" (Hunter 50). In the worst locations the river flowed with terrific force through narrow gorges. As many as a thousand men were required, with the help of steel blocks and tackle, to get the seven gunboats up the difficult cataracts.

Kitchener did not direct a battle in the way Napoleon did. "There seems little doubt that Kitchener left the direction of the fight, as he had done at Firket, to Hunter, not that a divisional or even brigade commander could give much direction in the general *mêlée* obtaining, once the zariba had been reached. Kitchener's main role, as he himself saw it, was to bring his troops in good shape up to the Atbara—a remarkable logistical achievement in itself. When appealed to for orders he said: 'I have been for three years bringing you face to face with these fellows, now go in and fight it out', and throughout the battle he never gave a single order leaving it to Hunter to direct the fight." (Hunter 86.) According to G. W. Steevens, war correspondent of the *Daily Mail*, Hunter was a brilliant general, though occasionally daring to the point of recklessness, but one who "never fails to plan and execute a masterly victory." Kitchener in his planning was never reckless, for having the fewest possible casualties on his own side was always the goal. Sir Henry Rawlinson, one of Kitchener's staff officers, said of Kitchener that "everything runs smooth and well as long as he is at the head of affairs but he does too much and may break down if he is not hit."

Kitchener would scrutinize all the contributing details that led up to a campaign. He tried to think of everything. This naturally led to what some called an "ability to visualize the future." Some Arabs credited him with "prophetic powers."

The march into the Sudan and to Khartoum led to the decisive battle of Omdurman (Khartoum is at the juncture of the Blue Nile and the White Nile; Omdurman is on the opposite side of the river from Khartoum). The battle began at 6:30 AM on September 2, 1898 and was decided by 8:30. The British machine guns and gunboats made up for the fact that they were outnumbered almost 3 to 1.

Hunter said of Kitchener: "He deserves all he gets. He has run the show himself. His has been the responsibility. Some of us have helped too."

Kitchener's Dream for the Sudan. Kitchener wanted to start a college in Khartoum for the sons of the tribesman, so that they would have "the intellectual force to act as governors of their own destinies." The College would serve all of Sudan, from the Moslem north to the "animists" or native people in the south. He wanted the college to be named the Gordon Memorial College in memory of Charles Gordon, since Gordon himself had done so much for the poor youth of England and the Sudan. Kitchener summoned the war correspondents to his office. He wanted the British public to know about his dream for the Sudan. His goal was to raise £65,000 for the college, but the correspondents wisely suggested that he ask for £100,000.

He made the journey to England in order to get the project launched. He said that he would "sooner fight a dozen battles than give a single speech", but he made the effort due to the fact that the cause that was so close to his heart. "The vast country," he said, "has been opened to the civilizing influence of commercial enterprise. I sincerely hope by the means of education and good government we shall be able to raise the standard of life of the inhabitants of that country, and that in the place of persecution, tyranny, and fanaticism, we may establish the reign of prosperity and peace." He was a great national hero; large crowds turned out to see him and hear him speak. He certainly did not like all the adoration, the hero worship, and wanted to escape back to the Sudan. But he went on touring the country and giving speeches: "How Gordon would have rejoiced had he known that by his death the blessing of education would be given to the people that he loved and among whom he died.... Those who have conquered are called upon to civilize...."

He touched the soul of the nation (Britain has a 2nd ray soul), and the nation responded generously—the £100,000 was raised.

Kitchener returned to Khartoum to apply himself as energetically to the work of rebuilding the nation as he had done to the work of conquering her. A new Anglo-Egyptian state was created, with the goal of working towards independence. Kitchener was appointed its first governor general.

Kitchener's Rule of Law in the Sudan. In the new Anglo-Egyptian Sudan Kitchener sought quickly to reestablish the rule of law, to settle land claims, and to reopen trade routes. Dervish prisoners were used in order to clear the rubble and to lay out a rectangular grid of streets. The foundation stone of the Gordon Memorial College was laid on January 4, 1899. It was Kitchener's habit to keep his immediate subordinates close to him and to encourage or require a free flow of discussion, information, and opinion. It should be noted that he considered "regulation to be for the guidance of fools." His style of governing encouraged creative problem solving within certain clearly articulated and meaningful principles. His subordinates were given far more free reign than was customary in British military or government administration. Kitchener looked for quality, ability, and genius, and then he allowed those qualities to experiment, experience, and express their innate gifts. This is more of a decentralized style rather than a pyramid style of governing. It is more of a round-table style.

Once again, one of his primary principles was not to impose foreign rule but to work with the natural or already established rule that existed within the country, people, and culture. His effort was to work "in harmony with the requirements of the Sudan. The task before us all, and especially the Mudirs and Inspectors, is to acquire the confidence of the people, to develop their resources, and to raise them to a higher level.... Our objective is to increase their prosperity... Once it is thoroughly realised that our officers have a heart, not only the progress of the country generally, but also the prosperity of each individual with whom they come in contact, their exhortations to industry and improvement will gain redoubled force. It is to the individual action of British officers, working independently but with a common purpose, on the individual natives whose confidence they have gained that we must look for the moral and industrial regeneration of the Sudan. By listening to outspoken opinions, when respectfully expressed, and checking liars and flatterers, we may hope in time to effect some improvement in this respect in the country. Courts of law should inspire the people with absolute confidence that real justice is being meted out to them."

He also advocated quick repression of insubordination. He wanted correction to be strict without being severe. There is a fine line here that Kitchener himself must have mastered over his years of experience. Kitchener also emphasized that it was critically important *not to interfere* with the Islamic religion. Mosques were rebuilt. At the same time, however, extremism or fanaticism, where the rights of others were threatened, was not allowed. Slavery, cruelty, interference with liberty were to be punished according to the rule of law.

Kitchener called before him all of his governors of the provinces and all inspectors—British officers, also Egyptian and Sudanese officers—to impress upon them these guiding principles. After Kitchener left the Sudan, these principles and directives continued to be the inspiration of the administrators, carrying the country right up to its day of independence 55 years later.

Kitchener also had meetings with leading Sudanese merchants. He allowed complaints to be aired openly without restraint. Some merchants complained that the government requisitioned camels and boats to haul building materials when they were needed to transport grain. Kitchener would immediately change government policy if he saw that it was interfering with local enterprise. He was keenly alert to foreign exploiters interfering with the well-being and developing autonomy of the country.

With these innovative attitudes he came in conflict with his immediate superiors in Cairo—Lord Cromer the British Consul General, and Eldon Gorst, Cromer's financial adviser.

Britain at this time was wavering between carefully expanding the empire (under Disraeli and Salisbury), or quietly withdrawing from earlier foreign commitments (under Gladstone. Gladstone felt that the expensive imperial policies weakened the empire by needless wars). In which direction policy was developed depended primarily on whether the Tories or the Whigs were in power. The financial burden of the empire was becoming weightier with each passing year.

Two regions, however, were particularly crucial to Britain's interests: One was the *Suez canal* and the other was *India*. Turkey was Britain's ally at the time. Turkey had a history of committing horrendous acts of barbarism and cruelty—including the atrocities committed against the Bulgarians in 1876. This greatly disturbed the idealist Gladstone, but Turkey's barbarism was ignored or minimized by Disraeli. *The conservative Tories feared Russia: If Turkey fell, the Suez canal would be a hop, skip, and a jump from Constantinople. Also, the only possible threat to India was by Russia via Afghanistan.* Britain and Turkey needed each other, for they both feared Russia. Britain's presence in Egypt was one of mutual benefit to Turkey, Britain, and Egypt, although the alliance was fragile. Egyptian nationalism was always brewing unrest at some level. Turkey had too many problems keeping her own house in order to worry about her diminishing influence in Egypt.

Britain, for the most part, had more of a civilizing effect in her colonial reach than an exploitative one, and Kitchener seems to be an excellent example of British influence at its best. Colonialism, however, was waning; independence and self-autonomy were on the increase. Colonial powers could either bleed the underdeveloped countries of their resources and then leave, or they could prepare the country for independence. Kitchener had in his mind *as a priority* the well-being of the underdeveloped nation, including the well-being of the peasant, native population. He clearly saw that it was in Britain's best interest to place the other nation first.

As a military man, though also an able administrator, Kitchener had a difficult time keeping up with the clever duplicity of some of the bureaucrats, politicians, and statesmen. Kitchener's criticism of Eldon Gorst, Cromer's financial adviser in Cairo, was that Gorst "is not and never has been straight.... He is the meanest little brute I ever met, professes all sorts of help and then leaves you in the lurch. We will have as little as we can to do with him." (Letter to General Sir Reginald Wingate, Feb. 1899.) Gorst took revenues from the railway and Dongola but did not return any of it for expenses in the Sudan. Among other complaints, army officers and men were not paid or housed properly.

War Clouds Gathering in South Africa. The Boer War 1899-1902 South Africa was colonized by both the British and the Dutch. The Dutch-descended population was known as the Afrikaners or Boers, and they controlled the republics of the Transvaal and the Orange Free State. Britain controlled the Cape Colony and Natal. Paul Kruger, President of the Transvaal (the South African Republic) envisioned an all Afrikaner South Africa. Sir Alfred Milner, Governor of Cape Colony, envisioned a South Africa that was under British control.

The conflict waiting to erupt was confused further by the discovery of gold (1884) and earlier diamonds. This brought a sudden influx of British miners and prospectors. The city of Johannesburg was created almost overnight. The Uitlanders (foreigners) were taxed but had no voting rights and had no representation in the Volksraads. The British did not like being treated as second class citizens in the Afrikaner republics. Hostilities grew as negotiations failed. Milner built up the British Army in the Cape Colony, and war was declared in October, 1899.

Initially, the Afrikaner forces overpowered the British. Reinforcements came for the British and these too were overpowered. British General Frederick Roberts replaced General Buller, and the tide of the war changed. Kitchener was brought into South Africa as second in command under Roberts. Within six months the British captured Johannesburg and Pretoria, the capital of the Transvaal. When the capital fell, the British thought the war was over, but this was not so. The Afrikaners launched relentless guerrilla warfare against the occupying British troops.

This changed the whole tone of the war. There was no army to defeat, just endless acts of sabotage (now referred to as acts of terrorism). Bridges were destroyed, telegraph lines cut, railways demolished, and troops were attacked in a hit-and-run fashion. Wherever any acts of sabotage occurred, Roberts had the nearest farms and farm houses burned, and he had the women and children placed in camps known as "government laagers" and "camps for refuge." Kitchener was initially opposed to these camps.

Roberts was promoted to Commander in Chief of the British Army, which took him to other parts of the British Empire, and Kitchener replaced Roberts as commander in South Africa. Roberts, confident in Kitchener's ability, also suggested that Kitchener become Commander in Chief of the Army in India when the Boer War was resolved. Queen Victoria wanted Kitchener in London in the War Office (Defense Department), because of his "remarkable qualities as an organizer." Kitchener abhorred the idea of working in the War Office with all its regulations and red tape.

Kitchener was promoted to lieutenant general, and he commanded a force of 230,000 men. As the war dragged on, it became increasingly unpopular in England. Many of the English saw the Boers as brave, rural farmers defending their homeland against the intrusion of the British Empire. The senselessness of the war was becoming evident.

In February of 1901 the Boers General Louis Botha sent word to Kitchener that the two generals should meet and discuss terms that would bring the war to a close. Kitchener was excited about the possibility. He agreed to a meeting with the intention of being fair and of not humiliating the Afrikaners.

Kitchener offered amnesty to the Boers for acts of war and he offered large sums of money for the restocking and rebuilding of their farms. Kitchener wanted to establish a generous peace so that the British and the Boers could quickly reestablish friendly relations. The keynotes of Kitchener's life mentioned earlier in the essay are recalled here: "So fierce in war, so gentle in religion, and *so fair in peace*." A fair peace was as central to Kitchener's thinking as a victorious war. The reason for this foresight we can only speculate. He might have observed the impracticality and the cost of a punishing peace that seems to do little more than postpone another war. His Cancer sensitivity might have helped him identify with the foe to the point of seeing, in the final analysis, very little difference between "them and us." His deep religious morality, fostered throughout his life in his work as a Freemason, might have helped him to see that we are indeed all brothers. Unfortunately, however, his views were not shared by other key players. Sir Alfred Milner, Governor of Cape Colony, thought the terms far too generous. Kitchener did everything he could to bring Milner over to a more conciliatory point of view, but Milner would not budge. Chamberlain, the Colonial Secretary at that time, agreed with Milner's position and even admonished Kitchener in Parliament for his overly generously terms.

As a result, the war dragged on. Milner left for England and Kitchener was appointed Acting High Commissioner. This made Kitchener both political and military ruler of South Africa. Back in England Milner said of Kitchener that he had "enormous energy" and that his weak point was controlling a large number of operations all at the same time. Milner also said that Kitchener had a "driving power and iron constitution for work. He is doing a terribly heavy bit of work with splendid zeal and devotion, and the least I can do is not to allow this side of the case to be forgotten." (Letter, Lord Milner to Lord Knollys, June, 1901.)

The war became more horrid with atrocities on both side. Kitchener complained that there was never any "straight fighting," and it must have been extremely difficult for him to carry on a war that he did not feel needed to be extended this far. He took "no pleasure in destroying a country." The "government laagers" and "camps for refuge"—used to house the homeless Afrikaner women, children, and elderly—came to be known as concentration camps. Conditions in the camps deteriorated; people died from a lack of sanitation and ensuing epidemics. A daughter of an archdeacon visited the camps and then returned to England to tell the sad tale. Newspaper accounts of the camps helped to increase the growing public sentiment against the war. The conservative Tories under Lord Salisbury were in power; the liberals claimed that the war was becoming increasingly barbaric. Both the Cabinet and Kitchener were blamed; Kitchener kept trying to find a way to end the war.

Kitchener managed to end the war by:
1) extending the blockhouses (8000 small fortresses in key locations throughout the country),
2) by raising regiments of surrendered Boers who agreed to fight with the British in order to end the war,
3) by allowing people in the "concentration camps" to leave,
4) and by arming native Black Africans. This is something the Boers especially feared. The Afrikaners had not always treated the natives respectfully, to put it mildly. The Afrikaners feared what armed and trained Blacks might do to them after the war.

As the war drew to a close, respect for Kitchener increased. Kitchener loathed drawing any kind of attention to himself. He was self-effacing rather than self-proclaiming. "Six months ago," an observer wrote, "I felt that the Government did not in the least appreciate his gigantic work, but I think now they are beginning to get a glimmering of what a great man they have got out here.... He is always the same, never irritable, in spite of all his trials, and always making the best of things however much he may be interfered with." (Conk Market's letter to his sister, January, 1902.)

Another observer commented that Kitchener appeared to be rock-like but he was really controlling with "an iron will" a highly sensitive nature.

Kitchener fought the Boers on one hand, and on the other hand he "fought" those in the British government who advocated a vindictive, unconditional, humiliating surrender. Kitchener won in both struggles. Kitchener's peace stipulated:
1) Financial loans to the Boers.
2) Their farms would be rebuilt primarily at British expense.
3) The British side would re-stock the farms.
4) And the British would also rebuild bridges and dams.
5) The Boers would have to become subjects of the King of England.
6) The Dutch language would be used along side of English in administration and court of law.
7) There would be no war reparations.

Milner complained about how much Kitchener was willing to give away.

The Boers also wanted self-government, but Kitchener persuaded them to postpone the demand for another two years. The Liberals were likely to win by that time, Kitchener told their leading general as he took him aside. And the Liberals were sympathetic to their cause. Kitchener wanted the vote to be given to the natives, but the Boers wanted this postponed until self-government was obtained.

One could not clearly say that Kitchener was either liberal or conservative; he merely took every situation that arose and tried to observe it free from any party prejudice. As a general, he was accustomed to getting along with whoever was in power, whether he personally liked it or not.

Rennell Rodd, a diplomat in Cairo, wrote a letter to Kitchener after the signing of the peace agreement: "Perhaps the greatest thing about it is the way in which you have succeeded in conquering deep seated animosities and making the end radiant with the spirit of conciliation and goodwill." Kitchener was promoted to a full general in the army.

Reforming the Army in India. Conflict with the Viceroy. After a short leave, Kitchener went to India where he spent the next seven years as Commander in Chief of the Indian Army George Curzon, the Viceroy of India, was pleased to get Kitchener. Curzon wanted the army to have more "controlled expenditure" and he wanted it to have more "system and method." There was a lack of "fiber and tone," and altogether too much "slackness and jobbery." Kitchener, he thought, would be the perfect man to put it all in order. He was the perfect man for the position, and he did put it in order, but not without coming into bitter conflict with Curzon himself.

In the comparison of Kitchener and Curzon, by Curzon's secretary Sir Walter Lawrence, we find some interesting first ray and seventh ray indicators:

> There was a likeness between these two remarkable men. They lived for work, and cared nothing for the susceptibilities of others. Neither could tolerate inefficiency nor be lenient to failure. Lord Curzon was the greater student and could work longer than Lord Kitchener. Both were equally impatient of criticism or opposition. Both loved pageantry, loved beautiful surroundings, and took an almost feminine interest in the details of domestic arrangements. Both were determined and acquisitive collectors, and both had an extreme reverence for rank. Lord Curzon loved debates and revelled in logical and masterly minutes. Lord Kitchener distrusted and despised all such official exercises. (*The India We Served*, Sir Walter Lawrence, 1928.)

The seventh ray type tends to like pageantry, since it is generally a kind of ceremony or ritual. The seventh ray may also play a role in the tendency to be a collector. Kitchener's first collection—started as a boy and carried through adulthood—was stamps. When stationed in Cyprus, Palestine, and Egypt, he began collecting ceramics, armor, carvings, screens, and antiquities. In India Kitchener had much opportunity to enhance his collection. Over the years he received many gifts from rajahs and sheikhs. As a means of relaxation, he enjoyed organizing and rearranging his prized collectibles.

Curzon was impressed with Kitchener's openness and honesty, his direct commonsense opinions. One learned quickly where Kitchener stood on any given issue. Kitchener eventually learned that Curzon could not be trusted and that Curzon's apparent honesty was simply subtle manipulation. Unlike Kitchener, Curzon was not direct and straight forward. With Curzon there were hidden agendas and unrevealed side issues.

While touring India, Kitchener's organizational eye immediately saw that there was no one, real Indian Army. There were many small little armies, which were very competitive with and jealous of each other. In time of war this lack of unity and cohesion could easily prove disastrous.

Kitchener's proposals for change were often denied by the Military Member of the Viceroy's Council. At first this was frustrating for Kitchener, eventually it became intolerable. Curzon almost always stood behind the Military Member's decisions. The Military Member was a post designed to be a civilian check on military matters. In theory it seemed at first an appropriate function. In practice, however, it weakened the power of the Commander-in-Chief of the army to the point of being ineffectual. The Military Member could veto anything that had to do with supply, transport, ordinance, or organization. The Commander-in-Chief of the army was responsible only for training and military operations. Instead of a single person at the head of the military, there was both the Commander-in-Chief and the Military Member of the Viceroy's Council, which came to be known as "Duel Control." Kitchener considered it an "unworkable farce." In Kitchener's view, the Commander-in-Chief had to have control of all military matters. The only civilian check on the military that was needed was the power of hiring and firing the Commander-in-Chief. There was the need to find a good Commander-in-Chief for the position, and then there was the obvious need to give him the power to do his job. If inadequate, he would be removed from office. This was Kitchener's straight forward view.

A case in point had to do with Kitchener's effort to make changes in how the regiments were named. Instead of 1st Bengal, 1st Madras, etc., there would be a sequence of 1st cavalry, 1st infantry, 2nd cavalry, etc. As well as a number, a name could also be chosen to designate location and tradition. By means of Kitchener's system a step would be taken to integrate the many armies into a single Indian Army.

Curzon's and Military Member's response was not directly to veto the idea but to file it away, which in effect was a veto. Curzon initially wanted to have more "system and method," but he considered Kitchener's suggestion a "tinkering" with the system. Kitchener felt, as he stated in a letter to Lord Roberts, Commander-in-Chief of the British Army, that it was "enormous and heartbreaking" to try to get anything done in the present system. Kitchener was rightly beginning to seek circuitous ways of reaching the Prime Minister's Cabinet, although protocol demanded that all complaints go through the Viceroy.

Curzon's response to Kitchener's effort to rename the regiments established a pattern of conflict that would be repeated many times over the seven years of Kitchener's duty in India. It is highly probable that the Military Member of the Cabinet either conferred with Curzon, or knew Curzon's mind, before he vetoed one of Kitchener's requests, because the Viceroy always backed the Military Member's veto. Curzon was in effect interfering in the running of the military. One of the motives behind this was a fear of the potential power of the military commander. Another reason was Curzon's own personal will-to-power.

Both Curzon and Kitchener were powerful, 1st ray people. There were a couple of interesting distinctions between the two men that became clearly evident as they came into relationship and conflict. Curzon saw himself as a "superior person." His poetic assertion while at Oxford seemed to still apply at 38 years of age in India:

My name is George Nathaniel Curzon
I am a most superior person,
My cheek is pale, my hair is sleek,
I dine at Blenheim once a week.

Curzon was aware that he was heir to an estate that "had been held by Curzons in unbroken male descent since Norman times, and to an old peerage, while Kitchener was merely the grandson of a tea merchant." (Pollock 245). Kitchener never thought of himself as a "superior person." He stood with the people. His priorities were duty to God, duty to humanity (which often meant the "natives" and the peasants, the ones that had no voice in government), and duty to country. He was not a person with a strong ego. He was a man of some strength who had to work awfully hard in order to do God's Will.

Another interesting distinction has to do with the third ray of intelligent activity. As noted above, Curzon "loved debates and reveled in logical and masterly minutes." Being articulate, being able to speak eloquently with intelligence and poise, is often an indicator of the presence of a developed third ray quality. It is a most valued quality in business, government, and politics, and helps one to rise in the establishment. Kitchener did not possess this quality, in fact, he distrusted it. Kitchener was clear, straight forward, and simplified matters wherever possible. It is interesting, in regard to the third ray, that Curzon accused Kitchener of "tinkering" with the intact system of organization of the army regiments when Kitchener proposed a different number-naming system. The truth of the matter is that Curzon was the one doing the "tinkering." The Viceroy was interfering in a purely military matter, not a matter of State. The Viceroy was playing a power game, or trying to put Kitchener in a clearly subordinate position, while Kitchener was trying very hard to improve a disorganized army. Kitchener complained to friends that Curzon had a way of twisting the meaning of things; Kitchener thought that Curzon should either have been a lawyer or an actor.

As we come to see, in the development of the pattern of this conflicting relationship, *Curzon was very much inclined to accuse Kitchener of the very thing that Curzon himself was doing.* This is a manipulative tactic. The third ray has great skill in clearly pronouncing the truth. On the reverse side, however, the person influenced by the third ray may also have great skill at making the false word appear true.

In the effort to resolve the dispute over the issue of Dual Control, it was suggested to Kitchener that he refrain from bringing the matter up for one year. Kitchener was to live with the existing system so that he might come to recognize its value. Further acquaintance with the system, however, had the opposite effect. Kitchener was able to see in greater detail just exactly why the system of dual control was unworkable.

At the end of the year, he produced a 32 page document, outlining his reasons why the Military Member of the Viceroy's Council should be eliminated (January 1, 1905). Two months later all the other members of the Viceroy's Council rejected Kitchener's proposal. The struggle between these two men of very strong will continued.

As the dispute reached London, Secretary of State John Brodrick tended to side with Kitchener. The Prime Minister Arthur James Balfour (replacing Salisbury in 1902) also tended increasingly to side with Kitchener. London's initial intent was to arrange a compromise that would prevent the resignation of either Kitchener or Curzon. The Prime Minister's Cabinet decided on May 30, 1905, that the Military Member of the Viceroy's Council would be abolished and that almost all the military departments (supply, transport, ordinance, military works) would be turned over to the Commander-in Chief of the Army of India, as Kitchener wanted. A Council of Military Finance and Stores (covering the remaining two military departments previously under the Military Member) was created to replace the Military Member but with much less responsibility and much less opportunity to interfere with the Commander-in-Chief.

Kitchener was pleased with the not complete but nevertheless substantial victory. Curzon tried to negotiate London's decision, as if he were an independent head of state instead of the Prime Minister's appointee. Curzon's cunning took elaborate twists, but eventually he resigned. By that time London, on to Curzon's ways, was content to see him go.

Curzon "warned" the new Viceroy of India, the Scottish Earl of Minto, about Kitchener, saying that Kitchener was ambitious, self-seeking, and difficult to work with. Minto, on the other hand, found Kitchener to be broadminded, easy to work with, and willing to look at matters from opposing points of view. After a year of working with the changes initiated by Kitchener, the Viceroy's Council found the new system a "complete success and an immense improvement." In 1907 Kitchener's term was extended two years, so that he could implement his reforms still further. In 1909 the Military Finance and Supply department was abolished, turning over the responsibility to the Commander-in-Chief of the Army, resulting in Kitchener getting everything he wanted.

In the Sudan and South Africa, Kitchener carried the responsibilities of military operations in his own head, that is in a centralized manner. In India, during a time of peace but readiness, Kitchener worked with administrative principles of decentralization. According to Viceroy Minto: Kitchener's "divisional system had removed so much work from army headquarters that K has little to do." (Letter, Minto to Biggs, July 21, 1909, Royal Archives.) This freed up Kitchener so that he could make tours and inspections of the various divisions. Field Marshall William Birdwood, commenting about Kitchener, said that he found it very "unusual to find highly organizing power and great personal driving force combined in one and the same individual."

Consul General in Egypt. Kitchener hoped to be appointed Viceroy of India at the end of Minto's term, but such was not the case. The home government thought it would be offensive to India if a military man had that position. This was a bitter disappointment to Kitchener.

In 1911 Kitchener was appointed Consul General in Egypt. Technically, the line of authority in Egypt started with the Ottoman Sultan in Constantinople, then the Khedive of Egypt, and then various diplomatic representatives of the Egyptian Khedive—the Consul General being one of them. The British Consul General, however, backed by the British Army, was for all practical purposes the true ruler of Egypt.

One of Kitchener's main projects or goals in Egypt was to improve the conditions of the poor. For the benefit of the Egyptian peasantry, he established the Five Feddan Law (a feddan being approximately an acre). This law enabled a peasant to keep a portion of his land and tools, no matter how high his debt. Kitchener also developed systems of public health and education, drainage and irrigation—all to benefit primarily the poor people. He also adopted the oriental custom of the ruler receiving people from all classes. Peasants as well as noblemen could request audience with him in order to have a grievance settled.

Kitchener's basic premise was: "I am here to administer Egypt for the Egyptians, not for the English." He was a popular ruler; indirectly his rule did much to raise British prestige.

The Great War in Europe. On July 28, 1914 Austria declared war on Serbia. Germany was poised to move into Belgium. The first days of World War I were underway. Kitchener was called to London and was appointed Secretary of State for War. The people and the press were overwhelmingly in favor of Kitchener being appointed to this office, and public opinion helped to bring it about. As one writer expressed it:

> No appointment could have produced a better effect upon the hearts of the British people and upon those of the Allies. The nation felt... that Lord Kitchener was holding its hand confidently and reassuringly in one of his, while with the other he had the whole race of politicians firmly by the scruff, and would see to it that there was no nonsense or trouble in that quarter. (F.S.Oliver, *Ordeal by Battle*.)

Kitchener's response to the appointment was: "May God preserve me from the politicians." His prayer was *not* altogether answered.

Kitchener's contribution to this important war effort was considerable:

• Kitchener realized at the outset that it was imperative that Britain stand behind France. If Britain did not stand behind France, Britain would lose all influence in Europe.

• Kitchener predicted that the war would last three years. Others said it would be over in a matter of months. Kitchener prepared for the long ordeal, which turned out to be critically important. He predicted that it would be primarily an Anglo-German war,
that would last three years, and that there would be no clear victory.

• Kitchener saw that in order to win the war Britain would have to raise a large new army. This surprised other members of the cabinet due to the fact that Britain had been primarily a naval power.

• Kitchener organized the recruiting and training of the new army in such a way that at the beginning of the third year—when other armies were wearing down—he would be able to send in fresh troops.

- Kitchener's responsibilities were many. He had to mobilize a slow and lagging arms industry. He had to recruit a large number of volunteers and postpone conscription as long as possible. He had to direct war strategy. All these factors were often made more difficult by other members of the Cabinet who did not have an understanding of war. In Kitchener's view: "Arguing with men equal in status but each with a departmental axe to grind was frustrating." (John Pollock, *Kitchener*.)

Kitchener was popular with the British people, but he suffered from the meddling of politicians in military matters. On several occasions he wanted to resign. He became something like a scapegoat among the cabinet members. If something went wrong, the tendency was to blame Kitchener. On the question of munitions, Kitchener proceeded carefully and thoroughly. The French had developed a quick, mass-production (fast-track) system of producing guns, with the result that many of the guns exploded when fired. Kitchener did not want the British to make the same mistake. Lloyd George seized a political opportunity to complain about slow production of munitions and eventually was able to head a Munitions Committee. Kitchener's motive on all matters was clearly *to win the war*. Other Cabinet Members, Lloyd George foremost among them, placed their own personal career above the selfless one of winning the war. Lloyd George wanted to be Prime Minister and, if this was not possible, then to move Kitchener out and to head the War Office. For purposes of his own hidden agenda, he had to make Kitchener look incompetent wherever possible. Kitchener thought he had an ally in Prime Minister Herbert Asquith, but such was not the case, although Kitchener never knew this. But again, Kitchener was popular with the people. The politicians had to play a most subtle game, appearing to be one way while surreptitiously moving in the exact opposite direction. Curzon (now seeing a chance to settle a score), Lloyd George, and Balfour were all together in their determination to oust Kitchener. His prayer "May God preserve me from the politicians" became more understandable.

Perhaps the major reason for Kitchener enduring his extremely difficult position was his wish to have some influence during peace negotiations. Kitchener wanted to have a peace settlement that would result in reconciliation rather than simply postpone another war. "I have no fear whatever about winning the War, what I fear greatly is that we may make a bad peace. Here I think I might be of some use. " (R. Churchill, *Lord Derby*.)

This, however, was not to be. It was arranged for Kitchener to visit Russia. Prince Youssoupoff on a recent visit to London had been impressed by Kitchener's knowledge of Russia and keen intellect. Czar Nicholas sent word that he would find a visit from Kitchener to be "most useful and important." Kitchener valued Russia in this particular war as a threatening presence in the East that would prevent Germany from concentrating her forces completely in the West. Also Kitchener seized every good opportunity to get out and away from the politics of the Cabinet in London.

On June 5th, 1916, he boarded a train for the Highlands of Scotland. At 4:45 PM he set sail aboard the *Hampshire*. A terrific north-western gale came up and pitched the ship violently on huge waves. There was an explosion. The battleship had hit a mine. Electricity went out and it became impossible to steer the ship. With the enormous waves it was useless to try to get into lifeboats. About twelve minutes after the explosion, the stern lifted and then the ship went down. Twelve sailors out of 600 managed to reach shore. Kitchener was not among them. He was last seen on the quarterdeck talking to the captain. He showed no sign of nervousness. His body was never recovered.

In grief, King George V wrote to his uncle that Kitchener's death was "a terrible blow to me, as besides being a personal friend of 30 years' standing, I had the greatest admiration for him and absolute confidence in his judgement. I shall miss him terribly and his guiding hand."

As newsboys shouted out the tragic headlines, people poured from busses to read the papers. Only a handful of officials had known that Kitchener had been on a secret mission to Russia. Many simply could not believe it; many hoped and prayed that he had somehow survived.

Britain and her allies eventually won the war. Some say, had Kitchener been alive, it would have ended sooner. The generals sorely missed Kitchener's support. Lloyd George became Prime Minister. Not a peace of reconciliation but a cruel and vindictive peace was forced upon Germany.

And the rest is history.

It seems very clear that Kitchener lived up to the tradition of the "grand old knights"—so *fierce in war and so gentle in religion*—carrying it all a most vital soul-step further: *SO FAIR IN PEACE.*

Summary of Soul Indicators.
Working for the long term, the future.
Working from a highly principled position.
A strong sense of morality.
Dedicated to selfless service.
Serving with a sense of humility, not superiority.
Standing with the people. Identifying with humanity.
Working for the well-being of others rather than self or personal career.
Knowing where one's contribution is and not interfering with the work of others.
A sense of true group work. Group consciousness.

Summary of First Ray Indicators.
Strength.
Capacity for hard work, great powers of endurance.
Personal driving power. A tough taskmaster.
Control and repression of emotion.
Being rock-like. Having an iron-will.
Demanding of others and being intolerant of inefficiency or failure.
Reverence for and clear recognition of rank.
Responding to and strictly adhering to hierarchical order.
Brief and to the point. Straight forward.
Identifying the simplicity of the power factor.
Diplomatic skills. Leadership skills.
Administrative skills.
Ability to handle men and measures.
Ability to command an army.

Summary of Seventh Ray Indicators.
Some skill in the scientific disciplines.
High organizing power.
Love of pageantry.
Love of beautiful surroundings.
Keen interest in the details of domestic arrangements.
Collecting art objects and antiquities.
Reverence for rank.
Deep interest in the symbolism and rituals of Freemasonry. (In India Kitchener joined the Himalayan Brotherhood Lodge. He was appointed District Grand Master of the Punjab.)
Being able thoroughly to master all details.
Ability to see how the parts work together in relationship to the whole.
Interest in city planning.

ALICE BAILEY
SECOND RAY SOUL

Alice Bailey's Childhood. Alice Bailey was born June 16th, 1880, in Manchester, England. She described her childhood as being "thoroughly unhappy," even though she was "surrounded by beauty" and had a life "full of variety", traveling and meeting many interesting people. "I never knew what it was to want anything. I was brought up in the usual luxury of my day and class; I was watched over with the greatest care---but within myself I hated it all." At first glance, it seems rather difficult to imagine just exactly why she hated it all.

Even though many people say that childhood is the happiest time, Alice did not believe this at all. There was physical comfort and luxury, to be sure. There were years of "freedom from all material anxiety but they were, at the same time, years of miserable questioning, of disillusionment, of unhappy discovery, and of loneliness." (*The Unfinished Autobiography of Alice Bailey* 9.)

As she speculated as to the possible reasons for this unhappiness, she concluded that perhaps it was not all that bad. Perhaps the sense of unhappiness is due simply to the fact that difficult times seem to stand out more prominently in one's memory.

Her mother died of consumption (tuberculosis) at the age of 29—Alice was six years old. Her father, a prominent engineer, died also of tuberculosis approximately two years later. Alice had no memory of her mother, except for a vague recollection of beautiful hair. She remembers her father as having "resentment over our existence, particularly, for some reason, over mine." Alice also had a younger sister. "He probably felt my mother would be alive if having two children had not drained her physical resources." "My father did not care for me and when I see the picture of myself when small, I can scarcely wonder—skinny, scared and startled looking" (*Autobiography* 16, 19).

Alice as a young child was spirited, a developed soul, somewhat feisty and rebellious. Except for the very early years, she was raised without a mother. She had a father who apparently showed no love to Alice at all and perhaps even resented her in some unconscious way. Even if it were true that the mother's constitution was weakened by having children, how can one assign any blame to the children? Evidently, the father provided for the two daughters' material needs. Emotionally and spiritually, however, he neglected them, and such neglect can have a very serious psychological effect on any child, particularly one as developed and as sensitive as Alice.

Yet Alice wondered why she was unhappy. She even made excuses for her father (as forgiving children so often do) by saying that it was "no wonder" he didn't care for her. After all, she was "skinny, scared, and started looking" as if these were somehow legitimate reasons for a father not to care for his daughter.

Yet her physical needs—her food, clothing and shelter, her education and cultural development, her need to acquire social manners and right conduct, etc.—were all dutifully met. That is to say, they were attended to with the utmost discipline. Her life was one of regimentation with a routine that reminds one of a military academy. Up at 6 AM (regardless of season or weather), piano practice at 7:00, breakfast at 8:00, prayers with the family and servants at 9:00, school lessons with the governess at 9:30 followed by a walk. The 8 AM breakfast was taken alone in a large room designated "the schoolroom."

"We were allowed to have lunch in the dining room but were not permitted to speak and our good behavior and silence were under the anxious eyes of our governess." Adults can all too easily do damage to the spirit of a child in their demand for so-called "good" behavior, when in effect they are only thinking of themselves. Evidently her governess was responsible for this lunch time, as well as the school lessons, for the grandmother would appear from time to time to make sure that conduct was proper, such as no elbows on the table—outer behavior, evidently, being *just about everything*.

After lunch they rested for an hour on a "flat sloping board whilst our governess read aloud some improving book" and then went for another walk. This was followed by more lessons. Up to the bedroom at 5 PM where the nurse and the maid tended to their more formal dressing—white dresses, colored sashes, silk stockings, well-brushed hair. They were then paraded to the drawing room, where the family and guests were sitting after tea. "There we stood in the doorway and made our curtsies and thus endured the misery of being talked to and inspected until our governess came to fetch us." Supper in the schoolroom at 6:30. More lessons till 8 PM, then bedtime.

Alice summed it up in this way: "There was never any time in those Victorian days to do anything which we, as individuals, might want to do. It was a life of discipline, rhythm and obedience, varied occasionally by spurts of rebellion and consequent punishment." (*Autobiography* 26).

"Discipline" without an inherent *meaning* will tend to foster rebellion. "Rhythm" without *beauty* quickly becomes something like a routine that is intelligently designed to appear to be perfectly reasonable when in effect it fails to address the true nature of the child. And "obedience"? Yes, to be sure, obedience—but the military sort, where orders are never to be questioned. The following of the order, the authority, becomes the highest value.

What was the Mood of Alice During this Time? A general sense of unhappiness has been mentioned, but there were much stronger psychological reactions. One of her reactions was a fluctuation between opposite extremes: "If I did not watch myself with the greatest care, I would always be either in the heights of happiness and exhilaration or overcome with despair and in the depths of depression." Her effort was to "live on a tableland", which is to say level and balanced. She learned to "repudiate both extremes." This was obviously not achieved overnight. One is incline to speculate as to the possibility of Alice having a fourth ray mind. The tendency to swing between dramatic opposites is suggestive of this. The first ray of her own personality, however, along with the strong first ray note sounded in the environment (Britain has a first ray personality), served to help Alice bring any dramatic imbalances under control .

Alice also said that at that time she did not like the "feel" of life. "I was morbid, full of self-pity, through loneliness, exceedingly introspective,...and convinced that no one liked me.... I was the unhappy, self-dramatized center of my little world." During her childhood, she made three attempts to commit suicide. The first occurred when she was five years old. She thought that she would die if she bumped down the steep stone kitchen steps. She was only battered and bruised. At eleven she tried to smother herself with sand. The third and last time, at fourteen years of age, she tried to drown herself in a river, but "The instinct to self-preservation was too strong" (*Autobiography* 21).

Positive Early Influences. Another somewhat depressing factor about Alice's life is that, as a child, she had "no real home." She and her sister were shuffled about between relatives and from governess to governess. A positive influence, however, was that every summer she and her sister lived with their aunt, Mrs. Margaret Maxwell, in

Scotland. "She gave me a keynote for living so that I feel to this day that any achievement which I may have had can be traced back to her deeply spiritual influence." During the months when Alice was not living in her household, Margaret wrote regularly to her, at least one letter a month, helping to orient Alice in a spiritual direction.

Another positive influence was a governess, Miss Godby, who came to Alice and her sister when Alice was twelve and stayed till eighteen. "She was the one person to whom I felt 'anchored.'" Miss Godby gave Alice a sense of "belonging and was one of the few people in my life at that time who I felt truly loved me and believed in me."

Master K.H. Visited Alice When She was Fifteen. There was no one in the house except Alice and the servants; others had gone to church. Master K.H. appeared, or walked into the room. He had a turban on his head, which was the most disconcerting factor for Alice. She was "petrified" and could not utter a sound. He told her that there was some work planned for her, but it would be necessary that she change her disposition very considerably. "I would have to give up being such an unpleasant little girl and must try and get some measure of self-control.... He said that if I achieved real self-control I could then be trusted and that I would travel all over the world and visit many countries, 'doing your Master's work all the time.' Those words have rung in my ears ever since.... He added that He would be in touch with me at intervals of several years apart."

Years later, when Alice was working with the Theosophical Society in California, she found out that this "visitor was the Master K.H., the Master Koot Hoomi, a Master Who is very close to the Christ, Who is on the teaching line and Who is an outstanding exponent of the love-wisdom of which the Christ is the full expression" (*Autobiography* 37).

This early meeting with the Master K.H. served, among other things, to bring about a dramatic change in Alice's behavior. There were no more "explosive displays," she controlled her tongue, and she became "smug, sweet, and sentimental." The change was in such stark contrast with her previous rebelliousness that the family thought there might be something seriously wrong with her.

The Background of Alice's Upbringing. The nineteenth century was a time of considerable change. England was digesting and assimilating some of the philosophical-social questions raised by the French Revolution. After the defeat of Napoleon, monarchies were restored, but the monarchies in the 19th century had to choose between *constant resistance* to the spirited change threatening to come from below upward and *concessions* to this new spirit of the people—a spirit that would simply *not go away*. Concessions meant government reform, which was a means by which change could be controlled from above downward, thus avoiding some of the bloody and terrifying mistakes of the French Revolution.

The industrial revolution was underway, which was also the beginning of the technological revolution. The railroad, telegraph, telephone, radio, photography, unified postal service, steam engines, inventions in the textile industry, new methods of drilling, draining, sowing, and fertilizing, road and canal building, etc., were changing lives and disrupting traditions.

Charles Darwin's *The Origin of the Species* was published in 1859. These theories were stretched and made to apply to the social realm. The phrase "survival of the fittest" was coined by Herbert Spencer (1820-1903), who was a major exponent of social Darwinism. The notion that the human condition was essentially a jungle in which only the fittest individuals, classes, and nations survived was accepted by many intellectuals of the day. The losers were seen as the ones who could not adapt, could not compete, could not survive. As serfs and slaves were emancipated, a new kind of slavery developed—but under a different name and different rationale. The poor lived in misery. Men and women labored in mines and factories for 12 to 18 hours a day. Child labor was widespread. Wages were at a starvation level. Vagrancy, homelessness, unemployment, epidemics of typhus and cholera were all common urban phenomena accompanying the prosperity and growth of the new industrialism. Organized crime grew in the urban congestion. Labor was forbidden to organize. (Trade unions were partially legalized in 1825). In 1800 two hundred offenses were punishable by death. By 1830 this number was reduced to about twelve. In describing the very wide distance between the rich and the poor, Benjamin Disraeli (Prime Minister 1868, 1874-1880) wrote the following in his book *Sybil*:

"Two nations between whom there is no intercourse and no sympathy; who are as ignorant of each other's habits, thoughts, and feelings as if they were inhabitants of different planets."

Charles Dickens (1812-1870) brought the plight of the poor dramatically before the public eye in such novels as *Oliver Twist* and *David Copperfield*. In his productive years, Dickens was the world's most celebrated writer. He had a special ability to tell the story that can stir the emotions and inspire compassion. Dickens felt the deep need to reform all England. He sought to do this through his novels, his weekly journal *Household Words,* and his magazine *All the Year Round.*

Britain: Both More Advanced and Less Advanced. According to the historian Norman Davies, Great Britain was

"both more and less advanced than its main rivals. On the one hand, Britain could fairly claim to be the home of 'the Mother of Parliaments', of the rule of law, of the Bill of Rights, and of free trade. British society was for long the most modernized and industrialized in Europe, and supposedly the most open to liberal ideas. On the other hand, ... the monarchy continued to reign according to rules and customs agreed in the seventeenth century, as if the French Revolution had never happened.... There were republican sympathies in Britain, but no serious move to abolish the monarchy or to introduce a constitution. Britain's ancient institutions were slow to reform.... The feudal privileges of the House of Lords were not even trimmed until 1911.... The British loved to pride themselves on their tolerance and liberalism; but much of their pride became outdated. In later decades they lagged behind France in domestic democracy, behind Germany in social legislation, behind Austria-Hungary in nationality policy."

Europe, A History 807, 810.

This duality of the British—to be somewhat liberal, open-minded, and innovatively eclectic on the one hand, while being bull-headed, resistant to change, and ultra-conservative on the other—may be related to the fact (according to the esoteric teaching) that Gemini rules the soul of the nation and Taurus rules its personality. Consider the following from *Destiny of Nations*:

In considering Great Britain, we note first that the ruling sign is Gemini from the standpoint of the soul of the people, and that Taurus governs the material outer form of the nation; it is this factor that has led her people to appear before the world under the symbol of John Bull, expressive of the British personality. ....It is the Gemini influence that has led to the constant movement and restlessness of the British people; which has led them to cross and recross the ocean and to stage a constant going out to the very ends of the earth, to return ever again to the centre from which they came. This is characteristic of the race. It is the Gemini influence which has produced — viewing the work of the nation from the personality or lower angle — the secret and oft devious diplomacy and subtlety which has in the past distinguished Great Britain's political activity. Gemini people are often distrusted, and the Gemini effect along this line makes of Great Britain no exception. Such distrust has been warranted in the past but is not as justifiable now, for the nation is old and experienced and is fast learning the lessons which she has had to master. As yet, from the higher angle, Gemini does not entirely control, for the soul of Britain is only now struggling for expression. For long ages Taurus has led the way with his material aims, his acquisitive desires, his arrogant will and his blind moving forward towards the possession of that which has been desired. Pervasiveness and movement are two qualities with which Gemini and Taurus have dowered the race.....Great Britain regards herself as the preserver of the balance of power among the nations and as the one to mete out justice and indicate the right methods of law and order; yet her Gemini nature at times offsets this, whilst Taurus frequently blinds her to the real issues.

Destiny of Nations 81.

Great Britain represents that aspect of the mind which expresses itself in intelligent government, based on just and loving understanding. *Destiny* 54-5.

Great Britain expresses the will-to-power but on account of age and experience, dearly bought, this is today mellowed by justice and a growing understanding of human need. This, in its turn, is the result of the control for many centuries in the past by the aristocracy, with its paternalism, conservatism and its method of slow adjustment.

Externalization of the Hierarchy 131

In the 19th century Britain had no lack of intelligently considering all the latest liberal, social, philosophical ideas and no lack of reflecting on the dramatic changes occurring on the continent. The Gemini influence would certainly aid this tendency. Balancing the rush of new ideas, however, was a cautious conservatism, augmented by the influence of the Bull of Taurus. Benjamin Disraeli served in Parliament for 44 years and was Prime Minister in 1868 and 1874-1880. According to Disraeli—who was something of a contradiction, for in some respects he wasn't at all British, while in other respects he deeply understand and identified with the heart and soul of British conservatism—according to Disraeli:

> England is the only important European community that is still governed by traditionary influences, and amid the shameless wreck of nations she alone has maintained her honour, her liberty, her order, her authority, and her wealth.... But it is said that it is contrary to the spirit of the age that a great nation like England, a community of enlightened millions long accustomed to public liberty, should be governed by an aristocracy. It is not true that England is governed by an aristocracy in the common acceptation of the term. England is governed by an aristocratic principle. The aristocracy of England absorbs all aristocracies, and receives every man in every order and every class who defers to the principle of our society, which is to aspire and to excel.
>
> Disraeli, *Lord George Bentinck.*

With the Gemini influence there is a circulation of ideas, an intelligent open-mindedness, an expansion through travel, willingness to adapt and change, and a flexibility-mobility-fluidity. With the Taurus influence there is the stability of tradition (related to achievement and excellence) and the stability of the conservative method of "slow adjustment."

Alice's Coming of Age in 19th Century England. A New Cycle of Work Begins. As mentioned, Darwin's *Origin of the Species* was published in 1859. Thomas Huxley (born May 4, 1825, Taurus) acquired the nickname of "Darwin's Bulldog" as he brought the new scientific theories into public debate. All England was processing the theory of evolution, as the new theory brought the Biblical paradigm of long tradition into question. Interestingly, there was a strong reaction to the theory that "man came from ape" and to the theory that an animalistic struggle to survive was an inescapable natural phenomenon applicable to the human condition. The reaction brought about a *growth in Christian and evangelical fundamentalism* and a growth in humanitarian enterprises, including charity schools, Sunday schools, hospitals founded at private expense, a huge increase in private charities, missionary work in the colonies, Bible-reading classes, and the International Red Cross (founded in 1867). Alice Bailey was drawn to the evangelical movement.

Up to the age of 21, Alice had lived a very sheltered and protected life, although, by means of tutors, she received "an exceedingly good classical education; I spoke fluent French and some Italian." During that time she had traveled much and met many people, but she had always been "accompanied by a chaperone, a relative or a maid."

Her education also included Christian Bible study, which included being of some help and service to less fortunate ones. "From the earliest possible time we were taught to care about the poor and the sick and to realize that fortunate circumstances entailed responsibility. Several times a week when it was time to go for a walk we had to go to the housekeeper's room for jellies and soup for some sick person on the property, for baby clothes for the new baby at one of the lodges, for books for someone who was confined to the house to read." She took this part of her education very seriously; she felt that "Christ was an ever-present reality to me." She never had any doubt on this matter. It is probable that the essential message of the Christian teaching sounded a note that resonated very deeply in Alice's soul.

At 21 Alice found herself in good material standing (the family was sufficiently wealthy to provide her with a regularly income), and in good social standing (she knew many of the right people in the upper classes). She was very attractive and she was well educated. Her sister went off to Edinburgh University to study medicine and had a brilliant career. Alice could have gone on to University for further study, or she could have circulated more socially in the effort to find the right marriage partner. Instead she responded to another kind of calling. She "furiously and frantically began to do good. I became an evangelist with the British army."

Her first spiritual tour of duty was in Ireland with a Miss Elise Sandes at a Soldiers Home. She worked at a Home in Belfast and learned all aspects of the work. She served men in the coffee shops (hundreds at a time), baked hundreds of buns, played checkers, befriended the men (in an impersonal way), and conducted Gospel meetings. After some difficult experiences, she steadily learned to speak in front of a large group of men. "I know that all things work together for good to those who love God, and this means that we do not love some far off, abstract Deity but that we love our fellowmen.

Loving our fellowmen is evidence—undefined, maybe, but just as sure—that we love God. Elise Sandes taught me that by her life and her love, her wit and her understanding."

Alice as an Evangelist in India. This 21-28 year cycle begins with enthusiasm, idealism, and also much naiveté—which is age appropriate. During this developmental stage, with its youthful zeal and energy, one breaks ties (at least psychologically) with parents, educators, and all previous nurturing authority figures. One goes out, blindly to be sure, into the world (literally or psychologically) to make one's own mark. It starts with enthusiasm (fools rush in where wise men fear to tread) As Alice put it: "In those days I was utterly fearless; I did not know what it was to be afraid. Part of this was a natural thoughtlessness, part of it ignorance, and part of it a surety that God would take care of me. Apparently He did, on the principle, I suppose, that drunken men, infants and fools are not responsible, and must be guarded." This 21-28 year developmental stage, as ideals and naiveté are confronted with "reality", can lead to some kind of failure, breakdown, or some sense of being overwhelmed. This is true particularly during the 21-25 crisis years of this cycle.

The woman who was in charge of several Soldiers Homes in India was unable to carry on with the work. Alice was sent to replace her. Years later, with self-effacement, Alice described herself then as being "a consummate prig, even if well-intentioned. I was almost too good to live and certainly holy enough to be hated."

Alice set out to work. Her life became very hectic. "I went from one Home to another, attending to the accounts, interviewing the managers, holding endless Gospel meetings, talking to the soldiers about their souls or their families, visiting in the military hospitals and dealing with the many problems which naturally arise when hundreds of men are stationed away from home and faced with the problems of life in a hot climate and an alien civilization. I became very well known to many regiments. I once totaled up the number of regiments I had worked with in Ireland and India and found I had worked with forty." The different regiments had various nicknames for her—"Granny", "China", "Benevolent Old Lady", and the most popular "Mother."

Sometimes, disgruntled and unruly soldiers would "break the place up" by spattering the walls with cocoa and eggs, turning the coffee house into an abominable mess. She learned to deal with this, not with condemnation and accusations, but with understanding and love.

A typical morning might include Bible study (14 sessions a week), correspondence, conferences with managers, and going over the accounts (they were feeding 600 men in each coffee shop every morning). Afternoons were spent in the hospital, usually where the need was the greatest, which meant in that section of the hospital where no nurses were available. Chaplains would send for her when the men were dying. "Death is not so awful when you are face to face with it. It often seemed to me like a kind friend and I never had the slightest feeling that something real and vital was coming to an end."

She developed, during this time, great skill as a public speaker. This skill and development was to serve her well in future years. Her first attempts at public speaking sent her from the stage in tears. But by sheer will and determination she quickly overcame the problem and went on to do extremely well. She recognized that part of the problem was "selfishness and self-centeredness: I was caring too much what people thought of me." Eventually, she came to a point where she was "happier on the platform than anywhere else." The secret of good public speaking, she concluded after many years, is to "like your audience, and then to put them at their ease by being just human. I have never attempted to lecture. I just talk to an audience as I would to one human being. I take them into my confidence. I never pose as a know-it-all." (*Autobiography*, 75, 78, 56, 57.)

She loved the work with the soldiers in India. Outwardly, she was attractive, young and energetic (albeit somewhat naive), well poised, well educated, well trained in an aristocratic demeanor. She had a deep sense of simply wanting to do good in the world, and this opportunity was certainly awakening, to some degree, her heart center. She was certainly extending herself in service to others. She was, however, beginning to suffer from incapacitating migraine headaches. She was also becoming more stressed. "I was handling problems for which I was quite unfitted and some of them were quite tragic. I had so little experience of life that when I made a decision I never was at all sure that it was the best or right one....This constant stream of emergencies finally broke me down."

The End of One Cycle and the Beginning of Another. The 7-year cycles are of great significance. Three 7-year cycles make up the larger cycle of 21 years. The unfoldment seems to be a 3-2-1 unfoldment, which is to say: First of all the form aspect—3rd aspect. Second the consciousness aspect. Third the development of will-purpose—1st aspect.

7-YEAR SUB-CYCLES, 21-YEAR CYCLES

```
63 _____
   1                    Maturity
56___           1       Purpose-Will (spirit)
   2
49___
   3
42 _____
   1                    Middle Years
35___
   2            2       Consciousness-Quality (soul)
28___
   3
21 _____
   1   intellect        Youth
14___
   2   astral    3      Activity-Form (personality)
 7___
   3   physical
 0 _____
```

The above diagram is discussed as some length in *Threefold Method for Understanding the Seven Rays*. The larger cycles of 21 years seem also to fall into the 3-2-1 or form-consciousness-will sequence of development. The first 7 year cycle, somewhat easier to see, begins with the focus of physical form development (0-7), proceeds to focus on sentient-emotional development (7-14), and is followed by mental development, or at least the opportunity for mental development (14-21). This sequence has far-reaching educational implications, which are fully realized by Rudolf Steiner's Waldorf education, and somewhat confirmed by Piaget (although Piaget does not recognize the spiritual overtones).

The first 21 year cycle is concerned with form development—the building of the physical body, the emotional or astral body, and the mental body. These three as a unit constitute the three aspects of personality. Each of the three major aspects seems to have a *threefoldness*. When viewing life with this paradigm, it must be remembered that unfoldment is not rigid or mechanical. Each unit and sub-unit is separate—as the heart, lungs, and liver are separate organs. But at the same time there is a vital relationship, a fluidity, and a flow of energy between the various units and sub-units. It must also be remembered that *in-between bodies* are built or developed. This is readily "observed" in the kama-manasic body, or emotional-mind, or that temporary body that is neither pure emotion nor pure mind. During the existence of the temporary and in-between kama-manasic (literally desire-mind) vehicle, emotion interferes with the mental processes. Eventually the soul-mind interplay supersedes the dominance of the emotion-mind interplay and a higher or subtler unit of consciousness is developed.

THREEFOLDNESS OF THE THREE MAJOR ASPECTS

1. spiritual will (atma, the Will of God)

SPIRIT   2. intuition   (buddhi)
God conscious
            3. higher abstract archetypal mind (higher manas)
- - - - - *(vehicle of buddhi-manas or intuition-mind)*
            1. sacrificial will

SOUL   2. love-wisdom
group conscious
            3. light of the soul
- - - - - - -   - - -   *(soul-mind vehicle)*
            1. intellect (lower manas)
                            (kama-manasic vehicle)
PERSONA   2. emotion (kama)
self-conscious
            3. physical-etheric

The 21-28 year cycle is the first sub-cycle—the *activity* cycle— of the larger 21-42 *consciousness* cycle. In other words, the 21 year consciousness cycle (21-42) begins with the activity of consciousness, proceeds to the wisdom or soul of consciousness (28-35), followed by the will of consciousness (35-42).

Alice Bailey, it appears, was "right on cycle", so to speak. During the 21-28 cycle there was the focus on the *activity* of consciousness expansion—the activity of going out on one's own away from the family nest and gaining experience, going out into the world, the activity of intellect as it tentatively explored new ideas away from the family traditions. She was beginning to broaden her mind through life experience, through her own experience. This sub-cycle often comes to a close, as mentioned, with a sense of failure, break down, or sense of being overwhelmed. There is actually a mini-crisis introduced at this time in order for the individual to *reduce the activity so that one might deepen the conscious awareness.* One must go into the *heart of consciousness*, so to speak. One must reappraise everything; look at everything anew. It becomes a matter of not doing more things but looking at things less superficially. Youth thinks it knows, and thus proceeds naively and enthusiastically, with good intentions but with more self-centeredness than it is willing to see or admit. This changes. As a new sub-cycle begins at 28 years of age, there is the opportunity to see the old things in an altogether new light.

The Five Points of Crisis. It might be helpful to mention here the crises of opportunity in a person's life. According to D.K., there are "five points of crisis" in the life of an individual, during which time the soul begins to appropriate one or other of the vehicles or subtle bodies.

"1. Appropriation of the physical sheath. This takes place between the fourth and seventh year, when the soul, hitherto overshadowing, takes possession of the physical vehicle.
2. A crisis during adolescence, wherein the soul appropriates the astral vehicle. This crisis is not recognized by the general public and is only dimly sensed, from its evidenced temporary abnormalities, by the average psychologist. They do not recognize the cause but only the effects.
3. A similar crisis between the twenty-first and twenty-fifth years, wherein the mind vehicle is appropriated. The man should then begin to respond to egoic influences, and in the case of the advanced man, he frequently does.
4. A crisis between the thirty-fifth and forty-second years, wherein conscious contact with the soul is established; the threefold personality then begins to respond, as a unit, to soul impulse.
5. For the remaining years of life, there should be an increasingly strong relationship between the soul and its vehicles, leading to another crisis between the fifty-sixth or the sixty-third years. According to that crisis will depend the future usefulness of the person and whether the ego continues to use the vehicles on into old age, or whether there is a gradual withdrawal of the indwelling entity."
Esoteric Psychology II, 52-3.

Tabulation of the Five Points of Crisis

Age............... Vehicle Appropriated by Soul

4 - 7 .... physical vehicle appropriated by soul

14-18........... astral vehicle appropriated by soul

21-25............mind vehicle, responds to soul influences

35-42........... personality, responds as a unit to soul impulse

56-63........... possibility of continued soul relationship

If we compare this tabulation with the earlier one on the 3-2-1 sequence of the 7 year sub-cycles and the 21 year major cycles, we find that *crises generally occur when the 1st aspect conditions a 7 year sub-cycle.* This is a significant factor, and it is one that should help anyone meet the particular challenges of a particular life crisis. Thus, 14 to 18, 35 to 40, and somewhere between 56 and 63 we find "points of crisis" and we also find the 1st aspect of power-will having a stronger influence.

Third Aspect: *Activity.* New activity. Beginning a new cycle through doing. New experiences. New adventures. New experiments.

Second Aspect. *Consciousness*. Reflecting on what has been done. Psychologically processing. Less activity, more thought. Refinement of activity. The art of activity. A finer *feeling* developing around the doing. Intelligence maturing into *wisdom*.

First Aspect. *Will-Purpose.* The crisis of bringing the personal concern under the guidance of the group good. The individual enters into the community and is required to follow the will of the larger whole. The personality hears the call of the soul and is presented with a choice or fork in the road. The experienced soul is presented with the opportunity of further self-sacrifice and the unique challenges of additional soul work, or with gradual decline.

Marriage and America. Alice Bailey pressed a lot of activity, work, and new experiences into the 21-28 year cycle. She concluded this cycle with a very strong need to withdrawal from the stress and intensity of the work. From a more esoteric angle, it seems that her soul was beginning to call her to another type of work—one of deeper reflection, developing of the "heart of consciousness" that would lead to greater wisdom and eventually to new activity on a higher turn of the spiral.

Of the hundreds of soldiers she had met, there was one with whom she was "intrigued" and with whom she "fell in love." "He had a brilliant mind and was highly educated and got soundly converted through my ministrations." The system was set up in such a way that the women who were running the soldiers homes had such an aristocratic background that marriage between them and the soldiers was "simply out of the question. The well defined caste system in Great Britain aided this position. They must not and they could not and usually they would not fall in love with a man in the ranks."

Alice and her future husband, Walter Evans, got over this social hurdle in the following way. Alice went to Edinburgh to consult with the head of the Church of Scotland deaconesses. The head deaconess paid for all of Walter's expenses so that he could go to the United States, study theology, and become a clergyman in the Episcopal Church. This, among other things, gave him enough social standing for a marriage between Alice and Walter to take place.

They got married, settled in Cincinnati, Ohio, and Walter studied at a Theological Seminary. They had a baby girl, the married couple found out they really didn't know one another, and Alice was introduced to all sorts of mundane household tasks for the first time in her life. "Up to that time I had never washed a pocket handkerchief, boiled an egg or made a cup of tea, and was a completely incompetent young woman." After graduation, they moved to California, and Alice had two more children.

The marriage in the long run did not work out. One of the problems was Walter's temper. He was well liked as a clergyman, but they lived in "constant terror" that members of the congregation would discover just how bad his temper was. When Alice was pregnant with her third child, Walter, in a fit of temper, threw her down the stairs. They separated (Alice was 34) and eventually divorced. Alice then supported herself with the small amount of money that she received from family in England, from raising a couple of hundred chickens, and working in a sardine factory.

Summation of this Stage of Development. From a personality perspective and from a form perspective this stage, like the previous one, seemed to end in failure. She had no career, she had a failed marriage, and she barely was able to support three little girls by working in a sardine factory. From the point of view of soul and of consciousness, however, it was an entirely different matter.

Several significant consciousness factors were occurring at this time. She was moving *from theoretical idea to actual experience.* Her Gemini (Air) Sun Sign brought her in touch with a variety of ideas, but these ideas are often human intellectualisms that become quite another matter when the sentient-emotional factor is introduced and when practical expression is sought upon the physical plane. An idea is one thing, living it is quite another. Theory is greatly modified when it reaches the full flowering of artistic and practical expression. Alice had been well educated in theory but had been insulated and protected from life experience. This is, however, age appropriate for inexperienced youth. Youth should be full of idealistic notions, for in that way it is able to touch something of the spirit of the changing times. Having an intimate relationship with a loved one, a partner in marriage, and bringing one's own offspring into the world, is one of life's most fundamental and most precious experiences. There is often (but not always) a deep sense of incompleteness when this is not experienced.

Moving from *theory to practice* and from *idea to experience*, Alice greatly *modified her belief system.* Youth is so sure of the ideals and the belief system in which it was raised, yet a few years into the more independent life cycles can see the whole structure of ideas being cast aside. Only one idea or belief remained from all her Christian fundamentals, and that was a very deep feeling in the existence of Christ. "I knew enough of theology to have lost my faith in theological interpretations and I felt that there was nothing left for me except a vague belief in Christ." The Church presented platitudes and authority, but the Church lacked the living Christ. As she began to think for herself, almost all the theological interpretations were relinquished.

Theory and idea, theology and belief system, are all actually part of the form aspect. As such they serve a temporary purpose—they nurture the young mind, giving it something to hold on to. One must, however, as one matures, enter into life itself, into actuality, into spirit. One must come to know not theoretically, which is the words of others, but one must know with the life, soul, and spirit of one's own being. There is something basically frightening about this, because spirit is a far different teacher than form. Spirit tends to have ironical and paradoxical sport with anyone who thinks they know something in an absolute and conclusive manner.

Another most important thing that was happening to Alice at this time had to do with *connecting more deeply with humanity*. This is an extremely important factor, the significance of which can be easily overlooked. The problem, at least in part, had to do with the fact that Alice "had been brought up in a rigid caste system and nothing in my life had tended to throw me on equal terms with those not of my own caste. I had to discover that behind all the class distinctions of the Occident and the caste system of the Orient there is a great entity which we call Humanity."

The *noblesse oblige* of the aristocracy "can degenerate into a stupefying paternalism." Even though she had played checkers and talked about family life with hundreds of soldiers in Ireland and India, there was still a "veil" between her and them. It was obviously necessary for her conscious development to replace this separative veil with more inclusive attitudes—no easy matter. As a minister's wife, she found herself being "snooty" and feeling that "nobody was good enough for me to associate with." Time and time again, however, there were occasions when some ordinary person, or some person of questionable moral value, would reach out and extend a helping hand to Alice. This always touched her very deeply and helped considerably to tear down the separative veil. One day Alice suddenly "woke up to the fact that the world was full of lovely people and that I had been blind all my life. I had moved further into the house of humanity" (*Autobiography* 103,113).

Doing humble, ordinary tasks also helped to teach her the lesson that she was in fact not aloof, not superior, but a part of humanity. Working in a sardine factory, she found herself "down among the people; I was just nobody and I had always thought I was somebody. I was holding down the kind of job that anybody could hold down. It was unskilled labor." She met people who helped her in little ways. "I had never done them a kindness in my life, but they were just straight good to me and I have never forgotten it." This experience of doing the most humble, mundane and unglamorous tasks "down among the people" helped greatly to bring about Alice's "unalterable and unshakable faith in the beauty and divinity of humanity." This heartfelt connection with humanity is an extremely important matter, for it constitutes the foundation of brotherhood upon which all spiritual work rests. How are we able to go to our brother in humble service if we think that we are in some way special or superior to them?

From a personality perspective, which measures success in terms of money, status, social rank, career, and material possessions, there was failure. From a soul perspective there was sure and steady progress. The mind was expanding as the theoretical structures were being relinquished one by one. "The limbs", one might say, were becoming more experienced as handkerchiefs were washed, diapers were changed, sardines were packed, eggs were boiled, and as young people fell in and out of love. And the heart was truly awakening as she experienced and connected with the hidden soul of the people. This cycle, as the previous one, was preparing her for the great labor of her life.

Foster Bailey and the Theosophical Society. The turning point in her life came when Alice was 35 years old. The 35-42 year sub-cycle, we recall, is the 3rd stage and 1st ray aspect of the larger 21 year cycle (21-42). "Much observation," wrote Alice, "had indicated to me that *thirty-five is frequently a turning point in many lives. If a person is ever to find their life work, if they are ever in any particular life to attain a measure of surety and usefulness, it will be at that age*" (italics added).

Two English ladies of aristocratic background were hosting a Theosophical lecture in their home in Pacific Grove, California. Alice went to the meeting primarily to meet the English ladies. One thing, however, soon led to another. Alice became friends with the ladies, they gave her books to read, and Alice asked many questions. In order to do all the reading, Alice led a very disciplined life of getting up early, tending to the many needs of three daughters, and working in the sardine factory. She managed to read while ironing, peeling potatoes, sewing, and mending. As she read, studied, and thought, her mind woke up in a new way. "I regard the hours of study that I expended over it [Blavatsky's *The Secret Doctrine*] as some of the most valuable hours of my life, and the background and knowledge it gave me has made all the best of my work along occult lines possible."

Alice joined the Theosophical Lodge in Pacific Grove and began to teach and hold classes. Perhaps one of the most significant things she was learning was that "the esoteric presentation of truth in no way belittled Christ." Christ was the "Master of all Masters and the Teacher alike of both angels and of men. I found that the Masters of the Wisdom were His pupils and disciples, just as people like myself were pupils of some Master" (*Ibid* 139, 140).

Alice moved to a location near the Theosophical Society headquarters at Krotona. Soon she was asked to run the cafeteria. She was admitted into the Esoteric Section of the Society, and it was in their Shrine Room that she, much to her surprise, saw a picture of the Master K.H.—that man whom she had seen when she was fifteen years old.

Alice was granted a divorce from Walter Evans. She met Foster Bailey, who was very active in the Theosophical Society. Foster was made National Secretary of the Theosophical Society in 1919, and Alice became editor of the sectional magazine, *The Messenger*, and chairperson of the committee that was running Krotona. The deeper they got into the Theosophical Society, the more they realized that the Society, like any organized group, was not able to escape entirely from competitive personality attitudes.

In November of 1919 Alice made her first mental contact with the Tibetan. She heard a voice which said: "There are some books which it is desired should be written for the public. You can write them. Will you do so?" At first Alice rejected this startling proposal, for she had some negative opinions in regard to psychics. The "voice" explained that Alice had a gift for "the higher telepathy" and that she should take time for consideration. Eventually, she agreed to do it on a trial basis.

"In the work that I do," Alice clarified, "there is no negativity" as there is in automatic writing. "I assume an attitude of intense, positive attention. I remain in full control of all my senses of perception and there is nothing automatic in what I do. I simply listen and take down the words that I hear and register the thoughts which are dropped one by one into my brain.... I do not always understand what is given. I do not always agree. But I record it all honestly and then discover it does make sense and evokes intuitive response."

Move to New York. Starting the Arcane School. In 1920 Foster Bailey was offered a job in New York in connection with the Theosophical Society. Alice followed soon after, and it is in New York that they got married. A new cycle of living then began. Alice was 40 years old. She was approaching the 1st ray (power responsibility) cycle (42-63). The first sub-cycle (42-49) begins with the *activity of power*. This is a cycle when one's previous work comes to fruition, a time when one assumes a greater level of responsibility. This may mean a rise to a higher career position, or a time when one begins one's own enterprise.

Foster made an effort through the Committee of 1400 to "swing the Theosophical Society to its original principles.... It was not a fight of doctrines; it was a fight of principles and Foster spent much time organizing the fight." One of the first things that Alice did in New York was to start a Secret Doctrine class. They rented a room on Madison Avenue where they could "hold classes and see people by appointment. This Secret Doctrine class was started in 1921 and was exceedingly well-attended."

For Alice and Foster there was the "intense pressure of the work to be done for the people and for the Masters," as well as the duties of running a household and looking after the education of her children. There was also the growing publicity, which she found the most difficult. "I have never been a lover of publicity. I've never liked the inquisitiveness of the general public or their feeling that because you write books and lecture on the public platform that necessarily you have no private life. They seem to feel that everything you do is their business and that you must say the things they want said and portray yourself to them as they think you should be." (*Ibid* 182.)

Alice gave a great many lectures, mostly in New York, and often to as many as 800 people. The work steadily grew and grew. A typical year would see her, with the help of her close associates, write as many as 6,000 letters to students, associates, and people interested in the new esoteric teaching. (*Ibid* 176.)

The first book that the Tibetan (D.K.) wrote through Alice was *Initiation, Human and Solar* (1922). Other books steadily followed, including: *Letters on Occult Meditation* (1922), *Treatise on Cosmic Fire* (1925), *A Treatise on White Magic* (1934), and *Esoteric Psychology* (v.1, 1936). The first book that Alice herself wrote was *The Consciousness of the Atom* (1923).

As the work expanded and as Alice received letters from all over the world, she and Foster organized the Arcane School in April, 1923. With all the other responsibilities she had, she added this one, which was "extensive and all-engrossing." As the School grew, senior students called "secretaries" helped with the correspondence work. "The basic training given in the Arcane School, is that which has been given down the ages to disciples.... Those ready to be trained in the spiritual laws which govern all disciples are rare indeed, though we can look for an increasing number.... It had seemed to me and still does that there is room in the world today for hundreds of true esoteric schools and that they should be able to work in cooperation with each other, supplementing each other and helping each other." (*The Unfinished Autobiography* 194, 195.)

The Rays of Alice Bailey. After the war in Europe, Alice and Foster made trips to England in order to reopen the British headquarters. She was able to make the trip in 1947, 48, and 49. Her last trip in 1949 was the year she died.

"In retrospect," Foster writes, "it is clear that A.A.B.'s greatest service was subjective. Those who knew her best and those closer to her personal evolutionary status, knew this full well. Others, perforce, recognized her in terms of physical comings and goings, as a lecturer and by the evidence of the physical effects. This subjective potency is naturally true of all senior disciples, but we all could increase our constructive effect in the world if we used our auras more consciously and our wills more definitely to meet the subjective needs of those who touch our lives. I have watched Alice time and time again take in inimical forces threatening the Arcane School, sometimes quietly and serenely letting them exhaust themselves against her poise and integrity, and at other times consciously transmuting them. However, she was at times willing to let the group suffer, up to a limited point, for the sake of a brother disciple or because of potential discipleship quality. It takes much wise discrimination to build an esoteric group and a type of impersonality often misunderstood." (Mary Bailey, *A Learning Experience* 11.)

Foster mentioned that Alice had a 2nd ray soul and a 1st ray personality. (Foster himself had a 1st ray soul and a 2nd ray personality.) The 2nd ray of love-wisdom is known as the "teaching ray." To quote from the earlier passage:

> "This is called the ray of wisdom from its characteristic desire for pure knowledge and for absolute truth—cold and selfish, if without love, and inactive without power. When both power and love are present, then you have the ray of the Buddhas and of all great teachers of humanity,—those who, having attained wisdom for the sake of others, spend themselves in giving it forth."   *Esoteric Psychology* I

The second ray is the ray of "all great teachers of humanity." They "attain wisdom for the sake of others" and they "spend themselves in giving it forth." This seems to aptly describe Alice Bailey.

The teaching energy or quality was evident early in her life. Teaching requires study; one of the vices of the ray is "over-absorption in study." Vices, in this sense, have to do with "good" qualities, or virtues, carried too far, or developed in an exclusive, imbalanced way. If study becomes something that separates us from our fellowmen, then we have "over-absorption in study." Alice's 1st ray personality always seemed to balance her 2nd ray soul. Her 2nd ray soul was *not* without power, therefore she was never "inactive," even when somewhat withdrawn from public work. She led a very active life, as a young person involved with overseeing the activities of the soldiers homes in India, as an evangelist, as a minister's wife in California, as a single mother raising three daughters, as a student in the Theosophical Society, and as a teacher of humanity in her 30 years work with the Tibetan Master D.K. and in her founding of the Arcane School.

Initially, her teaching energy had a decided 6th ray quality about it. She was forever trying to "save souls." Her early lectures on Christianity to the soldiers, from the indications that she has given us, were somewhat zealous. She described herself as an "unthinking fundamentalist." An observer at that time, might have speculated that Alice had either a 6th ray personality or a 6th ray soul. It is possible that Alice had a 6th ray astral body, but, at her level of development, it is more probable that she had a 2nd ray astral body. One could also speculatively attribute Alice's strong and developed 6th ray qualities to previous incarnations. Part of her work, it seems to me, is related to the general work of substituting the 2nd ray energy for the 6th ray energy.

Study and teaching, albeit with 6th ray undertones, were evident in Alice's youth. As the crisis of the 35 to 42 year cycle occurred and as the soul appropriated the personality, offering it new possibilities, both the study and the teaching *broadened considerably* (with the help of the Gemini influence) and sounded a very inclusive, profoundly wise and loving note. One can see that at this time there was something like a dramatic change (although it occurred over several years) as the soul took greater control of the personality.

As the soul quality matured in Alice's life, we see a very high sounding of the 2nd ray energy. And here we truly have to refer to Foster's remarks above to get some little feeling for the radiance and resonance of this note that was so helpful to so many. As to the expansion of Alice's study, Foster wrote: "She made a deep study of the writings of Blavatsky and mastered the essentials of the teaching in the *Secret Doctrine*. Her classes on the *Secret Doctrine* and *Isis Unveiled* were gems and her understanding of these two books phenomenal. She browsed in the current theosophical writings, including not only Annie Besant but also Steiner, Tingly, Heindel, Bhagavan Das, and many others." (Mary Bailey, *A Learning Experience* 13.)

Alice's 1st ray personality was no small contributor to her service work. It has been said that a 2nd ray soul *likes* a 1st ray personality. The 2-1 (and also the 1-2) ray combination is an especially beneficial combination for several reasons. In the case of 2-1, we find a love-wisdom that does not become inactive, that does not loose itself in study, and that does not withdraw from the world in order to live in some sort of "ivory tower." Alice said that she had a problem with fear. This can be a difficulty with the 2nd ray person (either soul or personality). Alice also had a will to overcome her fears, and her 1st ray personality undoubtedly aided her in this effort.

The 1-2 combination is also an excellent balance. The 1st ray soul can be fearless, somewhat insensitive, even cruel and ruthless, in the effort to establish one's will and to manifest one's plan. The 2nd ray of love-wisdom can soften the hardness of the 1st ray. It can learn to manifest its will in a wiser, gentler way. This can prevent unnecessary harm and destruction.

Alice's rays and Foster's rays complemented one another. Alice wrote of Foster: "I could have done none of this without the support and wisdom of my husband. I shudder to think of the mistakes I would have made, the errors in judgment of which I would have been capable and the legal end of it in which I would have found myself embroiled. His clear legal mind, his impersonality and his constant failure to get excited when I thought he should, has saved me constantly from myself." (*Autobiography* 193.)

Strong 1st ray qualities are evidenced here: The law deals with questions of power and order. The 1st ray is often a strong asset in this field. Impersonality, emotional control ("constant failure to get excited"), and poise tend to come more easily when the 1st ray is present in the psychological make-up.

Earlier in this essay I mentioned that I thought Alice might have a 4th ray mind. Foster wrote: "Alice did not have a 5th ray mind, but she was keenly interested in scientific exploration and in the field of theoretical physics." Alice gave a series of lectures in New York on the subject of the atom, which was later published in book form: *The Consciousness of the Atom.* It is possible, however, that she had a 1st ray mind. When working in India, she had a great deal of responsibility, which included ever increasing administrative tasks. Her writing seems to indicate an ability to go directly to the salient point. Her writing could not be described as colorful, rather it is brief and to the point. Having a strong sense of humor, which she claims "has often saved my life," suggests the 4th ray. Her tendency to take action, to be at the head of some teaching group wherever she lived, to assume ever greater levels of responsibility, suggests the 1st ray. We are sure of the soul and personality rays. The rest is speculation.

Summary of Second Ray Indicators.
Just and loving understanding.
Dedication to loved ones.
Sympathy. Compassion.
Patience. Forgiveness.
Love of learning and study.
Desire to "save souls" or to bring a spiritual quality into people's lives.
Tendency to become over-absorbed in study.
Putting oneself in the second position.
Humility. Self-effacement.
Selfless service.
Looking deeply into the world of meaning.
Replacing condemnation with understanding and love.
Supportive of others.
Sensitive to the quality of soul.
Ability to work soul-to-soul.
Ability to teach and to have an effect upon consciousness.
Ability to identify and work with a World Teacher.
Desire for pure knowledge and for absolute truth.
The ray of the Buddhas and of all great teachers of humanity.
Attaining wisdom for the sake of others.
Inclusiveness.

A.P. Giannini - Third Ray Soul

On May 6, 1870, Amadeo Peter Giannini, son of Italian immigrants, was born in San Jose, California. His father, an independent farmer, had been killed by a disgruntled, transient farm worker when Amadeo was six years old. Amadeo was the oldest of three sons. His mother, Virginia, was pregnant with the third son, when the father was shot and killed. The mother continued to work the farm after the death of her husband. Amadeo grew up quickly, worked hard, and assumed some responsibility. In those days farm produce was shipped by steamer from San Jose, along the rocky shoals of the peninsula's coast, down the Bay to San Francisco's waterfront. Each trip was an adventure filled with risk. Amadeo accompanied his mother on those trips, bringing the produce to sell to wholesalers at the waterfront. Four years after the death of her husband, Virginia remarried.

Lorenzo Scatena, a native of Genoa, was a real father to Amadeo. He was gentle and soft-spoken. The boys warmed up to him quickly and called him "Pop" and "Boss." Lorenzo was unable to make a success of the farm and orchard. This was due in part to the five-year draught at the time. They sold the farm. Lorenzo, following Virginia's advice, got a job working for one of the wholesalers on the waterfront. The wholesale firms were the middlemen, buying from the farmers and selling to groceries, restaurants, street markets, and pushcart peddlers. The competition was brutal, but the opportunity for making money was better at the wholesale level than at the production level.

Lorenzo worked 16 hours a day, beginning at midnight when the produce arrived, until early in the afternoon when the produce had been sold. Lorenzo did well and received a raise from $100 to $250 a month. Virginia told him to ask for $300. His boss refused. Virginia told him to quit and open his own wholesale business. Following her good advice once again, he quit, opened his own business and earned $1500 in the first month. The area in which they settled was North Beach, home of about 10,000 Italian immigrants. The Italians worked as longshoremen, stonemasons, pushcart peddlers, grocers, laborers, fisherman, shoemakers, and shopkeepers. They lived in small fishing shacks and cottages along narrow cobblestone streets. With the view over the Bay, they referred to the area as *un piccolo canto della patria* (a small corner of the mother country).

Getting About His Father's Business. It did not take long before Amadeo became fascinated with his step-father's business—L. Scatena and Company. He did well at school (spelling, penmanship, math) but he was more interesting in what was going on down at the docks. When he was twelve, he would spend afternoons at his father's desk, writing promotional flyers with his neat handwriting. He offered special prices and quick service to those who dealt exclusively with L. Scatena and Company. This was a new and creative approach at the time, and many responded to it. Soon A.P. was showing up at the docks not only in the afternoon, but also at night when the produce arrived. In order to do this, he had to carry his shoes when tiptoeing out of the house. He did not want to wake or disturb his mother. She was concerned about a young boy spending hours in a rough atmosphere with grown men. Above all, she wanted him to get an education. But once he set his mind on something, he was the immovable Bull of Taurus.

At fifteen he wanted to leave school so that he could devote full-time to his stepfather's business. His mother refused to allow this. His will, however, as usual, managed to find a way. He agreed to go to a three-month accounting course at Herald's Business School in downtown San Francisco. After six weeks, he asked for an early examination, and passed it. Once again he could devote most of his time to the waterfront business.

The docks were crowded not only with Italians but also with Greeks, Jews, Portuguese, Armenians, and Syrians—all clamoring in various languages to buy and sell at the best possible prices. Later, in an interview, Giannini said that these "nightly transactions deepened his addiction to business. He enjoyed watching the rough give-and-take among rival merchants, which he later said taught him a good deal about the art of survival in the world of commerce." (*A.P. Giannini, Banker of America*, Felice Bonadio, p. 9.) He knew at an early age that business was his work and that there was no sense in "putting it off" by going to school.

When a steamer of produce came, the frenzied competition began. There was the need to know prices, to know how to negotiate, to know how to size-up a person and tell if they were bluffing or not, and there was the need to know what was fair and when to hold firm. There was the need to hold one's own among people who were fighting for their economic survival. Later in the day, when out selling to the merchants, a second round of bargaining went on. Giannini showed an "unrelenting drive" and "inexhaustible energy." "I don't think he ever lost an account or a contest of any kind. No one could bluff, intimidate, or out-general him. In those price wars he had an extraordinary faculty for gauging just how long the other fellow could stand the gaff. No such salesman was ever known on the waterfront." ("A Real Romance of San Francisco: The Story of the Bank of Italy and A.P. Giannini" by Reed Hayes, in the *San Francisco News*, March 6, 1928.)

Early in his life we find three qualities that emerge with force and clarity:

1) First of all, there is the *third ray of intelligent activity*—the ray of energy and the ray that loves the bustle and the complexity of business enterprise. There was evidence of "inexhaustible energy." He thrived in the atmosphere of "incessant activity."

2) Secondly, this energy seemed to be coming from a very deep level. There was a feeling of *destiny*. Giannini did not spend a long time searching for his work; he *knew* what it was at a very young age. He did not always know the specifics of the work, but he knew that it was definitely in the field of business.

3) A strong will, an "unrelenting drive", is also evidenced early in life. His teachers commented on his "stubborn independence." His strength of will enabled him to work side-by-side with adults. He enjoyed the "entrepreneurial warfare." He would defy even his mother, whom he loved above everything else, in order to reach a particular objective.

Giannini was avidly interested in all aspects of the business. His success was linked to the success of the farmers. He rode out on horseback, traveling to the outlying farmhouses, to ask questions about soil, weather conditions, and up-coming plans for the next growing season. He was also well known for his remarkable memory. He remembered names, dates, faces, and numbers for many years.

There is a story that is often told to illustrate Giannini's aggressiveness or will. One day he was out soliciting business from various farmers. Giannini noticed a competitor of his who was further down the road and approaching the same farmhouse that he was headed toward. He quickly got down off of his horse, took a short-cut by swimming across a river, scrambled up to the farmer's house, and managed to have the farmer signing the sales agreement by the time the other merchant pulled up with his team of horses.

As in other business practices, there were always some who had questionable integrity and others who were downright fraudulent. Some wholesalers exploited the growers by not honoring contracts and by not sending the farmer all the money their crops had earned. Giannini quickly established a reputation for integrity. Some of the other merchants would not tell the farmers what the current market value was for their crops, in the effort to get them at a cheaper price. Giannini, on the other hand, would bring lists from San Francisco, showing the farmer what the prices were. He never forgot the farmer. He remembered well from his own childhood the great hardships that farmers had. His effort was always to do business by knowing what the fair price was and negotiating in an open and honest way. And he always made sure the farmers got their money in cash and on time.

Giannini devoted all his time to business. Hanging out with the boys, or going to dances, he considered, for the most part, an utter waste of time. One Sunday morning during Mass he noticed a young woman singing in the choir. At that point he "made up his mind that he would never marry any other woman." (Bonadio, p.15.) Clorinda was engaged to another man at the time, and Giannini, as usual, was completely engrossed in business. Nevertheless, through his determination, it all came about. "My courting days were a strenuous affair. I used to dress up mighty fancy and have never dressed up as fancy since. Many a time I went home after leaving her after a dance and changed to go to work—in those days we wore black formal clothes, long tails and all. But she was engaged to a doctor who was in Europe, and the big job I had then was to get her away from him." (Bank of America Archives, Giannini interview with Bessie James, Sept. 22, 1947.) After about six months of courtship, he married her on September 12, 1892.

A Sojourn into Politics. Giannini's drive, ambition, hard work, excessive energy, and reputation as a man of integrity resulted in a steady growth of business. By 1899 (when Giannini was 29 years old) L. Scatena and Company was the largest wholesaler in produce on the San Francisco waterfront. Giannini was known as "king of the waterfront." (Hayes, *A Real Romance of San Francisco*.)

During a time when cities and counties grew up almost overnight, the growth was accompanied by much political corruption. San Francisco was no exception due primarily to the "boss rule" of Christopher Buckley. When the opportunity came to challenge Buckley's rule, James Phelan, the reform Democrat mayor of San Francisco, called on businessmen from all over the city to help him out. The main task was to win voter approval for a new city charter, a charter that would bring more centralized authority to the office of mayor. Giannini, having already proved himself in establishing a successful business, was looking for ways of expanding his horizons or undertaking new challenges. Also the October-November campaign months were the time of year when his own wholesale business was slowing down.

Giannini jumped to the task with energy and an innate know-how. He rented an office, calling it the headquarters of the reform Democrats of North Beach. He spent most of his time meeting with local officials and volunteers, organizing political rallies, touring the district, and delivering speeches in Italian. One party worker described Giannini as having a "psychological something. Whatever it was, he could look a man in the eye and convince him that almost anything was possible." Giannini put it in business terms: "We were selling good government. I wanted the candidates to meet the voters and to convince them the same way a businessman does to buy goods." (Hayes, *A Real Romance of San Francisco*.)

Once again his will and his bullish nature pushed through every obstacle. As Giannini's campaign for "good government" gained momentum, Buckley sent out well-publicized warnings that anyone showing up at the polls would be met with physical violence. Giannini responded by hiring seventy-five wagons that transported voters to the polls. He also recruited a number of men armed with rifles to guarantee that there would be no violence.

After the election, Giannini went around to the districts to pass out cigars and personally to thank the people. "When election time came around next time we were remembered. When you sell people keep them sold. That applies to politics as well as business." (Hayes, *A Real Romance of San Francisco.*

A New Adventure. At this point Giannini could easily have gone into politics and public service. His real love, or his real calling, however, was in the world of business. He sold his shares in the Scatena firm to some of the employees and ventured into real estate. He was in the process of learning this business when his father-in-law died. His in-laws so respected his business acumen that, instead of dividing the million-dollar inheritance amongst a widow and eleven children, the family turned the money over to Giannini's management for a period of ten years. This estate included shares in a small Italian North Beach bank. It was here that he found what could very well be called his soul's work.

The Columbia Savings and Loan was the first Italian bank in North Beach. It had been opened in 1893 by Agenzia Fugazi. Fugazi and the board of directors were very conservative; they lent large sums of money to prosperous residents. They were not interested in small accounts for the ordinary Italian. Fugazi and the board also lent money to business ventures, such as real estate development, in which they themselves had a financial interest. The "little guy" was almost completely neglected by most bankers at that time. The small loan was considered a nuisance. Vast sums of money were being poured into the railroad, mining, public works, and also overseas investments.

Giannini, as he gradually gained knowledge of the banking business, wanted to move in an entirely different direction. He wanted to provide more services to the thousands of Italian immigrants who were thrifty, hard working, and who wanted to get ahead in the world. Many of the new immigrants could not speak English. Many hid their money in their mattresses. Many, unable to get bank loans, paid high interest to loan sharks. Many were intimidated by the formal setting of the large bank buildings. Everything about the banks—the large marble columns, the brass railings, the cold formality—seemed to cater to the well-to-do and to shun the average, hard-working person. Giannini grew up in the midst of the struggling immigrant. As he himself rose on the social ladder, he never ceased to identify with the pulse of the people. He never distanced himself from their concerns and their hardships. Also, he was never intimidated by wealth, so he almost always was able to devise some plan to confront those who neglected the interests of the common man.

At every board meeting of the Columbia Savings and Loan, Giannini brought up the same issues. Three of the board members came around to his view. Fugazi held firm. Disagreements turned into heated arguments. After five minutes into a board meeting, there would be an all-out shouting match. Giannini presented the ultimatum: Adopt his proposals or he would resign. Fugazi refused to budge. Giannini left the office and went down to see the banker with whom he had done business for many years when building the Scatena wholesale produce firm. He walked into his office and told him that he was going to start a bank and wanted to know how to do it. That was the summer of 1904. A.P. was 34 years old.

The Bank of Italy. In August Giannini obtained a certificate of incorporation for the Bank of Italy. He was able to lease the building that Fugazi's savings and loan was in. He opened his own Bank of

Italy in the same building, and at the same time he tripled Fugazi's rent. Fugazi was furious. Fugazi moved out and opened his bank across the street. Giannini hired Fugazi's best cashier, offering him twice the salary. The cashier was a man who treated the wealthy and the man in overalls with equal respect. In addition, all the women were crazy about him. Giannini's bank was modest. There were three wooden desks and a single teller's window. There were no private offices and no armed guards. Everything was out in the open, including the safe. Giannini was about to make a most significant contribution to the way banking was done in California and in the United States.

Friends and relatives helped to get the word out about the new bank. Giannini poured a tremendous amount of energy into the new enterprise, walking the docks after hours, bringing in old friends from the wholesale business, explaining the advantages of interest-bearing savings deposits, getting the Italian workers to bring in the cash stashed in jars, cans, and mattresses. "Giannini's pursuit of depositors was relentless. He was by temperament and experience a consummate salesman, driven nearly as much by intense personal satisfaction in his ability to attract new business as by his excitement in the possibilities of the bank itself." (Bonadio, *A. P. Giannini*, p. 30.) Most of the money he loaned went to individual real estate loans. He also loaned money without collateral ("character loans") if he believed the person to be trustworthy and a good risk. He also sought and obtained a large number of small stockholders who believed in him and could be counted on to be loyal to the Bank of Italy. He wanted long-term stockholders who understood what he was trying to do for the people.

The San Francisco Earthquake of April 18, 1906 could have brought ruin to everything that he had been building. He walked seventeen miles through rubble to get to the bank. Fewer than 300 of North Beach's 4000 homes were left standing. The bank had survived, and a couple of employees had protected it from looters. Giannini's bank was the first one to open for business, offering loans to rebuild San Francisco. His strength and confidence and energy inspired many to look beyond the disaster and start their lives over again. The newspaper *L'Italia* called Giannini North Beach's "most progressive businessman, bringing hope and confidence to so many people who had lost their homes in the fire."

Branch Banking. Giannini then sought to extend banking for the people through branch banking. His dream was to have a nation wide network of banks, stretching all the way to New York. Gradually and steadily, Giannini acquired other banks. His first expansion occurred primarily in northern California. Often he acquired banks that were ready to go under due to banking practices that had become illegal. Bankers would often loan money to their friends and relatives. These loans would be highly speculative—often real estate ventures—and not backed up with any collateral.

Giannini went into other communities, advertising: On parle français; Tobopn Ce Cphckkn, Si parla italiano, Man spricht Deutsch, Se habla español, Ome Laoymai Emhnika—as he branched out to more and more of the immigrants and to people of the working class. Another population that he thought was sorely neglected by most banks was the small farmer. In some areas he had his banks stay open every night until 8:00 PM and also on the weekends in order to accommodate the farmers. "The little fellow is the best customer that a bank can have," Giannini told the *San Francisco Bulletin*. "He starts with you and he stays with you to the end; whereas the big fellow is only with you so long as he can get something out of you, and when he cannot, he is not for you anymore."

By 1919 (ten years after opening up his first branch bank) Giannini's Bank of Italy had 24 branches with total resources climbing from $22 million to $100 million. The Bank of Italy was the fourth largest financial institution in the state and the first statewide branch banking system anywhere in the country.

The Opposition. William D. Stephens, elected Governor of California 1917, had the habit of taking out loans from various banks and then never repaying them. Banks had the habit of simply writing the loans off, in order to avoid negative publicity and embarrassment to the governor (and earlier to the mayor of Los Angeles and Republican congressman, when he held those positions). When Giannini took over the Park Bank in Los Angeles in 1913, he discovered an overdue loan to Stephens. Stephens at that time was a U.S. congressman, living in Washington DC. Giannini refused to write off the loan. He sent a man to Washington in pursuit of Stephens, and eventually Stephens paid.

When Stephens became governor, he placed Charles Stern in the position of superintendent of banking. Stern did whatever he could to prevent Giannini from expanding any further. Bank examiners claimed that Bank of Italy's bookkeeping was sloppy, that the earnings were inflated, and that the solvency of the institution was questionable. Stern referred to the Bank of Italy as a "house of cards." Giannini responded by joining the newly created Federal Reserve System and by opening up federal banks in addition to his state banks. His reputation grew to the point that he was not only considered a financial wizard but a person who had great skill in outmaneuvering his opposition as well.

He then opened a bank in New York, a small Brooklyn bank, serving predominantly working class Jews and Italians. This was followed by opening a bank in Naples, Italy. A bank in Naples was ready to fold, due to its tone of greed and incompetence. Giannini bought the bank, reorganized it, and instituted more efficient management policies.

The Social Services of the Italian Department. In California Giannini had set up what he called the "Italian Department" in his banks. This department originated in San Francisco but gradually spread to his other banks. The Italian Department had "missionaries" who, with almost religious zeal and dedication, canvassed neighborhoods for every possible Italian depositor they could uncover. Giannini's own energetic work habits ignited others with the same kind of energy and fervor. They kept 3 x 5 cards on many depositors, indicating whether or not they were good credit risks. Beyond the business of banking itself, however, this department and these "missionaries" did a lot more. They encouraged all Italians to become American citizens. They arranged for them to attend evening classes in local branch offices and they helped them with their naturalization papers. They helped them to find jobs. They translated official papers from English into Italian. They paid grocery bills for those who were unable to do so. They were even called upon from time to time to settle domestic disputes. "Before long the Bank of Italy became almost as well known among California Italians for its social as for its financial services." (Bonadio, *A.P. Giannini*, p. 77.)

Giannini also emphasized special services to children and women. Children could open an account with one penny. He felt that if a child opens an account with the Bank of Italy, he would stay with the bank for the rest of his life. He worked with the schools in developing the children's saving program, which expanded to 160 school in 41 towns. Most of Giannini's banks had a special teller's window for women in order to help them feel comfortable and to advise them on money matters. In 1921 he opened up a Woman's Bank that was staffed only by women. It was equipped with attractive furnishings and conference rooms. It offered free evening classes on business and financial matters.

Quoting from an article in the May 24th, 1924, *San Francisco Examiner*: "You would never guess which of all the banking institutions in America has the largest number of depositors. This bank is not located in New York or Chicago or Philadelphia or St. Louis or Detroit. The institution enjoying this unique distinction is the Bank of Italy with headquarters in San Francisco. This phenomenal achievement prompted me to delve into how it was done. The answer might be summed up thus: A.P. Giannini."

Continuing Expansion and Much Opposition. The larger the Bank of Italy became, the more formidable grew the opposition. The California League of Independent Bankers was formed in order to prevent the spread of Giannini's branch banking. They organized intense lobbying efforts in the Sacramento legislature to restrict additional branches. Fundamentalist ministers used their weekly radio sermons to "unleash a steady flow of inflammatory statements" against the Roman Catholic Italians. This propagandizing effort was secretly funded by the League of Independent Bankers. (Bonadio, p. 86.)

Giannini found new ways of outmaneuvering his opposition. He established a new state bank—Liberty Bank—with a branch system of its own. The board of the new bank was predominantly non-Italians. Giannini purchased two large banks in Los Angeles, one of which was the Bank of America—the name that would eventually be the one adopted when the various units were consolidated into one giant corporation. Commercial National was another one of his subdivisions.

Giannini helped Charles C. Young get the Republican Party nomination for governor in 1926. This was a critical move. Young defeated the Democrat, became governor, and appointed a new superintendent of banking. Under the new superintendent, the merger of the Bank of Italy and the Liberty Bank of America was allowed to go forward.

Financing the Movie Industry. When the movie industry was just beginning, Wall Street considered it a passing fad that was doomed to oblivion. Many movie producers had to deal with loan sharks in order to fund some of the early films or "flicks", as they were called. Giannini's brother, Attilio "Doc" Giannini, was in charge of their Brooklyn bank. He saw value in the new industry and considered it as sound an investment as barley, cotton, or wheat.

A.P. Giannini was also enthusiastic about the new industry, and, when its major center of production moved from New York to Hollywood, he was able to play a crucial and influential role. He brought producers, directors and well-known actors into the banking business as board members. This included such well-known movie producers as Cecil B. DeMille, Howard Hughes, Sol Lesser, Jack Warner, and Darryl Zanuck. "When Jack Warner's drinking and gambling problems threatened to ruin his career as head of one of Hollywood's largest studios, it was Attilio to whom Warner's wife turned for assistance. 'The Doc's been more than a banker to Hollywood,' said one movie writer. 'Everyone in Hollywood has cried on his shoulders.'" (Bonadio, p. 114.)

Refusing to Become a Millionaire. As the work to create a national network of banks got underway, and as large blocks of Bancitaly stock were being bought (1924), the corporation's annual profits increased dramatically. The *San Francisco Examiner* reported: "From all indications, Giannini is just getting a good start. Nothing succeeds like success. Hitch your wagon to a star."

In 1924 Giannini stepped down from being Bank of Italy's president. He did not accept any further salary. He was still president of Bancitaly but refused any compensation beyond business expenses and taxes. The directors of Bancitaly, in lieu of salary, voted to pay him five percent of the corporation's net profits, with a minimum of $100,000 a year. This would easily put him over the million-dollar figure. Giannini was annoyed by this, saying that he already had a half a million, and that is all anyone needs. He recommended that the money be donated to philanthropy. He wanted to see a research institute started that would promote the development of agriculture in California. The directors acquiesced and had the money donated to the University of California for the creation of a school of agriculture.

The *San Francisco News* reported: "By forming the foundation and putting his personal wealth to the use of California, Giannini strips himself of the title of millionaire.... The product of his financial genius has been dedicated to the helping of all Californians."

Giannini told a *San Francisco Examiner* reporter (January 24, 1928): "I don't want any more money. If I had all the millions in the world, I couldn't live better than I do. I enjoy work. What is called high society doesn't mean anything to me. I've always said I would never be a millionaire. Maybe this will convince some of the skeptics that I mean what I say."

Again, on May 6, 1945 when he resigned as Bank of America's chairman of the board (a day before his 75th birthday), he donated $500,000 to establish a Giannini Foundation. This Foundation would provide scholarships to Bank of America employees, and it would also be used to finance scientific research in the field of medicine. He told the *San Francisco News* that once again he felt that he was "in danger of getting into the millionaire class.... I've always vowed I'd never become a millionaire."

Ameritalia. In 1928 Giannini formed a $25 million corporation called Ameritalia. The purpose of this American-Italian corporation was to finance the rehabilitation of ailing Italian industries.

The great stock market crash on "Black Thursday", October 29, 1929 brought everything to a standstill. The economic house of cards came tumbling down. Needless to say, every aspect of human life was deeply affected by the market crash. Giannini's first response was to go ahead with business as usual, which meant continued expansion of his branch banking.

On the Verge of Losing Control. The name of Giannini's corporation that promoted nation wide branch banking at the time was Transamerica. Giannini wanted to go into semi-retirement at this point. He offered overall command of the corporation to Elisha Walker and Jean Monnet. Giannini's brother, Attilio, was more sensitive to the manipulations of some of the New York bankers. Attilio did not trust Walker and Monnet. In less than a year they were able to release false information and rumor to the press. Transamerica stock reached an all time low—a price which was actually far below its true market value. Giannini, who was trying to recuperate in European health resorts, finally caught on to Walker's intention of gaining complete control of the organization. According to Lawrence Mario Giannini (A.P.'s son), A.P. said: "This is all part of their plan to get price down and buy in so as to wrest control from the old crowd.... This sort of stuff will mean that the old crowd will stampede out and the new crowd will come into control"—the "old crowd" being the predominantly Italian stockholders who believed in Giannini's service oriented vision (a crowd that was in it from the beginning with the intention of staying in it for the long haul), and the "new crowd" being predominantly a New York crowd of financial wizards who had no apparent vision beyond their own personal power and wealth.

Preparing for the coming battle for control of the corporation, A.P. Giannini cabled his son Lawrence Mario with the brief message: "Don't let them ruffle you or get your goat. Maintain dignity keep cool and keep yourself in shape. Above all remember ours was institution with soul working solely interest stockholders. Its right and principle we are battling for and there's no compromise with right or principle regardless consequences. No sir, never my boy." (July 6th, 1931, AP. Giannini to L.M.G. Bank of America Archives.)

Giannini appealed to the thousands of stockholders who were from the old, original group. He called them "dissident stockholders" and created an organization (Associated Transamerica Stockholders) that would challenge Walker at the annual board meeting in Wilmington, Delaware (Feb. 12, 1932). "He regarded as unthinkable the possibility that a bank that he had founded to serve the financial interests of the people of California would 'fall into the hands of a small group of unscrupulous Wall Street bankers.'" (Bonadio, p.185.)

Giannini went up and down California, drawing huge crowds of stockholders and interested people. He informed them of the battle for the control of Transamerica and collected thousands of anti-Walker proxies.

Walker and Monnet, on the other hand, were focusing their attention on a small group of stockholders who held large blocks of stock. They were insisting that all bank employees prove their loyalty to management by submitting a signed Walker proxy. Employees who refused to sign were terminated. Giannini was once again able to outmaneuver them on the employee issue. He got the word to employees inside the bank to go ahead and sign the Walker proxies but to also sign a Giannini proxy a day or two later. The one with the more recent date would be the one counted in Wilmington.

This battle is said to be one of the most dramatic and bitter proxy battles in American financial history. Giannini had fears that Walker's men would try to steal the Giannini proxies en route to Delaware. Giannini had the proxies sealed in heavy wooden boxes and sent in a private railway car cross-country accompanied by armed guards.

The proxies were counted February 15, 1932. Giannini won an overwhelming victory. The *San Francisco Chronicle* called it "the greatest Wall Street defeat of all times." The *New York Times* wrote: "There was general admiration in the street [if not on Wall Street] for the fashion in which, at the age of sixty-one, Giannini had returned from retirement to wrest control of the huge holding corporation which he originally created from the men to whom he relinquished the management two years ago." (February 16, 1932.)

Confidence Building during the Depression. The goal was to restore confidence in the banks and to increase bank deposits on a large scale. Giannini chose to accomplish this through a radio campaign. He called it the "Back to Good Times" campaign. His weekly radio broadcast consisted of fifteen minutes of the finest music available, followed by fifteen minutes of an inspirational talk by various guest speakers (civic, political, and cultural leaders). These talks were reprinted for distribution in schools, libraries, civic organizations, and branch banks. Giannini was approached at this time to take the initiative in the building of the Golden Gate Bridge by buying part of the bonds. The bank bought the first $6 million and later purchased the remaining $323 million in bonds. It paid off both financially and in terms of public relations. At the end of the year of confidence campaigning, deposits had increased by $100 million dollars.

The Rays of A.P. Giannini. As an educated guess, we would suggest the following ray equipment for A.P. Giannini:

        Soul III
        Personality 1
           mental......... 4
           emotional.....6
           physical....... 3

The Third Ray of Intelligent Activity. Giannini's sense of destiny, his deep sense of purpose, was in the field of business. He responded to the activity of business at an early age (wholesale produce). At 12 years of age he was sitting at his father's desk; at 15 he was holding his own in the midst of aggressive and competitive adults. After a short interim in real estate, he devoted the major portion of his life to the business of banking. Several qualitative factors point strongly to the presence of the third ray of intelligent activity:

The sheer Amount of Energetic, Busy Activity. His day began at five in the morning and often ended at ten at night. When he went out into the countryside on a Sunday afternoon drive, he invariably included in this family outing the business activity of calling upon a number of farmers in order to solicit more business for the bank. At an early age, Giannini loved the "incessant activity and entrepreneurial warfare." He seemed to have "inexhaustible energy." (Hayes, *Real Romance of San Francisco*.)

Mental Activity. The presence of the third ray energy is often evidenced not only in an inordinate amount of physical activity (although this is not always the case), but also in intellectual and verbal activity. Talking fast and talking a lot is often an indication of the presence of the 3rd ray. When the 2nd ray is present, however, there is a tendency to slow everything down. Wisdom is slow, intellect is quick. Giannini was "gifted with a remarkable memory...he could digest huge amounts of technical and financial information at breakneck speed." (Bonadio, xxi.)

Mathematics. "Between the third and the fifth rays there is a close relationship. In the search after knowledge, for example, the most laborious and minute study of detail is the path that will be followed, whether in philosophy, the higher mathematics or in the pursuit of practical science." (Discussion of the third ray in *Esoteric Psychology*, v.1., 212.) The third ray, the fifth ray and also the fourth ray are associated with mathematics. Giannini had a natural gift in mathematics. "He could figure swiftly and keep figures and percentages in his recollection, even though a balanced personal checkbook was beyond him. He could remember the balance sheet figures of scores of banks from year to year, even though he never knew how much money was in his bank account." (Fred Yeates, *The Gentle Giant*, San Francisco.) Balancing his own checkbook was probably not "beyond him." It was more likely something that did not interest him, something that he did not have to bother with, and something with which he did not have to waste time. He was often irritated when others spent time on what he considered were irrelevant or trivial matters. When it came to giving a customer service, however, there was nothing that was too trivial or unimportant.

Competition. Giannini thrived in a competitive atmosphere. The quality of competition, it seems to me, can be ascribed to the third ray more than to any other ray. The presence of the first ray personality brought an additional fierceness, a fiery quality, to the more *clever* quality of competition. His first business experience on the docks was one of "brutal competition"—an atmosphere in which he thrived and excelled.

Manipulation. Skill with Words. The third ray is the master manipulator. The first ray works through power, force, and control. The second ray works through an "embrace," through the heart, through an appeal to what is right and just, through the commonly held feeling. The third ray works through manipulation—via the hand, the word, or the thought-form. One of the first skills that Giannini acquired when working on the docks was the "knack of sizing up men." He mentions this, in retrospect, as one of the most important things he learned during his first experience in business. This knowledge is essential for both the first ray and the third ray. The first ray is skilled at "handling men and measures"; the third ray is good at manipulating others. (It should be remembered that manipulation, in itself, is neither good nor bad—it all depends on the intent and, ultimately, the ability to recognize soul purpose and to cooperate with it.) It was said that he had "remarkable powers of persuasion," which indicates, in part, a special skill with words (3rd ray) and a forceful nature (1st ray). When Giannini sought to extend his banking enterprise into Los Angeles, he met formidable opposition. His achievement there was characterized as "stunning.... He moved with a combination of brilliantly calculated maneuvers and astonishing speed that had been overwhelming, and emerged with a banking system in Los Angeles larger and more powerful than any possessed by the city's well-established financial institutions" (my italics, Bonadio, p. 96). One of the methods of third ray manipulation has to do with doing complex things that are intelligent and doing them very quickly. By the time others figure out what has happened, it is usually too late. The third ray prefers out-maneuvering rather than confronting. (With a first ray personality, however, Giannini also used a style of direct confrontation.)

Economics, Finance. All the ray types can be found in the field of finance and economics, but the third ray plays a special and prominent role in this field. There are, we can recall from our esoteric studies, three aspects of divinity, manifesting through the "three great departments," each of which is responsible for certain evolutionary themes. One is known as the Department of the Manu. This has to do with "world government." The second is known as the Department of the Christ, which has to do with "world religions." The third is known as the Department of the Lord of Civilization, and has to do with "the social and financial order." (*Telepathy and the Etheric Vehicle* 186. See also *Initiation Human and Solar* and *Treatise on Cosmic Fire*.) These three major departments have a ray correspondence, the third department coming under the energy of the third ray. In the case of Giannini we see that "business consumed nearly the whole of his life." (Bonadio, p. 11.) "He was by temperament and experience a consummate salesman." (Bonadio, p. 30.) In the following characterization we see a three-one ray combination: "It was now that Giannini's reputation for cunning and financial legerdemain began to spread across the state. To his well-known image as a financial 'wizard' was added the reputation of a fiercely determined individual who would allow nothing or no one to stand in his way." (Bonadio, p. 70.)

Third Ray "Favored" Over First Ray in terms of Soul Energy. First of all, it seems evident that Giannini was of such a development that his soul was externalizing in a prominent-dynamic way through the personality Giannini. It seems also that it was a third ray soul working though a first ray personality and not the other way around. This we surmise for the following reasons:

Giannini's first sojourn or brush with politics came about when he was called upon to assist San Francisco's mayor, James Phelan, in Phelan's effort to bring about "good government." The work had to do with disempowering the corrupt "boss rule" of Christopher Buckley. Giannini described this interlude in the following way: "I got into politics because of a desire to help Phelan. It was a diversion. I had lots of energy and this gave me an outlet." (Hayes, *A Real Romance of San Francisco*.) He was between business activities at the time and was not sure of the next step ahead. In a deep way, he seemed to favor the *energy and activity* of business over the *power* of government. Politics was a "diversion" and clearly not his soul's work. He refereed to his activity in politics as "selling" good government. *This does not mean that there are no first ray souls in business and that there are no third ray souls in politics*. This is a point that needs to be emphasized. It Giannini's case, however, it does seem that we have the archetypal rule of a third ray soul in the area of business and finance.

Later he was accused by a democratic senator from Alabama as being a dominant figure in California politics. Occasionally Giannini would support a candidate, including Franklin Roosevelt in his first two terms. His supporting of a candidate generally related to how he was being treated by a state banking superintendent or by a federal secretary of the treasury. When he was accused of going into politics, Giannini's response was: "That's a lie. I am not in politics, never have been and don't expect to be. Whoever says I am is a liar." (*Santa Rosa Republican*, February 17, 1927.)

Interestingly, Giannini had a "fear of solitude." This is very unlike the first ray but possible with the communicating and talkative third ray. When Giannini's wife died, he was "overcome with loneliness." He wanted to sell his house and move into an apartment in downtown San Francisco. Eventually, however, he "persuaded his daughter and son-in-law to move in with him." (Bonadio, p. 275.) Had he had a first ray soul, the loneliness and solitude would not likely have been a problem. (This is simply one of several factors that seem to tip the scales in favor of the third ray as being the soul ray.)

The Quality of Soul. We continue to use the word "soul" not in a mystical way but in its technical sense. In differentiating between soul and personality there appears to be something that could be called a *reversal* of energy flow. Generally speaking, the effort-activity of personality is acquisitive. The effort is to get, to acquire, to accumulate. The soul, being group conscious, being conscious of the good of the whole, seeing the end from the beginning, not mistaking the part for the whole, shifts the getting and the acquiring into a giving and a serving. In the case of Giannini we see the soul attitude coming strongly into play, as indicated by the following factors:

Disregard for Wealth. A.P. Giannini had the opportunity to make millions. He never tried to accumulate wealth in any form. He purchased a home when working on the waterfront in his father's wholesale produce business and he remained in the same home to the end of his life. He did not accumulate other properties. He did not collect art. He did not have an extensive wardrobe. He had only four suits, none of which were tailor-made. When he died at the age of 79 (in 1949), he left an estate of approximately $500,000, which was *less than his net worth at the time he went into the banking business.*

A Man of Principle. Being a person of principle is a much rarer phenomenon than one is inclined to believe. People easily and often quote principles, but they seldom live by them. The principle changes for them, when the circumstances change, which is to say that they give lip service to whatever principle is convenient for them at the time. Most people live for self, whereas principle transcends self. Being honest, being a man of integrity, sharing wealth, not taking financial advantage of one's financial position, were some of the principles that Giannini followed. "His personal honesty was beyond question. He refused to accept gifts from admirers of Bank of America clients. When Louis B. Mayer, head of Metro-Goldwyn-Mayer, sent Giannini's daughter a lifetime gold pass to the studio productions, Giannini insisted she send it back. If, as occasionally happened, one of his executives used his financial transactions with a client to obtain gifts or favors, Giannini was quick to take action, regardless of how high the executive's position in the organization." (Bonadio, p. xx.)

As quoted earlier, in one of the battles he had with some New York bankers, Giannini cabled his son Mario: "Don't let them ruffle you or get your goat. Maintain dignity keep cool and keep yourself in shape. Above all remember ours was institution with soul working solely interest stockholders. Its right and principle we are battling for and there's no compromise with right or principle regardless of consequences. No sir, never my boy." These were ideas he *lived* but rarely articulated: He built an institution with *soul*, and he battled for *right and principle*. Self-centeredness and egotism hide behind and twist the recognizable principles of the culture. Giannini, on the other hand, clearly demonstrates the soul quality of embodying true principle, regardless of what effect it might have had upon the personal self. Needless to say, this was very upsetting to those who were not living such principles.

Deep Identification with Struggling People and the Family of Humanity. When Giannini was in the wholesale produce business, he called upon farmers in order to establish a business relationship. He could identify with the farmer probably because he remembered his own childhood and the struggle that his mother had trying to run a farm and to raise three boys. He was the oldest boy and a child of innate responsibility. He must have felt the difficulties of the struggling immigrant farmer very deeply. His whole life was dedicated to easing their burden. The farmer was easily exploited. Many of the wholesalers kept the farmer in the dark as to what the true market price of the produce was. Many wholesalers never paid the farmer for the produce they marketed. Giannini quickly established a reputation with the farmers as being a man of *honesty and integrity*. He kept the farmers informed of the fair market price. He always saw to it that the farmer got his money in cash and on time. In reviewing the life of Giannini, it seems that business for him was never the *happiness* of making money and of being successful, rather it was the *joy* of doing things the *right, fair, and honest way*, where everyone stood to benefit, particularly the little guy—the have-nots or the have-littles.

When Giannini died, letters of sympathy poured in from around the country. A typical letter: "I write so poorly but it is not often that a great man passes away and still rarer when it is someone like A.P. He is the first big businessman for who many people will grieve or shed any tears. While I have the greatest respect for Morgan, Vanderbilt, Rockefeller and our authentic big shots, A.P. was the only one who had any sincere interest in the average American or any love for the common people." (Quoted in *A.P. Giannini*, by Felice Bonadio.)

First Ray of Power and Will—the Personality Ray. That Giannini was a man of will, there is no question. Strength of will was one of the "faces," or "personas" that Giannini wore. This was a very visible side of him. We include below some first ray indicators:

Will and Determination. He demanded total loyalty from those who worked for him. He required that they adhere to the same ethical standards that motivated him. This first ray power-authority quality had some sixth ray overtones.

"Giannini thrived on incessant controversy and enjoyed nothing so much as a good fight. The more powerful and well-connected the opposition, the better he liked it. He could assault those whom he viewed as his enemies in language so violent as to frighten them into hiring bodyguards... In the face of threats, real or imaginary, he could not be satisfied with anything less than total victory." (Bonadio, p. xxi.) This first ray quality of sheer will and determination, and love for battle, seems to be mixed here with something of the fourth ray. The one-four combination finds exhilaration in conflict and battle. The rays of Italy are sixth ray soul and fourth ray personality. Both these rays—one of spiritual mission and the other of harmony, art, and conflict—seem to be present in Giannini. He was Italian and he totally identified with the Italian people. He resonated with them in a deep way. Many people are "connected" with the sixth ray of loyalty and devotion through the astral-emotional body and also through the development of this ray quality during many previous incarnations. All of us, in some way or another, developed the sixth ray in the Piscean Age. Giannini, it seems to me, includes a sixth ray devotional fervor as a contributing quality, but not as the main quality of his life. The same could be said of the fourth ray.

The Leader, the First, Rising to the Top, Ambition, Ruthlessness. There was often a tough and brutal quality to the business enterprises in which he worked, beginning on the docks and ending with the bank. The fourth ray loves a battle, but the first ray can stand the heat and the stress far more than the softer fourth ray. The fourth ray enters the battle sporadically; the first ray endures the battle on a daily basis.

As a student he had *the will and determination to rise to the top* of his class. He always wanted to be the leader. His motto was "be first in everything." Here too we find a strong indication of the first ray playing a dominant role. He was "ambitious" and he had an "unrelenting drive." "I decided what I wanted and then went after it hammer and tongs."

When he regained control of the bank after the bitter struggle with Walker and Monet, he proceeded ruthlessly to purge the bank, including all its branches, of those who were disloyal to him, those who had served Walker in his network of spies. Some described this as a "penchant for vendetta." In some cases his will went to considerable lengths in order to get even. One of his disloyal senior executives, Mount, submitted his resignation and went to another bank. Giannini bought the bank at considerable expense, so that he could fire him. Mount finally left the state of California altogether, telling a *Time* correspondent, "I'm not going to have Giannini gunning for me for the rest of my life."

Fourth Ray Mind. Often the ray of the mind is the easiest one to determine. This is not true in the case of A.P. Giannini. It is clear that he did not have a scientific fifth ray mind. He did not have the detached, observing quality of the fifth ray. He was primarily a man of action. Did he have a first ray administrative mind? Giannini seemed to be giving power away to others. He did not keep a tight control in a personal way of the organization. He set the standard, he set the keynote, he articulated the vision, and then, within certain guidelines and principles, he let others have a lot of authority in the implementation of the guidelines. He seemed to understand power, but he did not seem *to think* in a conservative way along power lines. There are some factors that seem to suggest a fourth ray mind.

Innovative, Creative. Giannini was characterized as an "innovative outsider in an industry not generally known for innovation." The quality of doing things in a new and different way, the quality of being creative in the field of business was present from the very beginning. He changed the way the wholesale produce business was done down on the San Francisco docks. He changed the way banking was done in the United States. It was also said that he had an intuitive sense about people. His management style was not that of "committees, organizational flow charts, and the mechanisms of corporate management." His style had to do more with enunciating clearly certain values and principles, giving others a lot of responsibility, and then working on a person-to-person basis. This human approach, this lack of structure or lack of excessive organization, suggests a fourth ray thinker. After his death, the L.A. Times wrote: "His unorthodox methods have been criticized, but also much copied. That he has changed banking in this state, if not in the nation, can never be denied."

Problem with Anger. He could use aggressive language at times. People became "the target of his fierce rage," when they got in the way of his decided course of action. The fourth ray mind tends to express emotion more readily than the first ray mind. The first ray mind likes to control emotion. He could inform people of their deficiencies in "devastatingly brutal language."

Warm, Charming and Self-Effacing. Giannini could get angry and he could apply a lot of pressure to people at times, but one could not call him a hard, bitter, stern, or cruel man. On the contrary, he could be very charming, humble, and self-effacing. The first ray type of mind tends more towards being in the subtle power position (through silence, or through having the superior point of view, or through perfect poise), whereas the fourth ray thinker tends more readily to gravitate towards the humble, the serving, the self-effacing position.

Enjoying the Battle, the Conflict. In retrospect Giannini gave the following reasons for leaving the wholesale produce business: "Our firm had absorbed or driven out of business all of the big commission houses. I suppose that's why I quit the produce business. There wasn't anyone around to fight me anymore." After driving out the competition, most businessmen would stay with the business to profit from the "monopoly" they had built. Giannini, on the other hand, seemed to enjoy the battle, the struggle, and the fight more than the goal itself. Here we seem to have the fourth ray working together with the first ray. He was very good at the struggle or the conflict. He never shied away from a fight, on the contrary, he went looking for battles. This is a very strong indicator of the fourth ray of harmony through conflict. The first ray likes power, but that does not mean that it goes out looking for battles. Each first ray type has its own particular style, depending on the other ray influences. The first ray, along with the fourth ray, likes the battle, the conflict. It thrives during the heat of conflict.

A Sense of the Dramatic. When it comes to power some people work behind the scenes, some manipulatively, some by stone-walling the opposition, some through developing a support network, some by sheer force of will, some through a lot of activity, some through developing power partnerships, etc. One of Giannini's techniques was to create dramatic events. He tended not to work quietly; he was visible and he was often dramatic. This too suggests the presence of the fourth ray.

The Psychological Factor—Image, Inspiration, Vision, Imagination. The dramatic event is designed to change consciousness. Consciousness is more the language of the 2-4-6 line of ray energies than the action oriented and form oriented 1-3-7 line. Giannini, unlike many business people at that time, seemed to have a good understanding of the role of consciousness and the psychological factor.

During the Great Depression, Giannini launched a radio program, designed to overcome the psychological fear, and to restore confidence in the economy. This did much to increase deposits in the banks and to get the money circulating again. Merryle Rukeyser commented: "A.P. Giannini has demonstrated anew his capacity to inspire confidence among bank customers. Bankers of the no, no school might well analyze this new development in mass psychology banking."

Conclusion. The life of A.P. Giannini is truly inspiring for we can clearly see a soul at work. His life was dedicated to the well-being of others. He used his specialized business skills to elevate the people, the family of humanity, around him.

As a little boy of eight, nine and ten years old, he would accompany his widowed mother on her trips by steamer to the San Francisco waterfront to sell their fruits and vegetables. Years later John Leale, the captain of the bay steamer *Reform*, would "remember the two Gianninis: a pleasant, attractive widowed woman and her small son sitting quietly together on the crowded deck of his boat as it moved through the cold, predawn darkness of the bay." (Bonadio, p. 5.) Imagine for a moment this little boy sitting quietly by his mother's side—the oldest boy among three, the boy without a father, the boy who at an early age began prematurely to bear the family burden of financial responsibility. He sat by his mother's side. He felt the desperate edge of survival, not only as it affected his own family, but as he could also see it affecting the struggling Italians and other immigrant farmers around him. He would take into the very depths of his soul many pictures and impressions of those predawn steamer trips—the steamer stopping at various ports and putting out its plank, the farmers carrying and dragging onboard sacks of potatoes and bushels of fruit. There would be the movement and bustle, the smells and the sounds of all the activity, as he sat quietly, wide eyed and alert, by his mother's side. We do not know what hopes he had or what vows he made as he quietly observed the undulating movement around him, but *we do know that he never forgot the little guy*—no matter what opportunity he had to separate himself into the world of great wealth—he never forgot the people. On the contrary, he dedicated his whole life to the elevation of their condition. He took his natural born gifts, developed them, and then dedicated and applied them to the betterment of the human condition—truly a great soul touching directly the lives of hundreds of thousands and reverberating through the lives of millions.

His funeral took place on June 6, 1949, at St. Mary's Cathedral in San Francisco. More than 25,000 people overflowed the cathedral. He had named his son, Mario, executor of his will. There was the relatively modest sum of just under $500,000. In his will was also a reminder to the Bank of America to administer "generously and nobly" the Giannini Foundation trust money. "Remember always human suffering. Let no legal technicality, ancient precedent or outmoded legal philosophy defeat the purpose of the trust. Like St. Francis of Assisi, do good—do not merely theorize about goodness."

Summary of Third Ray Indicators.
Aptitude for business.
Inexhaustible energy.
Knowing the price of things.
Skill at negotiation.
Efficiency resulting in a competitive edge.
Enjoyment of "incessant activity."
Enjoyment of "entrepreneurial warfare."
Selling ability. Verbal skills. Persuasive.
Great skill in outmaneuvering the opposition.
Gift in mathematics
Financial 'wizard.'

Summary of First Ray Indictors.
Unrelenting drive. Forcefulness.
"Stubborn independence."
Drive, ambition, hard work.
Ability to push through every obstacle.
Ability to handle men and measures.
Fiercely determined. Ruthlessness. A penchant for vendetta.
Leadership qualities.
Rising to the Top.   Ambitious.
Power and strength of endurance.
Going after what he wanted with "hammer and tongs."

Summary of Soul Indicators.
Intense drive to be of service to others.
A profound sense of destiny.
Self-sacrifice and self-effacement.
Not glamoured by wealth or power.
Achieving for the sake of others.
Working for principle, not for self.
Creating an enterprise "with soul."

Leonardo da Vinci, Fourth Ray Soul, and the High Renaissance

"However, all that I am positing about a ray Life may be equally well posited anent a human life, but it should be borne in mind that the pure ray type does not as yet exist, for there is not to be found that perfect form, mechanism or expression of the ray quality, nor that absolutely purified appearance in the human family, except in such rare cases as the Buddha, or Christ, and (in another field of expression) an Alexander or Julius Caesar. Leonardo da Vinci was an analogous expression."

Esoteric Psychology I, 74.

Leonardo, as a Child. Leonardo da Vinci was born April 15, 1452, in Vinci, Italy. Vinci is a small town in Tuscany at the foot of Monte Albano and 60 miles from Florence. His father, Piero d'Antonio, was a public notary (lawyer); his mother, Caterina, was a daughter of a farmer. Piero did not marry Caterina, for she was a peasant woman and below his social rank. Piero (25 years old) married his first wife the same year Leonardo was born. For the first five years of his life, Leonardo lived with his mother in the small farming community of Anchiano, 2 miles outside of Vinci. In 1457 the child Leonardo moved to Vinci to live with his grandfather. With this move, he became part of his father's family and was sent to school. Piero's first wife bore him no children. This is a possible reason why Leonardo was brought into the father's family at this time.

At school Leonardo learned to write, to read, to calculate. He learned geometry and some Latin. He probably applied himself very little to Latin, for he had to re-study this as an adult. (His famous notebooks were all written in Italian.) He showed a special aptitude for mathematics, music, and drawing. He sang well and played the lute and was called upon to entertain at family gatherings from time to time.

Leonardo, the Apprentice at Verrochio's Studio. According to the artist-writer Giorgio Vasari (*Lives of the Artists*), a peasant on the estate of Leonardo's father brought a shield to Piero one day, requesting to have it painted by an artist. Piero gave it to his son, Leonardo, who devoted considerable time and energy to it. He planed it, covered it with stucco, and then gathered a variety of animals and insects to serve as models. When finished, his father was so impressed with it, particularly with its realism, that he could not bring himself to turn it over to the peasant. He had a substitute shield made instead. Later the father sold the shield to an art dealer for a good price. The art dealer in turn sold it to the Duke of Milan at a considerable profit.

When Leonardo turned fifteen (1466), his father took him to Florence. In this important center of Renaissance activity, Leonardo began his apprenticeship years with the artist Verrocchio—a prominent Florentine artist. When his father brought Leonardo to Verrocchio, there is no doubt that he brought him to one of the very best art studios available.

The successful art studio-workshop at that time consisted of a small group of artists, including their apprentices, in which several creative artistic activities were going on simultaneously. One artist might be working as an architect, designing a church or a palace. Another might be painting a portrait or making a series of sketches for a commissioned oil painting. Another artist might be sculpting or casting a stature, another making floats for a festival procession, another working as a goldsmith, another making bronze doors for a church, another fashioning stain-glass windows, another cutting and setting precious stones. Verrocchio was accomplished in all these artistic areas, and Leonardo learned them all. Verrocchio's studio was in fact a large academy that became the principal center for the arts in Florence. Leonardo, from the point of view of a fourth ray soul, was born at the right time and studied in the right place. It was a time when the creative arts were flourishing in a most special way, and Florence, according to some historians, was the very center from which the Renaissance issued forth.

According to Giorgio Vasari, Verrocchio asked Leonardo to add an angel to his painting, *The Baptism of Christ*. It was common practice for a master to call upon the apprentice to help set up a project or to complete a particular work, so that the master could either begin a more important commission or could simply follow the creative flow that led in unpredictable directions. It was not uncommon for more than one artist to work on the same piece of work. Verrochio, it is said, was so impressed with Leonardo's angel that he gave up painting and devoted his time to sculpture from that point onward. Leonardo, the apprentice, within a few years had surpassed the master, Verrochio. This is a story that was handed down and may not be completely accurate, for Verrochio did do some paintings after that time. Nevertheless, the basic meaning of the story might well be true—Leonardo's skill as a painter surpassed Verrochio's own skill, which then affected the choice of Verrochio's subsequent work.

Admitted to the Guild. When Leonardo was 20 years old (1472), he was admitted into the guild of the Company of St. Luke. This guild or association consisted of physicians and apothecaries, as well as artists-sculptures-architects-goldsmiths. The headquarters of this association was in the hospital of Santa Maria Nuova—a situation that facilitated Leonardo's access to cadavers. One of Leonardo's half finished projects was a book on anatomy, which included detailed anatomic drawings that were far superior to anything that had been done before. This was never completed in Leonardo's lifetime, although many of the sketches and notes have survived.

"What is true of the early works of other great masters is also true of Leonardo's, that, if put in the right order, they show a coherent, logical, and rapidly moving development, such as can be expected only of a most talented artist, and that, besides, they were from the very beginning far superior to those of his fellow workers." (W.R. Valentier, "Leonardo as Verrocchio's Coworker.")

In 1477 (25 years old) he was offered a studio in the Medici gardens. In his youth Leonardo showed considerable talent, much versatility, intelligence, and the promise of genius. It is probable that Verrocchio recommended Leonardo to the powerful Medici family as being his most accomplished and promising student-apprentice.

The Powerful, Prosperous, and Cultured Medici Family. During the Renaissance, several families came to rule certain key Italian cities and their outlying areas. The Medici rose to power in Florence. Contrary to the more usual means of appropriating power (intrigue, force of arms, assassination, poisoning, subterfuge, etc.), the Medici used their considerable wealth (from banking and commerce) in an intelligent way to gain power and influence. The first was Giovanni de' Medici (1360-1429), who in 1421 became *gonfalonier* (the bearer of the *gonfalon*, the flag or banner)—the highest official. Interestingly, he endeared himself to the people by replacing the poll tax or head tax (a system in which the rich paid the same amount as the poor) with an annual tax that was based on income and capital. He was popular among the people, but the rich vowed vengeance on the Medici.

Giovanni's fortune was bequeathed to his son Cosimo (1389-1464), who extended the wealth and power of the family. He had branch banking houses in Rome, Venice, Geneva, London, and elsewhere, helping to make Florence the financial capital of Europe. He ruled Florence primarily from behind-the-scenes, making sure that all his favorite people got elected to the important political offices. He contributed much of his own money to public works and private charities. King Edward IV of England borrowed a substantial amount of money from him (and repaid it).

As well as judiciously managing wealth and power, Cosimo de' Medici was also very interested in literature, philosophy, and all the arts. Not only generously supporting many artists, architects, sculptures, scholars, and literary people, he also spent a large sum of money retrieving classical texts from Greece and Alexandria. Rediscovering the pre-Medieval works of art and cultural texts was a preoccupation of those who were resonating to the new energy which historians have termed *the Renaissance*. When Niccolo de' Niccoli, a prominent collector of ancient manuscripts, fell into poverty due to his collecting, Cosimo gave him unlimited credit at his bank. When Niccoli died, he left 800 manuscripts valued at 6000 florins (gold coins of Medieval Florence)—which was a considerable fortune. Cosimo acquired the collection through assuming Niccoli's debts. He then divided the texts between the library at the monastery of San Marco and his own library. Both libraries were open to scholars, students, and teachers without charge. When manuscripts could not be purchased, Cosimo hired copyists to copy them. According to the Florentine historian Benedetto Varchi: "That Greek letters were not completely forgotten, to the great loss of humanity, and that Latin letters have been revived to the infinite benefit of the people—this all Italy, nay all the world, owes solely to the high wisdom and friendliness of the house of Medici" (*Storia Florentina*, Köln, 1721). The historian Will Durant summarizes it this way: "In the patronage of learning and the arts the Medici have never been equaled by any other family in the known history of mankind" (*The Renaissance*).

During Leonardo's time it was Lorenzo de' Medici (Cosimo's grandson), also known as Lorenzo *il magnifico*, who became the ruling Medici. After barely surviving his first few years as virtual ruler of Florence, he quickly became an astute politician. He made alliances in Northern Italy with Venice and Milan, he appeased King Ferdinand of Naples, and he brought an angry Pope Sixtus around to his point. The Pope realized that a united Italy was his only security against an attack on the Papacy from Mohammed II, conqueror of Constantinople. Peace was what the people wanted, peace was good for business and the arts, and, at the risk of his own life (Lorenzo went to Naples unarmed and remained a prisoner for three months), peace is what Lorenzo secured for the people of Florence and Italy.

Lorenzo, in the tradition of his family, was a generous supporter of the arts. Following Cosimo's lead, he was also an avid collector of ancient Greek and Latin texts. Michelangelo designed a building to hold the collection. The library later was named Bibliotheca Laurentiana, in honor of Lorenzo. Scholars flocked to Florence, which was becoming know as the literary center of Europe. Translations into Italian of the ancient Greek and Latin letters were moving rapidly forward. The University of Pisa was enlarged. The Platonic Academy was formed, for there was rekindled interest in the thought of Socrates and Plato.

The Platonic Academy was not a formal college but an association of men gathered together to study and discuss Plato's writings. Minds were opening. The limitations of Medieval thought were being questioned; restrictions were being thrown off. Poetry, philosophy, the arts, music, architecture were all being rekindled. Commerce was expanding. The statesman was a man of multiple skills and learning. Lorenzo was not only a highly skilled statesman, an accomplished administrator of a commercial banking enterprise, but a discriminative supporter of artists, authors, and scholars, and he was also a writer of excellent poetry himself.

This gives us a little picture of the intellectual-spiritual atmosphere in which Leonardo became of age.

Significance of the Year 1400. According to esoteric history, the year 1400 has great significance.

> Since the year 1400 (a date to which I referred earlier) there have been constant appearances of lesser avatars, called forth in response to minor crises, to national dilemmas and religious necessity. They have taken the form of those men and women who have championed successfully some truth or some right cause, some human right or correct human demand. All these people have worked actively upon the physical plane and seldom received recognition for what they truly were; only history, at a later date, laid emphasis upon their achievement. But they changed the current of men's thoughts; they pointed a way to a better life; they pioneered into new territories of human achievement. Such a one was Luther; another was Columbus;

still others were Shakespeare and Leonardo da Vinci—to mention only four who so lived and thought and acted that they conditioned after events in some field of human living and are still recognized as pioneering souls, as leaders of men.
Externalization of the Hierarchy 297.

Leonardo's dates were 1452-1519 (he lived 67 years). This is the period generally recognized by historians as the High Renaissance (the early Renaissance beginning around 1350 or 1375). According to esoteric science, the years 1400 and 1425 were significant in the extreme. "When the Hierarchy withdrew behind the separating curtain in Atlantean times, it marked the beginning of an interlude of darkness, of aridity and a cycle of 'blank abstraction,' which persisted in its crudest form *until 1425 A.D....*" (*Discipleship in the New Age* II, 316). The Hierarchy withdrew "into the subjective side of life and focused itself on the mental plane (instead of the physical) during the days of ancient Atlantis and after the war between the Lords of the Shining Countenance and Lords of the Dark Face, as *The Secret Doctrine* calls it. For millions of years, as a result of the triumph of evil in those days, the Hierarchy has stood in silence behind world events...." (*Externalization of the Hierarchy* 519).

On the negative or "evil" side of this great conflict during the Fourth Root Race (Atlantean race), were those who were "renowned for their magic powers and wickedness, their ambition and defiance of the gods." They were called "Lords of the Dark Face," as mentioned above, and also the "Lords of the Dark Eye (the Evil Eye)." They were Sorcerers of much magical power and served "under the lunar gods." On the other side were the "Lords of the Shining Countenance," also called the "Lords of the Dazzling Face,"—ones who were adept at White Magic. They were "true to the Solar Gods." The latter were warned of coming cataclysms (of fire and water and great continental shifts) and they separated themselves from the former.

After the Great Flood there was the very long development of the Fifth Root Race. During this development there was an improvement in the human organism, the physical form, in respect to "texture and symmetry"—it was brought to a state of perfection. In this perfecting of the physical form, however, "every race became more material, the Soul stepping back to make room for the physical intellect" (*The Secret Doctrine*).

As the Hierarchy moves outward to walk among humankind once again, another "great choice" is being offered and presented. This one has to do with the direction of mind, or manas, and also with the development of a new race—the Sixth Root Race. The manasic plane is dual: There is lower manas (intellect) and higher manas (the plane of soul). Manas has the tendency to unite with emotional desire (and thus build the body of kama-manas), but it also has the ability to unite with the intuition (building the body of buddhi-manas). The search for Christ and Truth, for the spiritual sacrificial Will, for Love-Wisdom, for Beauty and intuition, and for the archetypal perception of higher mind, brings about the development of the subtler and more powerful buddhi-manasic vehicle. We find then something like a tension between those who deny the spiritual, who want to work in matter only, and those who want to render the form-material aspect of culture-civilization subservient to soul and spirit.

The Spiritual Hierarchy "withdrew behind the separating curtain in Atlantean times." We also read in *Externalization of the Hierarchy* that "for aeons, the Hierarchy has struggled alone to help and lift humanity and to stimulate the potency of the human planetary centre so that its vibratory activity would eventually be sufficiently powerful to swing it into the radius or magnetic field of hierarchical activity. This long task has at last achieved success. The Hierarchy and humanity are at last en rapport." (*Externalization*, p. 169.) Even though the Hierarchy "withdrew behind the separating curtain," humanity was never left alone. Quite the contrary.

We are given additional clues as to the significance of that time in history which we call the Renaissance. There was a "Centennial Conference of the Hierarchy, held in 1425" at which time "permission for the inflow of this force [the Shamballa force] was given...." (*Externalization*, 133). Also: "The third ray, which is one that has a very long cycle, having been in manifestation since A.D. 1425, has a direct effect upon the fifth root race." (*Esoteric Psychology*, v.1, p.67.) The Shamballa force has to do with that planetary center known as the Will of God and therefore brings a first ray energy of will and power. The third ray is the ray of intelligent activity. This ray stimulates commerce, intellectual activity of all kinds, travel, communication, education, diversity, etc. It would tend to be more active (or find greater interplay) within the fifth race than within the fourth Atlantean race. The Atlanteans had a greater affinity with astral magic, to be sure, whereas the fifth race is more intellectual, more commercial, more inventive, more scientific. The mental-intellectual science of the fifth root race would make little sense to the astrally sensitive fourth root race.

In the study of history, from the human perspective we tend to consider first and foremost the sequential unfolding of *outer events*. From the Hierarchical point of view, however, it seems that Their focus tends more towards the *quality of consciousness* and towards the stimulation of that consciousness through the manipulative inflow of certain ray energies that emanate from certain planetary (and extra planetary) centers.

The tremendous significance of the year 1400 and 1425 (and the "Renaissance" as we term it) can perhaps be appreciated if we realize that it may very well be related to a stage in the externalization of the Hierarchy. As the light of the personality and the light of the soul can be blended in the developed human being, so, on a planetary scale, the light of Hierarchy and the light within Humanity as a whole can be related in a more conscious way and eventually blended.

The Difficulties Just Prior to the Renaissance: The Plague. The long period of "darkness and aridity" was beginning to come to an end. A more direct and conscious relationship between Humanity and Hierarchy was becoming possible. The 1300's, the century preceding the Renaissance, was an extremely difficult time. Approximately 30 million people, one third of the population of Europe, died during the "Black Death" (1347-50). According to Matteo Villani, three fifths (60%) of the population of Florence succumbed to the bubonic plague in 1348. Death was so pervasive that "folk reckoned no more of men that died than nowadays they would of goats" (Boccaccio, *Decameron*). It was a commonly held belief that this was the end of the world, and that the Four Horsemen were in full stride.

Political Confusion. Politically, this was a time of the feuding noble families, vying for power and control within the city-states. The political power of the Church was being questioned everywhere from all salient perspectives. The progress that had been made in Italy towards democratic republics was eroded as the *signoria* (the despotic rule of a particular individual) came to power. The feuds were filled with murder, intrigue, the clashing of small armies, the siege of castles and strongholds. Fighting was the norm.

The peasantry was often exploited to the edge of revolution. Popular uprisings against overlords for excessive taxes, low wages, and oppressive laws became more common throughout Europe. The revolts, when successful, could not be maintained for any length of time. The nobles with their royal armies regained power. This was often followed by increased suppression. After the Black Death, there was a shortage of labor. Some peasants organized to demand higher wages and better working conditions. The Jacquerie in France (1358) and the Peasants' Revolt in England (1381) protested the exploitation of labor. Both of these protests failed and the status quo was restored.

The Decline of the Church. The Papacy had steadily become more a government than a religion. Funds were obtained more through taxation than through contribution. Positions in the Church hierarchy were sold. Purgatorial punishment was avoided through the payment of indulgences. The market for religious relics was prolific and lucrative. The popes had to be statesmen, diplomats, administrators, and dukes, rather than saints or contemplatives. The position of pope was not awarded to the most spiritual devotee, or the greatest imitator of Christ, or the true spiritual leader, or the initiate. Quite the contrary. The placement had much more to do with questions of material wealth, of maintaining of the status quo (anti-reformation), and of political advantage among complex warring factions, both within Rome itself, among various Italian city-states, and among European regions of growing national identity. Morality, being a religious question, was not much of an issue. After all, traditionally, certain spoils of war always went to the victor, or to those who think primarily of the power questions. What happened at the top, quickly trickled down to the cardinals, bishops, priests, and even the monks and nuns. Wealth, political power, pomp and circumstance, ostentatious edifice and ornament were all greatly valued by this government-religion or theocracy.

There was no lack of criticism of these practices, and there was no lack of an effort to reform the Church. The reformers either criticized from a saintly distance or became fanatic zealots who were able to gather a following for brief moments before being extinguished as traitors, heretics, witches, pagans, or as being in league with the Devil or with the infidel. Petrarch referred to the Church as "hell on earth, the sink of vice, the sewer of world.... Old men plunge hot and headlong into the arms of Venus; forgetting their age, dignity, and powers, they rush into every shame, as if their glory consisted not in the cross of Christ, but in feasting, drunkenness, and unchastity.... Fornication, incest, rape, adultery are the lascivious delights of pontifical games." (*Cambridge Medieval History*.) "The whole Church might be reformed if the Church of Rome would begin by removing evil examples from itself.... That the whole Christian folk take from the clergy pernicious examples of gluttony is clear and notorious, since the said clergy feast more luxuriously and splendidly, and with more dishes, than princes and kings." (Guillaume Durand, Bishop of Mende, reporting to the Council of Vienne, *Life in the Middle Ages*, Coulton.)

The Papal Schism: Two Popes, then Three. We have the further political and religious confusion occurring when Philip IV of France defied Pope Boniface VIII in 1302. The Pope issued a bull (*Unam Sanctam*) reaffirming the supremacy of the pope over secular rulers. Philip responded by sending an army to capture the pope and force him to resign. Boniface slipped away but died soon afterward. In 1305 the college of cardinals elected a Frenchman, Clement V, as the new pope. Philip pressured Clement to move his residence from Rome to Avignon in the South of France. This became the home of the popes (seven altogether) from 1309 to 1377. Gregory XI in 1377 returned to Rome.

When Gregory died, a crowd of people outside the Vatican threatened to kill the French cardinals if they did not choose an Italian pope. They chose Bartolommeo Prignano, who became Urban VI. He quickly restored order in Rome. His intention was to appoint Italians to the college of cardinals and to reform the Church, beginning at the top. All the cardinals fled, elected a new pope, Clement VII, and returned to Avignon. Now there were two popes—one in Rome, one in Avignon. The situation quickly took on additional political dimensions: France, of course, supported the French pope, as did her allies Scotland and Spain. England, the enemy of France, supported the Italian pope in Rome, as did Flanders, Germany, Poland, Bohemia, Hungary, and Portugal. Appeals were made at various times for one or the other or both popes to resign for the sake of unity. They both refused.

A general council of clergy and laymen was organized to resolve the conflict. The council met at Pisa, disposed of the two existing popes who refused to come before the council, and elected a new pope, Alexander V (1409). Now there were three. Alexander V died in 1410 and John XXIII took his place. John had a bad history, charges were brought against him (as a pagan, oppressor, liar, seller of Church offices, traitor, lecher, and a thief), and he was forced to resign. Gregory resigned, Benedict died, and a new pope, Martin V was elected, and the schism was resolved in 1417. Once again there was one pope, who happened to be from Rome.

The Humanists. Many attribute the beginning of the Renaissance to the humanists. The humanists were avid scholars who spent much time, money, and energy recovering the Greek and Latin classic writings (history, philosophy, drama, poetry, science, mathematics, astronomy), learning the ancient languages, translating classic works, and teaching about the scope, breadth, and profundity of these relatively ancient works. They were known as *umanisti* because they called the study of classic culture *umanità*—the humanities. They studied less of God and more about the human being. They turned the focus from religion to philosophy—the former depending on *inspiration* from above, the latter depending only on one's own ability to *reason*. They turned from heaven to earth, from the brooding on the after-life to intelligent study of this life. If one were to identify a location for the beginning of the Renaissance, it would have to be Florence. Most of the humanists either came from Florence or graduated from Florence. Gradually the movement spread throughout Italy and then throughout all of Europe.

The Esoteric Conditioning Energies. We see at this time something new, vital, and energetic, strongly affecting the course of human history. We see a *re nasci*, a re-birthing, a renaissance. Under (or within the context of) the 2000 year umbrella of the Piscean Sixth Ray of Idealism and Devotion, we see (with the help of the indications given in the esoteric literature), something dramatically "new", something dynamic, something that kindles greater awareness. There was 1) the first ray energy (or the "first faint indications" of this powerful energy; 2) a third ray energy (cycling in, beginning 1425), and 3) there are also suggestions of fifth ray energy—one of the rays of the fifth race—which was beginning to bring about a greater capacity for humanity to observe and ask questions. The authority of the Church and the authority of the prince, king, or emperor were all brought into question. The rulers were revealed as being all too human. The intelligent thinkers now had increased *power* to *search* things out for *themselves* and to *know* things for themselves.

The first ray energy brings about immediate change. With the first ray energy, it is never business as usual. Formidable obstacles are swept away; a new thrust forward commences in an unequivocal manner. The *first ray energy* was evidently stimulating *third ray activity* at that time. Some of the beneficial activities of the in-flow of the third ray of intelligent activity following the year 1425 can be seen in the following areas:
1) Banking, commerce, travel, the great voyages of exploration.
2) The Reformation, which means less devotion to the established authority and a more intelligent questioning.
3) Intellectual awakening as evidenced in philosophy and the arts. 4) Government, or the thinking about new and different forms of government. We have to remember, however, that all this is still under the "umbrella", so to speak, of the larger cycle of the Age—*Sixth Ray energy of Piscean Age.*

Banking, Commerce, Travel, Exploration. When the social structure consists of a sharp division between the very rich and the very poor, one finds a static condition. The ruling class rules through fear and through some form of established abuse and slavery. When there are predominantly two classes, the upper class promotes division and separation in its own self-interest. Labor is forced or coerced; there is no fluidity between the two classes. On the other hand, the rise of an increasingly prosperous middle class erodes class distinctions and facilitates in countless ways a much more fluid society—more class mobility.

In the fifteenth century Venice and Florence were the wealthiest cities in Italy. Northern Italy has traditionally been more industrial than the agrarian South. Italy was commercially located and had trading links to the Greeks, Arabs, Jews, Egyptians, Persians, Hindus, and Chinese. The financial-banking skills of the Medici family greatly played into the flow and stimulation of the new spiritual impulse. Florence was the financial capital of Europe from the 13th through the 15th centuries. A system of insuring ship cargoes was adopted in Italy approximately 250 years before England did the same.

The Reformation: Rethinking Fundamental Doctrine. In the first half of the Piscean Age the Church sought to establish the Christian faith in Europe. This was done politically through the power of the pope and his office (*the first administrative-power aspect* of the Church). It was also done pedagogically through the monks who established monasteries, tilled the soil, drained the swamps, cut roads, built bridges, brought literacy, established modest libraries, organized schools, copied manuscripts, and developed small industrial centers (*the second aspect—the building and teaching aspect*—of the Church). The monks brought, with energy and zeal, a *new moral teaching* to people who were often displaced (as a result of the innumerable wars) and who were often in a cultural limbo.

D.K. gives the rays of the Catholic Church in the following paragraph from *Discipleship in the New Age*:

> "The Catholic Church is governed by the first ray as its soul ray, and by the third ray as its personality ray. Hence its love of politics and of temporal power; hence also its intensely commercial and financial preoccupations. The mental ray of this Church is sixth ray. Hence its narrow one-pointedness; its emotional body is also sixth ray in quality, whilst the physical ray of the outer organisation is seventh."   (DNA II, 506-7.)

Soul	1
Personality	3
mind	6
emotion	6
physical	7

The disheartening factor here is that the second ray of love-wisdom, the primary ray of the Christ is absent in the psychological make-up of the Church. Often then we find a kind of 6th ray devotion to dogma, rather than a 6th ray that leads to the 2nd ray of love.

As the Church became more established, various forms of corruption tended to infiltrate the organization, followed then by calls for reform. At the time of the Renaissance, the movement towards reform received enough will energy to combat such a powerful institution as the Church. On several occasions popes had been displaced by kings, with the help of their armies, but to combat the Church on theological grounds was a question of a different order. Thinkers were generally not well organized. They tended to appeal to reason. Martin Luther (1483-1546) considered Rome to be the seat of sodomy and the Beast of the Apocalypse. Luther's dispute with the practices of the Church were intelligent and comprehensive. He was also politically connected to the Elector of Saxony, who was willing to protect and hide him when necessary. The protestant movement grew during this time. Huldrych Zwingli in Switzerland denounced indulgencies and claimed that each local congregation had the democratic right to control its own affairs. The Frenchman, Jean Calvin, brought in a particular kind of reform that included simplicity of living and strict moral conduct. John Knox brought this to Scotland where it became Presbyterianism. King Henry VIII of England desired a separation from the political interference from Rome, which eventually resulted in the Anglican Church. It could be claimed that the third ray of intelligent activity helped to bring *diversity* to the spiritual quest and practices, and helped to open people's minds to new ways of thinking. The 1st ray soul and the 3rd ray personality of the Catholic Church were met head-on by a 1st ray and 3rd ray energy cycling in during the Renaissance. The "new" energy was quickening souls with the new ideas and directions. The old was confronted and at least partially destroyed.

The Mental Awakening: Literature, Philosophy, the Arts. We have already mentioned the dramatic new impulse to uncover some of the ancient Greek manuscripts that had been hidden away in monastic libraries, gathering dust and totally ignored for centuries. The perusal of the great variety of ancient texts served to dissolve some of the rigidity of Church dogma. Some humanists considered the Christian myths to be merely helpful for the uneducated population. *Others saw value in both the Greek philosophy and Christian theology, and they sought to reconcile the two.* It has been noted that the third ray of intelligent activity augments the faculty of reason. This faculty was being emancipated. On the other hand, Christianity was and is multi-layered. At one level there is emotional devotion and faith. At another level there is the intricate and often tortured reasoning of theology (the Scholastics being an example). At still another level we find the mystics who seek to arrive at the Vision that far transcends reason. Reason, like the 3rd ray, is closely related to communication. The humanists rekindled an interest-skill in rhetoric, grammar, letters, language, as well as law, medicine, history, and philosophy. Reason helped to free medicine from religion and from superstition. When a plague came, it wasn't necessarily due to God's condemnation of humanity's sins in a moralistic sense. The search was on for other cause-effect relationships. Leonardo, as we shall see, responded heart and soul to the new impulse.

The Great Swiss Born Philippus Aureolus Paracelsus (1493-1541) might be considered both a Renaissance man and something beyond. He proposed to learn from practical observation and developed techniques of amputation, antisepsis (preventing decay and putrefaction), a therapeutic use of baths, and homeopathy, to mention a few areas. He questioned most medical practices of his times. Instead of rigidly adhering to traditional means, he introduced practical observation and empirical methods. He also studied alchemy (one of the forerunners of modern chemistry), astrology, and the treatment of illness through the use of herbs. After being rejected by the orthodox medical establishment in Basel, he traveled extensively into Spain, Portugal, Russia, Poland, Scandinavia, Constantinople, and the Crimea. He associated with the protestant sects of the Reformation (Anabaptists, the Brothers of the Free Spirit). He was almost executed in Salzburg for supporting a peasant uprising.

The First Ray Impulse and Centralized Government. Just prior to the High Renaissance of Leonardo's time, many changes were already underway. The Italian peasants were tenant farmers who had some democratic say in the election of local village officials. They were no longer feudal serfs subject to the will of the landlord. The feudal landowning aristocracy had been overthrown by the developing, powerful, and wealthy middle class of the prosperous city-states and their surrounding regions—Milan, Florence, Naples, Rome, and Venice. The vote had been established for those who were strong and prosperous enough to organize into guilds—the bankers, merchants, professional men (doctors, professors, skilled craftsmen, architects, etc.), and other skilled workers. Occasionally, the unskilled workers (such as textile workers) attempted to organize, but there were generally unable to hold for any length of time whatever gains they managed to accomplish.

Interestingly, with the impulse of the first ray force in 1400 and 1425, responding governments did not move towards a consolidation-expansion of democratic rule, rather they moved towards stronger centralized governments. The wealthy and politically ambitious families within the city state struggled for control—in Florence the Medici rose to power, in Milan it was the Sforza family. Democracy was not altogether eliminated—there were constitutions (which were frequently changed), guild members had some voice, and there was a ruling, governmental body (Signoria or municipal council). Behind the scenes, however, the ruling family kept control and everyone knew it. There were plenty of attempts to overthrow the particular family, but this did not come from a dissatisfied populace, rather it came from another politically ambitious family.

There were capable rulers who were brought to the fore during this period of dynamic growth. Some of the rulers were cleverly ruthless in their rise to power (such as Caesar Borgias and his re-establishing of the Papal States under the rule of the Pope—in this case, his father, Pope Alexander VI). Others were accomplished entrepreneurs, supporters of the arts, and able statesmen who used their own wealth for the benefit of the community (such as Lorenzo de' Medici of Florence), and others fell somewhere in between (such as Lodovico Sforza of Milan). Leonardo worked for or served all three of these rulers.

The vision of a united Italy emerged more clearly at this time. The strong, centralized city-states began to realize that their future life depended on mutually beneficial alliances. Spain, France, Austria, and Turkey were attracted to Italy at a time when the borders of slowly developing nation-states were not at all fixed. The embryonic nations of loose federation (such as Italy and Germany) became the political playground of the more unified nation-states. Italy's power was in her culture, her great works of art, her commerce and banking, and also in the political power of the Roman Catholic Church. (The nation-state of Italy that eventually did form has a 6th ray soul and a 4th ray personality. Italians could tolerate some corruption in the Church, for they knew that behind it all there stood a true spiritual endeavor, and there were always the true living saints to prove it. As a result of her 4th ray personality Italy exudes art and beauty and creativity. This is readily apparent in its music, its opera, its architecture, its painting, sculpture, literature, poetry, drama, crafts, etc.)

The power of the pope, at the time of the Renaissance, was lessening. Emerging nation-states did not like papal interference. Too many corrupt popes, too many inquisitions, and too much avarice brought about the quest for more self-reliance on the spiritual-moral questions. As borders shifted, France, Spain, Turkey, and Austria saw Italy as rich in the spoils of war. This was at a time when war was a habit. Mercenary troops were paid in loot and Italy was a treasure. It became increasingly clear that Italy had to work towards unification, and, if we can accept the message of the Renaissance political writer-thinker Machiavelli, this had to be done *no matter what the means.*

As the Spiritual Hierarchy began its work of externalization, the Western Hemisphere received a special focus, Europe became the leader in the new civilization, Italy was alive to the new energy in a special way, and Florence was a dynamic focal point for the new life that spiraled in, giving inspiration on multiple levels.

Service in Milan: 1482-1499. Leonardo's Letter to Sforza. At 30 (1482) Leonardo was ready (or probably over-ready) to leave Florence and work in another part of the country. He had heard that the Lodovico Sforza, Duke of Milan, was looking for an artist-architect and military engineer. Leonardo made application. He wrote a long letter, listing the skills he had that might be of some use to the Duke.

Leonardo advertised himself more as a military engineer than an artist. He had developed an "extremely light and strong bridge, adopted to be most easily carried, and with them you may pursue, and at any time flee from the enemy...." He knew how to make an "endless variety of bridges, and covered ways and ladders, and other machines pertaining to such expeditions."

Some say that Leonardo designed the first tank, termed here "covered chariot." " I will make covered chariots, safe and unattackable which, entering among the enemy with their artillery, there is no body of men so great but they would break them. And behind these, infantry could follow quite unhurt and without any hindrance."

It must be remembered that in the days when art and engineering, art and architecture, were not separated, Leonardo's drawings and designs were most impressive. *He could put his ideas to paper in a brilliant way*. At the age of thirty, he appeared somewhat bored with art—having mastered drawing and painting in several media—and was seeking to develop and apply his skill in larger projects—projects that required state or church funding.

The art historians of recent times look back and say in effect: What a shame that the genius Leonardo left so few finished works. There were many reasons why so many of his projects never reached fruition. Some of them appear to lie within his own character, and others lie with those who failed to recognize his genius or *failed to know how to work with genius in a right way*.

Like so many people of creative genius, Leonardo appeared to be far more interested in learning and self-development than in the repetition of accomplishment. Those artists who paint portrait after portrait (something that Leonardo could have easily done) usually do this for financial reasons rather than growth and creative reasons. To the true creative genius, this would seem almost like a living death, something to be avoid at all cost.

We have here also a very strong 4th ray quality of creativity. If something is turned into a business, there is the necessity for repetition, for mass production, and for marketing. The 3rd ray excels in such endeavors with its qualities of efficiency, energetic activity, intelligence, and communication-marketing skills. These qualities, however, often tend to grate on the sensitivities of the 4th ray type. To the 4th ray type, every endeavor is not a repetition of an earlier work but something completely new. Once a problem has been solved the artist wants to move on to new challenges. This is demonstrated again and again in Leonardo's life. The inner relationship with the Muse is more important than the outer relationship with the market place.

In Leonardo's letter to Lodovico Sforza, Leonardo mentioned his "catapults" (used in order to hurl large rocks at castle walls), which must have been an improvement upon Medieval artillery. He also said that he designed "other machines of marvelous efficacy and not in common use."

"In time of peace," he continued, "I believe I can give perfect satisfaction and to the equal of any other in architecture and the composition of buildings public and private; and in guiding water from one place to another."

Leonardo devoted a substantial amount of time to gaining knowledge about canal building and could easily be designated as one of the most prominent hydraulic engineers of his time. His nature, however, would not let him settle too long in any one area. One might conclude that his 4th ray soul won out over his apparent 5th ray of science, one of his secondary rays.

Some of his greatest proven accomplishments were last on the list: "I can carry out sculpture in marble, bronze or clay, and also in painting whatever may be done.... Again the bronze horse may be taken in hand, which is to be the immortal glory and eternal honor of the prince your father of happy memory, and of the illustrious house of Sforza."   *The Notebooks of Leonardo da Vinci.*

Leonardo's Notebooks. Leonardo began working on his notebooks when he was thirty-seven years old (1489). Up to this point, life and learning must have seemed to Leonardo to have no end. During the crisis years of 35-40, however, one thinks about selecting certain paths and eliminating others. One begins to face the fact that the particular life-cycle does not go on forever. Indeed, this is a good time to start compiling one's learning into some kind of book form.

His notebooks were sketches, ideas, theories, discoveries, notes, and outlines of his planned books. None of his books were completed and none of his writings were published in his lifetime. What has come down to posterity are the notebooks—the rough drafts. The plan evidently was to write something like forty books.

He was a little defensive as he began to write, worrying a trifle over a critical audience. "I know that many will call this useless work:...men who desire nothing but material riches and are absolutely devoid of that wisdom, which is the food and the only true riches of the mind... So much more noble are the possessions of the soul than those of the body. And often, when I see one of these men take this work in his hand, I wonder that he does not put it to his nose, like a monkey, or ask if it is something good to eat."

LEONARDO'S FORTY BOOK PLAN

Book on the Practice of Painting. "Many are they who have a taste and love for drawing, but no talent; and this will be discernible in boys who are not diligent and never finish their drawings with shading.... It is indispensable to a painter who would be thoroughly familiar with the limbs in all the positions and actions of which they are capable, in the nude, to know the anatomy of the sinews, bones, muscles and tendons so that, in their various movements and exertions, he may know which nerve or muscle is the cause of each movement and show those only as prominent and thickened, and not the others all over, as many do who, to seem great draftsmen, draw their nude figures looking like wood, devoid of grace; so that you would think you were looking at a sack of walnuts rather than the human form, or a bundle of radishes rather than the muscles of figures...."

The Importance of Experience. One of the major themes that emerges in Leonardo's approach to life has to do with *learning from experience*, which is also a major theme of the Renaissance. Learning from one's own experience was gradually to supersede the unquestioning dependence on the authority of Aristotle, the Bible, and the Church. In his draft of a book on the *Practice of Painting* he expressed it in this way:

> Studies [for later compositions] should be taken from natural actions and made from time to time, as circumstances allow; and pay attention to them in the streets and *piazze* and fields... The adversary says that to acquire practice and do a great deal of work it is better that the first period of study should be employed in drawing various compositions done on paper or on walls by divers masters... to which I reply that the method will be good, if it is based on works of good composition and by skilled masters. But since such masters are so rare that there are few of them to be found, it is a surer way to go to natural objects, than to those which are imitated from nature with great deterioration, and so form bad methods; for he who can go to the fountain does not go to the water jar.
>
> *Notebooks of Leonardo da Vinci*

In the introduction to his writings, he expressed the idea more generally: "Many will think they may reasonably blame me by alleging that my proofs are opposed to the authority of certain men held in the highest reverence by their inexperienced judgments; not considering that my works are the issue of pure and simple experience, who is the one true mistress."

A Meditative Approach: Clear Thinking, Companions of Similar Study, Avoiding Projection. .

> A painter needs... the absence of all companions who are alienated from his studies; his brain must be easily impressed by the variety of objects, which successively come before him, and also free from other cares. And if, when considering and defining one subject, a second intervenes—as happens when an object occupies the mind, then he must decide which of these cases is the more difficult to work out, and follow that up until it becomes quite clear, and then work out the explanation of the

other. And above all he must keep his mind as clear as the surface of a mirror, which assumes colors as various as those of different objects.

A painter who has clumsy hands will paint similar hands in his works, and the same will occur with any limb, unless long study has taught him to avoid it. Therefore, O Painter, look carefully what part is most ill-favored in your own person and take particular pains to correct it in your studies. For if your are coarse, your figures will seem the same and devoid of charm; and it is the same with any part that may be good or poor in yourself; it will be shown in some degree in your figures.

Notebooks of Leonardo da Vinci

No Sooner is Virtue Born than Envy Comes into the World to Attack It. Notes for an allegorical representation:

Envy must be represented with a contemptuous motion of the hand towards heaven, because if she could, she would use her strength against God; make her with her face covered by a mask of fair seeming; show her as wounded in the eye by a palm branch and by an olive-branch, and wounded in the ear by laurel and myrtle, to signify that victory and truth are odious to her. Many thunderbolts should proceed from her to signify her evil speaking. Let her be lean and haggard because she is in perpetual torment. Make her heart gnawed by a swelling serpent, and make her with a quiver with tongues serving as arrows, because she often offends with it. Give her a leopard's skin, because this creature kills the lion out of envy and by deceit. Give her too a vase in her hand full of flowers and scorpions and toads and other venomous creatures; make her ride upon death, because Envy, never dying, never tires of ruling. Make her bridle, and load her with divers kinds of arms because all her weapons are deadly.... *No sooner is Virtue born than Envy comes into the world to attack it*; and sooner will there be a body without a shadow than Virtue without Envy...

Notebooks of Leonardo da Vinci

As the Master Artist in Residence in Milan under Lodovico Sforza, Leonardo was called upon to do many tasks, including making floats and the decoration of the castle for various festivals. The communal festivals were major events, filled with months of decorative art and musical designing-preparation. The above note on the figure of Envy probably refers to a three-dimensional decorative piece to be used in one of the processions.

One can only speculate as to the amount of envy that Leonardo had to endure. Being a prominent, if not *the* most prominent, artist-engineer (with his 4th ray soul and probably 5th ray personality and/or mind) applying for patronage and favor at the high courts of the Medici in Florence, Sforza in Milan, and Borgias in Rome, Leonardo must have often felt "the arrows of the quivering tongue of Envy." Leonardo himself, so superior in talent and so elevated in soul, seemed to be far above the negative emotion of envy. He also, with his "cup" running over with inspired ideas, was far too busy with creative projects and things to learn to be concerned much with rank and position. The 4th ray developed type is very much concerned with the opportunity to create and with alignment with muse.

Six Books on Light and Shade. These books are technical and they are illustrated with several diagrams.

> The lights which may illuminate opaque bodies are of four kinds. These are: Diffused light as that of the atmosphere; direct light, as that of the sun; reflected light; the fourth is light which passes through transparent bodies, as linen or paper or the like, but not transparent like glass....
>
> A single and distinct luminous body causes stronger relief in the object than a diffused light; as may be seen by comparing one side of a landscape illuminated by the sun, and one overshadowed by clouds, and so illuminated only by the diffused light of the atmosphere.
>
> The lights which are produced from the polished surface of opaque bodies will be stationary on stationary bodies even if the eye on which they strike moves. But reflected light will, on these same objects, appear in as many different places on the surface as different positions taken by the eye.
>
> *Notebooks of Leonardo da Vinci*

For the exacting painter, these very careful observations by a scientific-artistic thinker are very instructive. The emotional painter would prefer not to be troubled with such analysis. Both types of painter-artists can make beautiful contributions to the world of art. Leonardo was a very thoughtful artist. His mind sought for reasons, for causes, and for laws. His artistic skills were able to bring them forth and produce them, especially when not troubled by the politics of the court and the ego of the patron. His extensive notebooks were an effort to pass on to others the knowledge and penetrating insights he was able to acquire over long years of work and study.

Book on the Theory of Colors.   His ability to think and observe scientifically, enabled Leonardo to see subtleties of perspective, form, light, shadow, and color that would probably escape the attention of most artists. "Of several colors, all equally white, that will look whitest which is against the darkest background. And black will look intensest against the whitest backgound. And red will look most vivid against the yellowest background; and the same is true with all colors when surrounded by their strongest contrasts."

Anatomical Studies: Overcoming the Fear of Living in the Night Hours with Corpses.

Book on Anatomy.   Leonardo indicated that he had written 120 manuscripts. Only 50 remain. Among those lost were the ones on the anatomy of the horse. These studies were thorough and excelled anything that had been gone before. He also was one of the forerunners in the study of comparative anatomy with his detailed illustrations of the limbs of man and animal. He began one of his works on anatomy with the following words:

I wish to work miracles. It may be that I shall possess less than other men of more practical lives, or than those who want to grow rich in a day.... You who say that it would be better to watch an anatomist at work than to see these drawings, you would be right, if it were possible to observe all the things which are demonstrated in such drawings in a single figure, in which you, with all your cleverness, will not see nor obtain knowledge of more than some few veins, to obtain a true and perfect knowledge of which I have dissected more than ten human bodies [10 at the time of the writing, but later there was a total of 30], destroying all the other members and removing the very minutest particles of the flesh by which these veins are surrounded, without causing them to bleed, excepting the insensible bleeding of the capillary veins; and as one single body would not last so long, since it was necessary to proceed with several bodies by degrees, until I came to an end and had a complete knowledge.   This I repeated twice, to learn the difference.

And if you have a love for such things, you might be prevented by loathing, and if that did not prevent you, you might be deterred by the fear of living in the night hours in the company of those corpses, quartered and flayed and horrible to see. And if this did not prevent you, perhaps you might not be able to draw so well as is necessary for such a demonstration; or, if you had the skill in drawing, it might not be combined with knowledge of perspective; and if it were so, you might not understand the method of geometrical demonstration and the method of the calculation of forces of the strength of the muscles; patience also may be wanting, so that you lack perseverance. As to whether all these things were found in me or not, the 120 books composed by me will give verdict Yes or No. In these days I have been hindered neither by avarice nor negligence, but simply by want of time.

Notebooks of Leonardo da Vinci.

There is indicated here a very definite presence of the 5th ray scientific quality of making painstaking observation, overcoming several obstacles in the process, in order to contribute to a body of knowledge. The artistic quality is seen in the highly developed ability to draw, an ability that has in its hand the touch of beauty. The drawings are not simply technical renderings devoid of that intangible something we call art. They are works of art.

Book on Zoology and Comparative Anatomy. His notebooks were sometimes instructions for others and sometimes they were notes to himself. Usually the brief notes and the more careful writing were interspersed and flowed one into the other. He would often begin with instruction, as if he were writing to others, and end with notes to himself as what his procedure should be or what studies he still needed to do.

Describe the various forms of the intestines of the human species, of apes and such like. Then, in what way the leonine species differ, and then the bovine, and family birds; arrange this description after the manner of a disquisition....

Describe the tongue of the woodpecker and the jaw of the crocodile....

Of the flight of the 4th kind of butterflies that consume winged ants. Of the three principle positions of the wings of birds in downward flight...

The walking of man is always after the universal manner of walking in animals with 4 legs, inasmuch as just as they move their feet crosswise after the manner of a horse in trotting, so man moves his 4 limbs crosswise; that is, if he puts forward his right foot in walking he puts forward, with it, his left arm and vice versa, invariably.

Book on Physiology.
I have found that in the composition of the human body as compared with the bodes of animals the organs of sense are duller and coarser..... I have seen in the lion tribe that the sense of smell is connected with part of the substance of the brain which comes down the nostrils, which form a spacious receptacle for the sense of smell, which enters by a great number of cartilaginous vesicles with several passages leading up to where the brain comes down... Death in old men, when not from fever, is caused by the veins which go from the spleen to the valve of the liver, and which thicken so much in the walls that they become closed up and leave no passage for the blood that nourishes it.... To keep in health, this rule is wise: Eat only when you want and relish food. Chew thoroughly that it may do you good. Have it well cooked, unspiced and undisguised. He who takes medicine is ill advised..... I teach you to preserve your health; and in this you will succeed better in proportion as you shun physicians, because their medicines are the work of alchemists.

Book on the Three Branches of Perspective. His notes and drawing on this rough draft were extensive. He divided the subject into three sections: 1) Linear Perspective. 2) The Perspective of Color. 3) The Perspective of Disappearance.

Book on Painting. These are instructions from the master painter. Here we find the master instructing the apprentice, correcting common errors, revealing his secrets of the fine art. An essential in painting is "appropriate action and a due variety in the figures, so that the men may not all look like brothers." One could say that a great many paintings of the era "fail" on these two fundamental important points.

Book on Astronomy. In his book on astronomy there were, of course, many errors: "In my book I propose to show how the ocean and the other seas must, by means of the sun, make our world shine with the appearance of the Moon, and to remoter it looks like a star.... The moon is cold and moist. Water is cold and moist. Thus our seas must appear to the moon as the moon does to us...."

Flying Machines. "Remember that your flying machines must imitate no other than the bat, because the web is what by its union gives the armor or strength to the wing. If you imitate the wings of feathered birds, you will find a much stronger structure, because they are pervious; that is, their feathers are separate and the air passes through them. But the bat is aided by the web that connects the whole and is not pervious.... You may see the air in motion over the sea, fill the swelling sails and drive heavily laden ships. From these instances, and the reasons given, a man with wings large enough and duly connected might learn to overcome the resistance of the air, and by conquering it, succeed in subjugating it and rising above it."

Book on Canals. "That river which is to be turned from one place to another must be coaxed and not treated roughly or with violence; and to do this a sort of floodgate should be made in the river, and then lower down one in front of it and in like manner a third, fourth, and fifth, so that the river may discharge itself into the channel given to it...."
Leonardo Concerned with the Probable Misuse of His Knowledge.
Book on Naval Warfare. Below is a list of various matters related to naval warfare that he intended to elaborate in a book.

How an army ought to cross rivers by swimming with airbags... How fishes swim; of the way in which they jump out of the water, as may be seen with dolphins... Of the swimming of animals of a long form, such as eels and the like. Of the mode of swimming against currents and in the rapid fall of rivers. How is it that animals which have not long hind quarters cannot swim. How is it that all other animals which have feet with toes, know by nature how to swim, excepting man. In what way man ought to learn to swim. Of the way in which man may rest on the water.... How by means of a certain machine many people may stay sometime under water. How and why I do not describe my method of remaining underwater, or how long I can stay without eating; and I do not publish nor divulge these by reason of the evil nature of men who would use them as means of destruction at the bottom of the sea, by sending ships to the bottom, and sinking them together with the men in them.

Architectural Designs. This planned book had preliminary sketches and discussion on plans for a town, plans for canals and streets, plans for small castles and villas, studies for a form of church most proper for preaching, a design for a mausoleum, palace architecture, a theory for constructing domes, plus several other architectural related items.

Book on Physical Geography. This rough draft included "the nature of water itself in its motion." Also to be included were "A book of driving back armies by the force of a flood made by releasing waters. A book showing how the waters safely bring down timber cut in the mountains. A book of boats driven against the impetus of rivers. A book of guarding against the impetus of rivers so that towns may not be damaged by them. A book of the way a tempest may of itself clear out filled up seaports. A book of the formation of hills of sand or gravel at great depths in water. A book of controlling rivers so that the little beginnings of mischief caused by them may not increase."

Other Books. Some of his other rough-draft books include: *Book of Useful Inventions.* This was to include instructions as to how to dig a canal. *Book of the Science of Mechanics. Book on the Proportions of the Human Figure. Botany for Painters and Elements of Landscape Painting. Topographical Writings,* which include notes on buildings in Milan, notes on North Italian lakes, notes on places in Central Italy, the Alps, France, notes on the Germans, the Red Sea, the Nile, plus many more topics. His book *Mechanical Appliances* included notes on a flying machine. He also wrote *Fables and Humorous Writings.*

How Do We See His Notebooks Today? The *artistic minded* and abstract philosophical thinker will probably be disappointed in Leonardo's *Notebooks*, for Leonardo avoids discussion of his feelings and innermost thoughts. He also does not tell personal stories or anecdotes. He does not reveal his religious views. The inquisition was active in Spain and more tolerant in Italy. Nevertheless, Leonardo chose to avoid discussion of the religious subjects. Obviously, he made the politically correct choice. In much of his art work he chose religious themes, which blended easily with the themes of his day. He surpassed others with the perfection of his technique.

The *scientific person* would probably have no reason to read the *Notebooks*; science has come very far since Leonardo's time. We must remember however, that for those of us who have no scientific inclination, although we may drive cars and use computers, Leonardo's scientific capabilities of 550 years ago far exceed our own. We are living in a scientific age; Leonardo was not. This should help us appreciate his extraordinary capabilities and genius.

From an *historical perspective*, the Notebooks become most interesting. In the historical context, we begin to see the grandeur and the genius of the man.

Leonardo's Fourth Ray and Fifth Ray Combination. Leonardo was eager to *gain knowledge* on a great variety of subjects, and he was eager to *work in some creative fashion.* The scientific attitude was strong, even when the field, such as painting, was essentially an artistic field. He explored the cutting edge in a variety of fields; he wanted to make a contribution in the furthering of knowledge in many of those fields.

Leonardo had a 4th ray soul, that is given. It seems clear from his writings on many scientific subjects that he had a 5th ray personality. The question is: what was the ray of his mind? His general avoidance of psychological and philosophical and literary themes and his careful adherence to form-detail suggest that he might have had a 5th ray mind as well as a 5th ray personality.

The architect-artist-writer Giorgio Vasari (1511-1574) wrote a ten volume book called *Lives of the Artists*, which included accounts of Leonardo, Michelangelo, Fra Filippo Lippi, Lorenzo Lotto, Andrea del Sarto, and many others. Of Leonardo he wrote: "The most heavenly gifts seem to be showered on certain human beings. Sometimes supernaturally, marvelously, they all congregate in one individual.... This was seen and acknowledged by all men in the cases of Leonardo da Vinci, who had an indescribable grace in every effortless act and deed. His talent was so rare that he mastered any subject to which he turned his attention.... He might have been a scientist, if he had not been so versatile."

D.K. includes Leonardo in a list of inspired men, overshadowed by divinity. "Oft, down the ages, men have been overshadowed by divinity and inspired by God to accept positive leadership, and so make divine purpose a fact in conditioning world affairs. Had they not so responded to the influencing impression, and had they not accepted the responsibility imposed upon them, the course of world affairs and world events might have been very different. I refer not here specifically to spiritual leaders but also to leaders in other departments of human living—to such expressions of the divine will as Moses, the Lawgiver, Akbar, the warrior and student, Leonardo da Vinci, the inspired artist, and to other great and outstanding figures who have determined the basic trends of human civilization."

Externalization of the Hierarchy 260.

Charles d'Amboise, France's governor of Milan for a short period, had this to say about Leonardo: "The excellent works accomplished in Italy and especially in Milan by Master Leonardo da Vinci, your fellow citizen, have made all those who see them singularly love their author, even if they never met him....For ourselves, we confess that we loved him before meeting him personally. But now that we have been in his company and can speak of experience of his varied talents, we see in truth that his name, already famous for painting, remains comparatively unknown when one thinks of the praises he merits for the other gifts he possesses, which are of extraordinary power.... If it is fitting to recommend a man of such rich talent to his fellow citizens, we recommend him to you to the best of our ability, assuring you that everything you can do to increase either his fortune and well-being or the honors to which he is entitled would give us as well as himself the greatest pleasure, and we should be much obliged to you."

This was a letter from Charles to the Florentine city fathers, dated December 16, 1506, indicating the great admiration that the French had for Leonardo.

Leonardo spent the last three years of his life in the palace of Cloux at the invitation of Francois I, King of France. This palace was the King's residence at Amboise. There was in fact an underground passage that connected Leonardo's house to the royal palace. The King could visit his favorite painter-engineer whenever he wished. According to Benvenuto Cellini, the King enjoyed Leonardo's conversation and considered him to be "a great philosopher," and the most cultivated man alive.

The Coming Spiritual Renaissance. In this essay on Leonardo we have attempted to enter into the spirit of the Renaissance. We have done this not only to catch a glimmer of the backdrop of Leonardo's life but also because there is a relationship between that time and our own. We are told that we are about to go through a *profound spiritual renaissance* that will recreate the civilization in which we live. It is always difficult to see the forest because of the trees. It is difficult to see the larger picture, due to the plethora of distracting details that surround the little personal life. It is important, however, to realize that we may very well be on the verge of profound and meaningful cultural changes, a period of dynamic new creativity. The beneficial new ways are always brought in through the leadership of great souls. It behooves us to be alert to the new dimensions and new directions—both within us and within the world around us, so that we too might experience something of the *joy of renaissance*.

"They [educators] must prepare for a *renaissance of all the arts and for a new and free flow of the creative spirit in man*. They must lay an emphatic importance upon those great moments in human history wherein man's divinity flamed forth and indicated new ways of thinking, new modes of human planning and thus changed for all time the trend of human affairs."

Education in the New Age 47, italics added.

"*A spiritual renaissance is inevitable* and is nowhere more needed than in those countries which have escaped the worst aspects of war. *For this renaissance we must look and make preparation*."

Problems of Humanity 40, italics added.

"We have touched upon the physical and psychological rehabilitation of the children and youth of the world. We have suggested that the textbooks be rewritten in terms of right human relations and not from the present nationalistic and separative angles. We have also pointed out certain basic ideas which should be immediately inculcated: the unique value of the individual, the beauty of humanity, the relation of the individual to the whole and his responsibility to fit into the general picture in a constructive manner and voluntarily; we have sought to have the futility of war, of greed and aggression emphasized and *that we prepare for a great awakening of the creative faculty in man once security is restored; we have noted the imminence of the coming spiritual renaissance.*"

Problems of Humanity 47, italics added.

Summary of Fourth Ray of Harmony Through Conflict Indicators.

Talent in the creative arts.
Sensitivity to beauty.
Creative self-expression.
"teaches the art of living in order to produce a synthesis of beauty."
A worker for harmony, unity.
Love of harmony, love of beauty, love of beautiful things.
Love of color.
Love of melody.
Rich imagination.
A tendency to have an intense, somewhat mystical, interior life that that can lead to intuitive insight and creativity.
An "ordered sense of color and proportion." (*Discipleship in the New Age* I, 647.)
A longing for harmony and divine assurance.
"The refiner, the producer of perfection within the form." (*Esoteric Psychology* I, 50.)
"The Corrector of the Form." (*Esoteric Psychology* I, 71.)
"The way of the seeker, the searcher and the sensitive reflector of beauty." (*Esoteric Psychology* I, 134.)
Quickness of intellect and perception. (Mercury is a 4th ray planet.)
"This produces a livingness through death, a harmony through strife, a Union through diversity and adversity." (*Esoteric Psychology* II, 92.)
Effort to harmonize the new ideas with the old.
Revelation of the world of meaning (related to intuition).

Summary of Fifth Ray of Science Indicators.
Skill in mathematics.
Keen eye for detail.
Detailed anatomical studies.
Studies of physics and engineering,
Keen interest in "machines of marvelous efficiency."
Powers of observation.
Detachment.
Extensive search for cause and effect relationship.
Inventive solution to physical plane problems.
Thorough mastering of a field of knowledge.
Interested in advancing a body of knowledge through original research.

Thomas Edison - Fifth Ray Soul

"A group of scientists will come into incarnation on the physical plane during the next seventy-five years who will be the medium for the revelation of the next three truths concerning electrical phenomena. A formula of truth concerning this aspect of manifestation was prepared by initiates on the fifth Ray at the close of the last [nineteenth] century, being part of the usual attempt of the Hierarchy to promote evolutionary development at the close of every cycle of one hundred years. Certain parts (two fifths) of that formula have worked out through the achievements of such men as Edison and those who participate in his type of endeavor, and through the work of those who have dealt with the subject of radium and radioactivity. Three more parts of the same formula have still to come, and will embody all that it is possible or safe for man to know anent the physical plane manifestation of electricity during the fifth sub-race."
Treatise on Cosmic Fire 455-6.

Edison as a Youth. Some say that the childhood of every great person is blessed with a loving, nurturing, and understanding mother. That would certainly hold true in the case of Thomas Edison, born February 11, 1847, in Milan, Ohio. He was born with a large (but not deformed) head. The doctor speculated "brain fever"; his mother prayed for him. Years later Edison remarked: "My mother was the making of me. She was so true, so sure of me, and I felt I had someone to live for, someone I must not disappoint."

When Thomas was two years and some months old, he would sometimes visit his married sister on a near-by farm. On one such visit, the sister and her husband awakened to the fact that neither one of them had seen Thomas for several hours. The barn was a likely place to find him, for he was very curious about the animals. There he was, sitting in a straw-filled nesting box on some goose eggs. They thought at first that he had soiled his pants. He had seen the chickens sitting on eggs to hatch the little ones, he tried to explain. He was trying to do the same with the goose eggs. This probably was not his first scientific experiment.

At the age of seven, Thomas was enrolled in a Christian school (Family School for Boys and Girls) and also in a one room public school. The public school teacher thought Thomas to be too dreamy and disturbingly non-responsive to the rote recitations. Years later Thomas recalled: "I heard the teacher tell the visiting school inspector that I was addled [confused, muddled], and it would not be worthwhile keeping me in school any longer. I was so hurt by this last straw that I burst out crying and went home and told my mother about it."

His mother, Nancy, brought him back to school, and she told the teacher that Thomas had more brains than the teacher did. She took Thomas out of school and taught him at home. Thomas Alva Edison, the genius of invention—a man who ranks high on the list of those who most influenced the century—spent a total of three months in school.

Thomas started reading Thomas Paine, one of his favorite writers or essayists, at the age of 13. He also read Gibbon's *Decline and Fall of the Roman Empire*, David Hume's *History of England*, Sears's *History of the World*, *The Dictionary of Sciences*, and R. G. Parker's *A School Compendium of Natural and Experimental Philosophy*. He became an avid reader. Eventually, his personal library numbered over 2000 books. Whenever he became interested in something, he wanted to obtain every available book on the subject.

Thomas's First Job. Also at the age of 13, Thomas got his first job. He became the newsboy on the Grand Trunk railroad between his hometown of Port Heron, Michigan, and Detroit. He left at 7:00 every morning, had a stopover in Detroit for most of the day, and then returned at 9:00 PM. Thomas had set up a chemical laboratory in his basement and wanted to earn money in order to purchase more chemicals. On the train he sold newspapers, magazines, fruit, sandwiches, cigars, candy, and peanuts. Eventually he included sweet corn, radishes, onions, parsnips, and beets from his father's acreage. He was definitely energetic and enterprising, for he fashioned a small flatbed proof press, wrote and printed his own single sheet newspaper (calling it *The Herald*), and used a corner of a baggage car for a chemistry lab. For his news stories, he obtained the latest information from telegraphers at stations en route to and from Detroit. It was a three hour ride each way. The train clicked along at about 20 miles per hour.

The enterprise expanded. He was able to buy fresh produce in Detroit and other towns along the way at wholesale, transport it freight free, and sell it in Port Heron at a profit. He hired two boys to tend the fruit and vegetable stand in Port Heron.

His first adventure into the world came to an abrupt end when one of his chemical experiments started a small fire in the baggage car. The conductor evicted Thomas at the next station, along with all his printing and chemical supplies.

Ray Indications at an Early Age. During his early teens, two ray energies seem to be relatively developed and prominent. One, clearly, is the fifth ray of science. The presence of the 5th ray energy is evidenced in his curious nature, in the asking of endless questions as to the cause and the function of things, in an avid interest in reading scientific subject matter, and, most dramatically, in his fascination with chemistry and the setting up of his own chemical laboratory. The other ray that seems definitely present is the third ray of intelligent activity. This ray is evidenced somewhat in his interest in history, in his general energetic nature, and more specifically in his enterprising activities of starting a newspaper, selling of wares, and beginning his own produce business.

The fifth ray in other combinations would be expressed differently. Had he had a fifth ray and second ray combination, for example, he probably would have been content to pursue science at home. He would not have been so eager to enter so energetically into business activities. He might have appeared more the pure scientific thinker and less the entrepreneurial inventor eager to establish a strong and successful business presence in the world.

Western Union and the Telegraph. Tom taught himself Morse code, took apart and reassembled a telegraph so that he knew exactly how it operated, and hung out at the Mount Clemens railroad depot just north of Detroit. One day, a three year old child had crawled onto the tracks without anyone noticing. An oncoming rolling freight car was heading for the child, unable to stop. The brakeman yelled out. Alert Tom heard the call, ran out onto the tracks, and scooped the child up in his arms to the relief of a near hysterical mother. The father of the child happened to be the station master himself. So overjoyed was the father that he offered Tom an opportunity to learn telegraphy. This was exactly the opportunity that Tom was hoping for. In three months time Tom mastered all its skills, applying himself with his usual amount of energetic enthusiasm.

His first job as a telegraph operator was at Micah Walker's jewelry store in downtown Port Heron, which included a Western Union office. He worked there during the day, read scientific journals when not busy, and returned to the office on his own time after dinner in order to increase his proficiency. This was in the fall of 1862. The Civil War was in its last phase, and Tom was 15 years old.

Looking for greater challenges, he obtained a position on the night shift (7:00 PM to 7:00 AM) as telegraph operator at Stratford Junction, some 75 miles north of Port Heron—his first job away from home. He was accustomed to catching short naps while sitting in a chair. During one little nap, a train went through the station and almost collided with another train. The station master was reprimanded for hiring such a young man in such a responsible position. Tom was fired and he returned home.

Soon he found another night job at Lenawee Junction, 50 miles southwest of Detroit. Tom lost this job when he tried to break into a transmission with an urgent message. The person on the other end of the line was a superintendent. The superintendent was so enraged with the interruption, that he fired Tom at the first opportunity.

His next job was in Fort Wayne, Indiana, for six months, and then onto Western Union in Indianapolis. He continued working extra hours on his own time, trying to master the more difficult press wire work, which dealt with receiving the news dispatches.

An Early Invention. His next job was night operator at the main Western Union office in Cincinnati, Ohio—a growing metropolis. Here he met Ezra Gilliland, who was to be a friend and business associate for 25 years. They shared their interests in mechanics and invention. Gilliland had been trained as a gunsmith. Edison had developed a telegraph repeater that was one of his first inventions. Some messages that came over the wire were easy to record, such as information about the arrival and departure of trains and also short individual messages. The difficult messages were those of the news service—they were longer and more complicated. Edison's telegraph repeater automatically relayed a message to a second line. The second instrument slowed down considerably the 40 words per minute rate of the first register. This made reading much easier.

Other inventions in various stages of development included a little steam engine made out of brass tubing with an ingenious valve motion. He was also working on a means of sending two messages over the same wire at the same time but in opposite directions.

Edison received a promotion, became a first class operator, and a salary of $125 per month. A friend told him of a job in Memphis, and off he went. He was dismissed from this job for unclear reasons. He got a job with the Associated Press Bureau in Louisville, Kentucky. The office was small, cramped, extremely untidy, and disorganized. Intoxicated personnel stumbled into the office at odd hours. He applied himself diligently to learning Spanish, for he had read about a need for operators in Brazil. This adventure, however, was never realized.

Tom was fired from the Louisville job when he spilled some sulfuric acid, which ate through the floor to the manager's office below. He returned to Cincinnati.

The Invisible Hand of Destiny, Which Becomes "Visible" in Retrospect.. One can almost identify an interesting pattern in his apprenticeship years. He was definitely not meant to remain at some obscure railway junction in Michigan, but he was too young to realize that. He had to get fired at the right time in order to move on. Eventually, however, when he began to see the wisdom of the move, he no longer had to get fired in order to move on to new learning experiences. A new job every six months became more of a *selected* pattern, rather than an *enforced* pattern.

This type of apprenticeship, however, was not to go on indefinitely, and it was definitely not to lead him to Brazil. Brazil might have had a romantic lure to a young man, but it was not the center of invention and of business enterprise that his soul was seeking to experience. His work, his soul's destiny, did not lay in the direction of Brazil. He was soon to find both his work and its right location, the latter being just as critical as the former. Also the Southern sojourn had its limitations. It was definitely time to move on, which in this case at this time meant moving back to Cincinnati.

His Self-Education and His Soul's Work. Being a telegraph operator had been an avenue of growth and development, but now he was being lead to something else. He would fain illness so that he could skip out of work and spend time in the Mechanic's Library and the Cincinnati Free Library. He studied the conductivity of various metals, magnetism, acoustics, everything related to electricity, and everything he could find related to the telegraph. Earlier he had worked extra hours without pay in order to learn all that he could. Now he skipped out of work to go to the library in order to learn all that he possibly could. He had an insatiable desire to learn as much as possible in scientific fields.

During the formative stages of development, often a young person will find certain role models or heroes. When one happens to find such a mentor, there is often some kind of immediate recognition. One reads and hears about many people, but one or two people suddenly stand out. Some person, or even some word or phase or historical event suddenly quickens awareness and arrests the attention. One becomes momentarily keenly conscious. In the midst of a crowd or in a classroom or library one becomes still and unnoticeably quiet with a marvelous little vivifying thread into the world of meaning. There is nothing arbitrary about this. This is not a chance happening. It is a touch of soul, and it has to do with the beginning stages of the soul's appropriation of the lower vehicle.

Many of us are able to look back and see quite clearly those moments in our own lives that proved extraordinarily meaningful, guiding, and pivotal. Those moments bring little hints of a direction, of the coming labors of love—not without blood, sweat, and tears—that lead eventually to what might be called one's destined work.. In the case of the young Thomas Alva Edison there seems to have been two special heroes during this early stage of soul unfoldment. One hero was Thomas Paine, and the other was Michael Faraday.

Edison's Hero: Thomas Paine. Thomas Paine (1737-1809) was an English-American political philosopher, whom Edison started reading when he was 13 years old. Paine's pamphlet *Common Sense* aroused public opinion in the American colonies to move towards independence from England. In came at a critical time when many colonists were undecided and hesitant to break with England. During the War of Independence, Paine wrote a pamphlet entitled *The Crisis*, beginning with the famous words: "These are times that try men's souls." George Washington ordered it read to all the soldiers in his army.

In 1787 Paine returned to England, wrote a pamphlet entitled *Rights of Man*, which strongly favored the French Revolution—not a popular position to take in England at the time. His criticism of the monarchy led the government to indict Paine for treason.

Paine fled to France where he was elected a deputy to the National Convention. When the question arose concerning either the banishment or execution of King Louise XVI, Paine chose banishment. The dictatorial Robespierre had Paine imprisoned for this. Paine escaped the guillotine, however, when Robespierre fell from power.

While in prison in France, Paine started writing his book *The Age of Reason*. This is the book that resonated deeply with Thomas Edison. At the time of its first publication the book generated a lot of criticism both in Europe and the United States. It was seen as essentially atheistic. It is true that the book is anti-church or anti-organized religion, but Paine was not an atheist. He was in fact a deist. Deism is a system of thought that advocates a natural religion based on human reason rather than revelation. As a scientific thinker, Edison probably had some philosophical differences with the church of his upbringing. His mother, Nancy, was a devout Presbyterian.

In *Esoteric Psychology* v. 1, we find two methods of approach to truth that seem to apply to Edison's path. "The method of approaching the great Quest, for this ray type [third ray type], is by deep thinking on philosophic or metaphysical lines till he is led to the realization of the great Beyond and of the paramount importance of treading the Path that leads thither." "For the fifth ray, the method of approaching the Path is by scientific research, pushed to ultimate conclusions, and by the acceptance of the inferences which follow these." Reason and scientific thinking were methods of approaching the great Quest that were evident in Edison's life.

Edison's Hero: Michael Faraday. Another hero of Edison's was the British scientist Michael Faraday (1791-1867). Faraday discovered that an electrical current could be generated by mechanical means—by moving an electrical conductor (copper wire) through a magnetic field. This was known as electromagnetic induction.

Michael Faraday was born on the 22nd of September, 1791, in Newington Butts, England. He was of humble origin and he grew up in extreme poverty (his father was a blacksmith). One day his older brother Robert took the very young Michael to a new school. The stern schoolmistress, upon examining Michael's abilities, soon determined that he could not pronounce his "r's" properly. He would pronounce "Robert" as "Wobert." The harsh school-mistress sent Robert out with a halfpenny to buy a cane so that little Michael could be properly flogged. This so incensed Robert that he took the halfpenny, threw it over a wall, and went home to tell his mother. Their mother went immediately to the headmistress and removed the two boys from school. Thomas Edison could readily identify with Faraday's humble origins, with the damaging school experience, and with having an understanding mother. Michael did go to another school to learn the basics of reading, writing, and arithmetic until he was thirteen years old.

Michael was taken on as an errand boy for a bookseller in London, which served as a preliminary trial for the position of apprentice. His duties included delivering (loaning) papers on Sunday, then going around to pick them up again. When he was told that the person had not yet finished reading the paper, he would beg to have it, since the next pick-up might be a mile off. After a year, he was accepted as an apprentice to learn the trade of bookbinding, stationer and bookseller. Here was an opportunity to read a variety of books, his favorite being the *Encyclopedia Britannica* (where he first read about electricity) and *Conversations on Chemistry*. He became fascinated with these two subjects. He was also able to attend lectures on natural science with the help of his brother Robert (a shilling was required for admittance). He made careful and comprehensive notes of all the lectures attended, and then he bound his notes into books. A very special event occurred when a customer at the bookshop gave Michael tickets to four of Humphry Davy's lectures. Sir Humphry Davy was one of the most prominent scientists of the day. These lectures were to be the great inspiring catalysis of Michael Faraday's life.

The lectures inspired him to leave the profession of bookbinding and to seek some employment in science. Within a few months and a fortunate twist of events (someone at the Royal Institution of Science was fired), Michael was given a position as assistant to Sir Humphry in the laboratory at 25 shillings a week, along with two rooms at the top of the house. This was March, 1813. Michael was 22 years old.

The following year, Michael wrote to a friend: "When Sir Humphry first made proposals to me to accompany him in the voyage [travels through Europe and into Asia], he told me that I should be occupied in assisting him in his experiments, in taking care of the apparatus, and of his papers and books, and in writing, and other things of this kind; and I, conceiving that such employment, with the opportunities that traveling would present, would tend greatly to instruct me in what I desired to know and in things useful to life, consented to go." Great Britain and France, however, were still at war. They wrote Napoleon, requesting permission to travel through France and neighboring countries. Napoleon, always an enthusiastic patron of the arts and sciences, made a special dispensation in Sir Humphry's favor. By the time they got to Italy, however, Napoleon's regime had fallen.

The group—Sir Humphry, Lady Davy, Lady Davy's maid, and Michael—met many prominent French scientists on their journey. One Frenchman, Jean Baptiste Dumas, later appraised the meetings in this way: "Davy's laboratory assistant, long before he had won his great celebrity by his works, had by his modesty, his amiability, and his intelligence, gained most devoted friends at Paris, at Geneva, at Montpellier. Among these may be named in the front rank M. De La Rive, the distinguished chemist, father of the illustrious physicist. At Montpellier, beside the hospitable hearth of Bérard, the associate of Chaptal, Faraday has left memories equally charged with an undying sympathy which his master could never inspire. We admired Davy; we loved Faraday."

The Rays of Edison and Faraday Compared. This character sketch, as well as the gentle tone of Faraday's letters, suggests either the humility of a Virgo or the social graciousness of a Libra or both (he was born on the 22nd of September, right on the cusp). Both Edison and

Faraday seem to have 5th ray souls. The secondary ray, however, was different; their styles were not at all similar. Edison was very enterprising; his research and inventions had a most practical intent. He sought to capitalize in a large way on his discoveries, which suggests the strong possibility of the 3rd ray as the secondary ray. Faraday, on the other hand, was more the pure scientist who preferred to stay in the laboratory, leaving the exploitation of the discoveries to others. The ray suggested by this quality, as well as his disposition, is the second ray. When visited by members of the Royal Institution, the common remark about a particular experiment was "But what's the use of it?" Faraday would borrow an answer from Benjamin Franklin: "What's the use of a baby? Some day it will grow up!" One day Mr. Gladstone, the Chancellor of the Exchequer at that time, inquired about this thing called electricity: "But, after all, what use is it?" "Why, sir," Faraday replied, "there is every probability that you will soon be able to tax it!"

Of the French people Michael Faraday observed: "The continued talk and chatter of people together when they are at work, whether in the house, or in the street, or in the air, as upon some of their cathedral scaffolds, is quite remarkable. The French must be a very thinking race to have so much to say." Quite a good observation and far more profound than he realized. France has a 5th ray soul and a 3rd ray personality. These two rays stimulate thinking, especially with both of them together. The 3rd ray is especially responsible for the verbal activity and the verbal skills.

Eventually Faraday moved out of the shadow of Sir Humphry and became a notable scientist in his own right. When he was offered a professorship of chemistry at the University of London, he turned it down: "I think it is a matter of duty and gratitude on my part," Faraday replied, "to do what I can for the good of the Royal Institution in the present attempt to establish it firmly." While occupying a chair of chemistry at the Royal Institution (a lifetime appointment) he took on additional duties as guest lecturer at other institutions. Lecturing and doing laboratory research along lines that he felt were intriguing and important were his main activities. Once important key discoveries had been made, he preferred to let the manufacturing sector develop the more practical and marketable implications of the discoveries. His lectures indicated a "love of accuracy and the cautious approach to questions of conjecture," which characterize the 5th ray type.

The Birth of Electrical Engineering. Faraday did research on optical glass that lasted five years, working primarily with heavy and fusible glasses. A telescope that was made from his optical glass had considerable magnifying power. When presented with the opportunity and the request to make a piece of such glass the largest size possible, Faraday had to choose between being "rich and miserable, or poor and happy." He chose the latter.

Faraday is credited with making the first electric motor and with being the first person to produce a continuous electric current from magnetism. Professor W. Cramp, an electrical engineer in London, described Faraday's findings in this way: "The paper [of Faraday's research] contains far more than is noted in his diary, and shows what hard thinking he must have done during those three weeks [of research in seclusion]. He sees clearly that there are two sets of phenomena. The first is that in which a varying current in one coil produces transient currents in a second coil. These he calls 'volta-electric induction'. They underlie every transformer (whether for power or for wireless), every coupled circuit, every induction coil that has been made. The second set, in which the relative movement between a magnet and a coil or disc produces a current, he calls 'magneto-electric induction', and these underlie every dynamo, alternator or motor since constructed. Thus then was born the industry of electrical engineering." These discoveries were made in 1831—sixteen years before Edison was born.

"Very few inventors of Victorian times did trouble to dig into Faraday's *Collected Researches*. It was not until 1868, the year after Faraday's death, that a young man of twenty-one, Thomas Alva Edison, purchased a residue set of Faraday's works in Boston and discovered that he had made his most profitable investment. He could understand Faraday's simple, non-mathematical explanations; he could repeat Faraday's clearly described experiments; he with his limited education regarded Faraday as his master. Nobody, he remarked later, did anything in electricity at that period except telegraph operators and manufacturers of cheap apparatus for school science classes." (*Michael Faraday*, by James Kendall. Roy Publishers, New York.)

Michael Faraday, Second Ray Personality: Faraday loved *pure research* and chose that path over the one leading to manufacturing and to entrepreneurial activities. The deeper he got into research, the fewer contacts he had with the outside world. He was a *generous* man. When he had additional funds from lecturing, he would make anonymous donations to church and individuals. He liked the format of *lecturing*. He took great pains to understand what constitutes a good lecture. He thought that a lecture that took over one hour was beyond the ability of the audience to assimilate in a comfortable manner. Lecturing, of course, is a *form of teaching* chosen by some 2nd ray types. The 2nd ray enhances the 5th ray's desire to develop and master a complete body of knowledge. The 2nd ray promotes something like an abundance of knowledge, and the fifth ray scrutinizes the kind of knowledge that can be known with exactitude.

Edison's Third Ray Personality. Edison, like Faraday, loved scientific research, but he was also very much attracted to entrepreneurship and the *activity of business*. For him, scientific research had to have a *practical application*, which meant manufacturing a *useful product*. He had a *lot of energy*, working nights and well as days, and sleeping very little. With every new invention there was a rush to the patent office and then the setting up of a new business and a production line. With the 3rd ray influence there is often a tendency to "bite off more than one can chew" or to be imbalanced on the activity side of the triangle of life. One of the negative aspects of Edison's over-activity was the almost complete neglect of his family life (two marriages) not from the material but from the psychological angle. Working night and day and sleeping in or near the workshop-factory, he generally saw his family once a week on Saturdays. This pattern had a very negative effect particularly on his first wife and on his children from both marriages.

First Patent. In 1867 Edison was working at Western Union's Cincinnati bureau and was skipping out of work whenever possible to devour books on electricity, magnetism, acoustics, and telegraphy. He was 20 years old. He was still following his apprenticeship pattern by staying at a particular job somewhere between 6 months and a year. When a job opened up at Western Union office in Boston, he immediately applied for it.

He began his new job on his favorite night shift, and his primary duty was to receive the press wire news from New York City. Edison began to build his reputation as an inventor by writing articles for Western Union's corporate newsletter, the *Journal of the Telegraph*. His articles and letters recorded his technological improvements and inventions. His first of over 1000 patents was for an electric vote recorder. This was designed to accelerate the roll-call process in a legislative body. (This was *not* utilized, because the legislators of the time preferred the delay.)

His Own Telegraph Business. Always pushing himself towards new horizons, he quit Western Union and started a stock quotation service. This included running his own wires to select businesses in Boston, giving them the latest, up-to-the-minute stock market quotations. It was a private-line dial telegraph system that used the alphabet instead of Morse code. He began to attract financial backers. His first business was not a thriving enterprise, to say the least. But no matter to Edison—it was all a learning experience. After being in Boston for about a year, he left for New York.

In New York he became superintendent of the Gold & Stock Reporting Telegraph Company, which did just that—it gave price quotations for gold to bankers and brokers around New York. Edison was much too innovative to settle into any routine for any length of time. Along with another ex-employee of Gold & Stock, he started Pope, Edison & Co., which leased lines to businesses, installed burglar alarm systems, and drafted patent applications. This led to Newark Telegraph Works with 50 employees.

Conflict Between Science and Business. An on-going archetypal conflict developed between financial backers (demanding quick results, interfering in research programs, keeping tight control of assets) and the inventors under Edison's direction (the team of electrical and mechanical engineers and their assistants). A series of "failed" experiments were most troubling to the financial supporters. To Edison, who labored from 7:00 A.M. to 2:00 A.M., there was no such thing as a failed experiment. Every experiment brought knowledge. In his words: "The manufacture of mechanism is a slow operation being legitimate, and all legitimate businesses are slow but sure, and the slower the more sure." One of the backers "says that some of our experiments were useless. But, after he has had more experience in this business, he will find that *no experiments are useless*." (*The Papers of Thomas A. Edison*, v. i, The Edison Papers Project.)

Here we have an interesting archetypal conflict between the 5th ray (in pursuit of knowledge for the sake of knowledge) and the 3rd ray, or that aspect of the 3rd ray that functions in the economic domain. From the business perspective one is looking at financial investment, efficiency of operation, marketing of product—all eventually resulting in profit. There is a definite time-table here, and there are definite limitations. The investment capital is limited. A need in the market place *today* may either evaporate or be taken over by the competition *tomorrow*. If we look at the situation from the point of view of the economic domain (where the 3rd ray of Intelligent Activity plays a critical role), then the above considerations are of critical importance.

From the 5th ray point of view, however, it is another matter. From the 5th ray point of view there is no time-table, there is only knowledge. Pure science functions outside of time, as every contemplative person knows. Business is concerned with product and form; pure science is concerned with idea and principle. Form is very much limited to the cycle of time. Idea and principle stand outside of time, beyond its limitations.

Edison had a Foot in Both Worlds. In a certain sense, pure scientific research is part of the cultural domain (funded by private contribution and government grants) and is not a business. The pressures of business can easily interfere with pursuit of pure scientific knowledge. Edison had a foot well-planted in both realms. He could move with skill in either domain. He understood many things about the market place and the economic domain. He was frequently racing with his competitors to bring out the product first. He controlled his inventions through patents and lawsuits. He enjoyed the process of inventing something that had efficiency and expediency as its primary purpose. But he was also the pure scientist discovering idea and principle.

One could almost say that when the developed Edison was a scientist, he was a scientist, and when he was a businessman, he was a businessman, and he enjoyed both worlds. That is why he succeeded financially, whereas others, like Nikola Tesla, with his superior alternating current, had a much more difficult time capitalizing on his inventions.

When Edison said "The manufacture of mechanism is a slow operation, being legitimate, and like all legitimate business they are slow but sure", he was incorrect. The *manufacture* of mechanism is not slow; it is efficient. Research and development are slow. When he said the above, and when he said "no experiments are useless" he was not speaking as a businessman; he was speaking as a scientist.

The businessmen, the financial backers, did not want to hear it. They thought the genius Edison could come up with the invention *just like that!* Indeed, he had come up with several ingenious inventions; to the backers it seemed like it must be a matter of a few hours or days. Edison, the scientist, however, knew it was a matter of months, if one was fortunate, and, more often than not, a matter of years—long and arduous years.

To appease his backers, as well as the business side of himself, he worked 18 hours a day. He also closely supervised and directed two shifts of engineers. Eventually it was productive; it proved successful, both from the scientific side and from the business side.

At 23 years of age Edison had a shop called the Newark Telegraph Works with 50 men working under him. They designed and manufactured transmitters, perforators, ink recorders, and typewriters for automatic telegraphy. The universal stock printer they manufactured sold for $125 each. Edison was also developing a domestic telegraph system so that a homeowner could send an emergency message to a local fire department or police station.

London born Charles Batchelor was one of Edison's most important engineers and scientific thinkers. Charles wrote to his brother in England: "We work all night experimenting and sleep till noon in the day. We have got 54 different things on the carpet and some we have had for 4 or 5 years. Edison is an indefatigable worker and there is no kind of failure however disastrous affects him." (Walter Welch, *Charles Batchelor, Edison's Chief Partner.* Syracuse, 1971.)

Electricity: What is it?   As means of generating electricity were discovered and applications of electricity were sought, no one was sure exactly what electricity is. In 1600 the English physician William Gilbert used the term *electric* (from the Greek *electron,* or amber) to name the force exerted when some substances are rubbed. In 1745 the Dutch physicist Peter van Musschenbroek of the University of Leyden developed the Leyden jar—a simple form of an electrical capacitor (a device used to store an electrical charge). Benjamin Franklin made many electrical experiments, including the well known lightening-kite-key experiment. He developed a theory that electricity is a *fluid* in nature—the "excesses and shortages" of this fluid would account for its flow.

The British chemist Joseph Priestley (1766) identified the law that the electric force between electric charges varies inversely with the square of the distance between the charges. The French scientist Charles Augustin de Coulomb did further research into electricity in the 18th century, followed by Michael Faraday in the 19th century. The Italian physicist Alessandro Volta in 1800 developed the "voltaic pile"—a device that produced a steady stream of electricity and was a forerunner of the electric battery. In recognition of his contributions to science, Napoleon made Alessandro Volta a Count in 1801. In 1819 the Danish scientist Hans Christian Oersted demonstrated the fact that a magnetic field exists around an electric current flow.

Michael Faraday carried this work further with his induction coil. James Clerk Maxwell (18431-1979), born in Edinburgh, Scotland, is best known for his work connecting light and electromagnetic waves. According to Maxwell, light is propagated in two waves (one magnetic and one electric) which vibrate perpendicular to each other. This was followed by the Italian engineer, Marconi (inspired by Maxwell's wave theory), who produced the first practical radio signaling system (wireless telegraphy).

Electricity is defined as "A fundamental entity in nature consisting of negative and positive kinds composed respectively of electrons and protons, or possibly of electrons and positrons observable in the attractions and repulsions of bodies electrified by friction and in natural phenomena (as lightening or the aurora borealis), and usually utilized in the form of electric currents." (Webster's Dictionary.)

Another definition: "Electricity is a class of physical phenomena resulting from the existence of charge and from the interaction of charges. When a charge is stationary or static, it produces forces on objects in regions where it is present, and when it is in motion, it produces magnetic effects. Electric and magnetic effects are caused by the relative position and movement of positively and negatively charged particles of matter." (Microsoft Encarta Encyclopedia.)

According to the *Secret Doctrine*, electricity is not a fluid (as all now recognize):

"There are fluids of various kinds. Electricity is called a fluid, and so was heat quite recently, but it was on the supposition that heat was some imponderable substance. This was during the supreme and autocratic reign of matter. When the latter was dethroned, and MOTION was proclaimed the sole sovereign ruler of the Universe, heat became 'a mode of motion.' We need not despair: it may become something else to-morrow." *Secret Doctrine.*

"An Occultist would even object to electricity being called a fluid—*as it is an effect and not a cause.* But its *noumenon*, he would say, *is a conscious cause.*" *Secret Doctrine.*

A True Unknown Force. In 1875 Edison (28 years old) seemed to be on the verge of finding "a true unknown force." In a race with Alexander Graham Bell, Edison and some of his now 120 employees were endeavoring to develop a "speaking telegraph." Edison focused on experiments with various metals, in order to determine which was best suited for the vibrating diaphragm. In the process, some strange phenomena were noticed. Bright sparks were observed jumping across metals even when the metals were not conducting currents. "A true unknown force" is how he recorded it in his notebook, which he said might be "nonelectric" energy in space. "Sparks can be drawn from iron bodies in a magnetic field, and these sparks or force can be transmitted over metallic conductors and do not follow the laws of either voltaic or static electricity."

He was criticized by many in the press, as they claimed that the discovery was nothing new and that in the past it led nowhere. George Beard—a New York physician who experimented with the treating of disease with electricity (diseases of the skin, eating and drinking disorders, whooping cough) and who became known for his work on the nature of electrical forces within the human nervous system—thought otherwise. Beard considered this new force to be "a radiant force, somewhere between light and heat on the one hand and magnetism and electricity on the other." Was this "etheric force?" Beard offered the term "apolia" since lack of polarity was its leading fact.

The scientist in Edison was always intrigued with penetrating into the unknown realms of pure knowledge, regardless of how long it would take or where it might lead one. The practical and business side of Edison, however, won out after a few months. "By the spring, Edison had dropped attempts to further validate etheric force, or to develop practical channels for it, although he remained in touch with his soulmate, George Beard.... Edison later regretted the decision to move on so precipitously; but, being irrepressible, the *idea* of penetrating new territory always captivated him..." (Baldwin, *Edison, Inventing the Century*, 65.)

Edison's Workshop-Laboratory-Factory at Menlo Park. Edison purchased a secluded tract of land for the site of his new laboratory-machine shop. Menlo Park, New Jersey, was a farming village 12 miles south of Newark and 25 miles out of New York City. This provided the seclusion he needed for the scientific work. Located on the Pennsylvania railroad running between New York and Philadelphia, he was also commercially connected with important trade and industrial centers.

Inventing a time-clock probably never crossed Edison's mind. His dedicated employees worked along natural and irregular work rhythms. They were truly on the cutting edge of the new technology, and they must have loved it. Several key men stayed with Edison for over 25 years. Edison was the indefatigable worker who outpaced them all and who was the main source of inspiration.

Edison's laboratory developed the phonograph or "speaking machine", which became a huge success. The first machines were tinfoil cylinder phonographs that sold for $100. Soon afterward he developed a plate machine, using a flat disc instead of a cylinder, with a megaphone-type attachment that amplified the sound.

Col. Olcott of the Theosophical Society Visits Edison at Menlo Park. Helena Petrovna Blavatsky was living in New York City at this time. She sent to Edison at Menlo Park a copy of *Isis Unveiled* (published in the fall of 1877). She included in the mailing an application form for membership in the Theosophical Society, which Edison signed: "Please say to Madame Blavatsky that I have received her very curious work and I thank her for the same. I shall read between the lines!"

In December, 1878, shortly before leaving for India, Blavatsky and Olcott arranged to make the short trip to Menlo Park to visit Edison. At the last minute, Blavatsky, due to a minor illness, was unable to make the trip. Henry Steel Olcott (Co-Founder of the Theosophical Society) described his visit with Edison in his book: *Old Diary Leaves*:

On the 5th of April, T. A. Edison sent me his signed application for membership. I had had to see him about exhibiting his electrical inventions at the Paris Exposition of that year; I being the honorary secretary to a Citizens' National committee, which was formed at the request of the French Government, to induce the United States Congress to pass a bill providing for our country taking part in the first international exposition of the world's industries since the fall of the Empire and the foundation of the French Republic. [With France having a 5th ray soul and 3rd ray personality, one can imagine that the French had a very keen interest in the electrical discoveries and inventions of the day.]

Edison and I got to talking about occult forces, and he interested me greatly by the remark that he had done some experimenting in that direction. His aim was to try whether a pendulum, suspended on the wall of his private laboratory, could be made to move by will-force. To test this he had used as conductors, wire of various metals, simple and compound, and tubes containing different fluids, one end of the conductor being applied to his forehead, the other connected with the pendulum. As no results have since been published, I presume that the experiments did not succeed.

It may interest him, if he should chance to see this record, to know that in 1852 I met in Ohio a young man named Macallister, an ex-Shaker, who told me he had discovered a certain fluid, by bathing his forehead with which he could transmit thought to another person employing the same fluid at an agreed time, however distant the two might be apart. I remember writing an article on the subject under the title of "Mental Telegraphing" to the old *Spiritual Telegraph* newspaper, of the late Mr. S. B. Britten.

Having been acquainted with several noted American inventors, and learnt from them the psychological processes by which they severally got the first ideas of their inventions, I described these to Edison and asked him how his discoveries came to him. He said that often, perhaps while walking on Broadway with an acquaintance, and talking about quite other matters, amid the din and roar of the street, the thought would suddenly flash into his mind that such a desired thing might be accomplished in a certain way. He would hasten home, set to work on the idea, and not give it up until he had either succeeded or found the thing impractical.

Old Diary Leaves: A History of the Theosophical Society, 466-8.

The above passage indicates that Edison was a scientist with an open mind. He was willing to explore subtle phenomena that some of his colleagues might have thought strange to the point of bringing one's scientific reputation into question. Also we see here something of how the lower concrete mind (the intellect) reasons or thinks to a point of exhausting all known possibilities, and then, while relaxed or away from the concentrated thought, new ideas suddenly drop into the conscious mind. A clue as to what this is may be found in the following passage: "Your mental body is on the fifth ray, giving you your grip of facts and your grasp of the contours of the occult sciences. But this mental body must be guided into being an instrument of illumination and not simply a recorder of facts; this only becomes possible when head and heart vibrate in unison."

Discipleship in the New Age I, 540.

Edison Considered "Incandescent Electric Lighting and Power System" to be His Greatest Invention. The word "incandescent" comes from the French: *incandescere,* to become hot, and from *candere* to glow. The effort began with Michael Faraday's mentor, Humphry Davy, who attempted to bring about a prolonged glow of a platinum filament. Dozens of scientists worked on the challenge for over 80 years. Edison experimented with many filaments, looking for one that would not burn out at high temperatures. He settled on a filament with a carbonized thread, horseshoe shaped, providing 100 hours of light. Air was drawn out of the bulb, producing a vacuum, which slowed the deterioration of the filament. A year later, a bamboo filament brought 900 hours of light.

There was another apparent conflict between Edison's fifth ray demand for the perfect invention and his 3rd ray rush to communicate. Edison would communicate to the public and his financial backers a new discovery when the discovery was proven in principle but not in all its details. For Edison, there was no doubt about the validity of the invention; it was just a matter of time. This conflict surfaced on a regular basis and brought some stress to his Menlo Park scientists, who were nicknamed by some journalist the "insomnia squad." Working out the points of refinement always took much longer than anticipated. The patience of many people was not very long, and he was called charlatan on many an occasion. The pure scientific 5th ray nature (exhibited by Michael Faraday) tends to understate and down-play the discovery. The statements are generally strictly accurate, without any fanfare. Edison announced his findings in scientific journals, took inventions to New York for demonstration, had a steady stream of people come out to Menlo Park to see with their own eyes, and readily gave interviews to curious journalists. This served to 1) heighten anticipation, 2) bring financial backing in the short run, 3) increase pressure from the financial backers in the longer run, and 4) increase the effort of the competition to get there before he did. Edison was obviously not the quiet, reclusive type of researcher who prefers to be completely out of the public eye.

Edison's Enterprises Steadily Expand. In 1881 (34 years old) he outdid his competitors at the International Electrical Exhibit in Paris. He received five Gold Medals, and his international reputation, already substantial, was enhanced. He received the prestigious offer to provide lighting for the foyer of the Paris Opera. This was followed by an offer to do the same for La Scala, in Milan. Two Edison companies were established in Paris for marketing and patent protection purposes. A three story generating station—the largest in Europe—was built in Milan on the site of one of Leonardo da Vinci's canals. The American in charge of the enterprise, John William Lieb, became so fascinated with Leonardo's artistic and scientific achievements that he became an avid collector of Leonardo's manuscripts and eventually a lecturer on "Leonardo—The Master Mind of the Renaissance."

Edison was also doing public relations work in London at this time. Some of his engineers were lighting a half mile strip along the perimeter of the City of London. Three years earlier (1878) his phonograph had been demonstrated at the Royal Institution where Faraday had given his famous lectures. Alfred Lord Tennyson was at the phonograph demonstration. He heard his own verse, "Come into the Garden, Maud" being phonographically recited.

Edison's phonograph continued to be developed and refined. By 1900 the Edison Phonograph Works employed a thousand workers. Although Edison experimented with a revolving plate (disc or record), he stayed with the cylinder (finer grooves, longer play) until the competition from Victor and Columbia forced him to go with the more popular flat disc.

"Good" electric lightening was aggressively marketed to replace the "evils" of gas lighting. Clean energy was replacing the hazards of the open flame.

Edison developed the motion picture with the primary inventive skills of William Dickson. Many inventors in Europe and the U.S. were working on this project, but with Edison's capital, large team of technicians, and Dickson's genius, he was able to stay ahead or outdistance the others. Edison's intention was to develop an instrument "that would do for the eye what the phonograph does for the ear, which is the recording and reproducing things in motion." The first motion pictures were viewed by looking through a viewing hole in a box known as a "kinetoscope." Edison felt that the wave of the future would be one viewer per machine. William Dickson saw it differently. His idea was to have images thrown upon a screen. Another factor that helped Edison beat out the competitors was his extensive experimentation to come up with a relatively refined product. The motion picture of other companies were very jerky in comparison to his own smooth images.

Another major invention of Edison's was the storage battery. The lead battery was heavy, cumbersome, and corrosive. His team of technicians experimented with thousands of combinations of elements and alkaline solutions for a period of three years to come up with iron for the negative pole, a super oxide of nickel for the positive pole, and potash as the electrolyte in a water solution. The battery had a high electrical capacity per unit weight. Extending this vision, Edison really wanted to see an electric car developed. Edison considered this one of his greatest inventions. Reporters frequently asked Edison what he thought his best invention was. It was a difficult question for him to answer. Nothing was every complete. Further refinement was almost always in progress. The greatest invention was always just around the corner.

The Noumenon Behind the Phenomenon—The "Unknown Force."
Earlier we noted that as pure scientist, Edison was indeed intrigued by a possible truly *unknown force*, which might be *non-electric energy in space*. In his mature years the reach of his inventive intuition was

displaced by the more Saturnian concerns of maintaining his manifold business enterprises. He was "regrettably" unable to go back and retrieve all the teasing threads of possible new discoveries of a phenomenal nature. Was there an electrical energy in space that was neither positive, nor negative, but neutral? Perhaps there was another person who was able to penetrate the etheric space and find the third factor.

According to the *Secret Doctrine*: "Neither the nature of electricity, nor of Life nor even of Light, are to this day understood. The Occultist sees in the manifestation of every force in Nature, the action of the quality, or the special characteristic of its noumenon; which *noumenon* is a distinct and intelligent Individuality *on the other side of the manifested mechanical Universe.*"

Man explores phenomenon, the world of appearances, but neglects to realize that a world of consciousness (noumenon, soul, quality) stands behind the world of appearance (the mechanical universe) and sets it all in motion. To quote from *Cosmic Fire*: "The tangible objective exterior, negative, receptive, and occultly unorganized, is without form and usefulness *apart from the inner energy*." The inner energy brings the form world (phenomenon, appearances) into manifestation, not the other way around.

Circulation of Energy Between Two Planes. The following quote from the *Secret Doctrine* raises additional questions:

> It may serve to elucidate the meaning if we attempt to imagine a neutral centre—the dream of those who would discover perpetual motion. A "neutral centre" is, in one aspect, the limiting point of any given set of senses. Thus, imagine two consecutive planes of matter as already formed; each* of these corresponding, to an appropriate set of perceptive organs. We are forced to admit that between these two planes of matter an incessant circulation takes place; and if we follow the atoms and molecules of (say) the lower in their transformation upwards, these will come to a point where they pass altogether beyond the range of the faculties we are using on the lower plane. In fact, to us the matter of the lower plane there vanishes from our perception into nothing—or rather it passes on to the higher plane, and the state of matter corresponding to such a point of transition must certainly possess special and not readily discoverable properties. Such "Seven Neutral Centres,"* then, are produced by Fohat, who, when, as Milton has it—"Fair foundations (are) laid whereon to build . . ." quickens matter into activity and evolution.

* Such, we believe, is the name applied by Mr. Keely, of Philadelphia, the inventor of the famous "Motor"—destined, as his admirers have hoped, to revolutionize the motor power of the world—to what he again calls the "Etheric Centres."
The Secret Doctrine.

The suggestion above seems to indicate that the "neutral centers" (so-called by certain scientists who were able to identify a very subtle force that seems to be related to electricity, yet is non-polar—neither positive nor negative) the "neutral centers" are the same as (or related to) what the occultists have called the etheric centers. If these centers exist within the etheric body of an individual, then they must also exist in the etheric body of the planet. The planet itself must have an etheric body, that is, a body of *vitality* (energy) drawing upon the pranic energy of the sun. According to esoteric science, the spleen center (not one of the seven major centers) is the center which stores up "the rays of radiatory light and heat [prana] which are secured from the sun and transmits them... to all parts of the physical body" (*Cosmic Fire*, 57).

Does atomic matter of the lower planes appear to vanish at a certain point? At "the point" where two planes meet there is an energy ebb and flow, the higher either vitalizing or withdrawing from the lower. The withdrawal or ebb is only an apparent "vanishing" to limited sight. The point at which two planes meet would hold mysteries of power or of possible energy release and utilization.

Negative Planetary Electricity and Positive Solar Electricity. The following quote from *A Treatise on Cosmic Fire* seems to answer some of our questions to a degree but also raises additional rather abstruse questions:

Only when the substance aspect is studied by the scientist *in its triple nature* will truth be approximated, and the true nature of electrical phenomena be comprehended; then and only then will electricity be harnessed and utilized by man as a unity, and not just in one of its aspects as at present; the *negative electricity of the planet is all that is as yet contacted for commercial purposes.* It must be remembered that this term is used in the sense of negative in relation to solar electricity. When man has found out how to contact and utilize *positive solar electricity in combination with negative planetary electricity*, we shall have a very dangerous condition brought about, and one of the factors which will eventually manifest in the destruction of the fifth root race by fire. At that great cataclysm—as the Bible says "the Heavens will melt with fervent heat." This will be seen in a still greater degree in the next round, and will cause that destruction by fire of the forms of the men who have failed, which will liberate the lives on a stupendous scale, and thus temporarily 'purify' the Earth from elements which would tend to hinder the evolutionary process. As the cycles pass away, the balancing of these fiery currents will be gradually brought about, and will result in a planetary condition of harmony, and of esoteric equality, which will provide ideal environment for harmonious man. [Italics added.] *Cosmic Fire* 524.

Again, there are several questions that are raised here. Planetary electricity is negative, and solar electricity is positive. Is there anything about the nature of this positive solar electricity that can be discovered now, or is this far in the future? Are the "neutral centers" mentioned above the same as or related to "positive solar electricity"?

Another important question is: Who is "Mr. Keely of Philadelphia", as mentioned in the *Secret Doctrine*? Again, quoting from *Cosmic Fire*:

Electric fire passes from atom to atom according to law, and 'fire by friction' responds, being the latent fire of the atom, or its negative aspect; the process is carried on through the medium of *solar fire, and herein lies the secret of transmutation* and its most mysterious angle. Fire by friction, the negative electricity of substance, has been for some time the subject of the attention of exoteric science, and investigation of the nature of positive electricity has become possible through the discovery of radium.

Keely, as H. P. B. hinted, had gone far along this path, and knew even more than he gave out, and others have approached, or are approaching, the same objective. The next step ahead for science lies in this direction, and should concern the potential force of the atom itself, and its harnessing for the use of man. This will let loose upon earth a stupendous amount of energy. Nevertheless, it is only when the third factor is comprehended, and science admits the agency of mental fire as embodied in certain groups of devas, that the force of energy that is triple, and yet one in the three worlds, will become available for the helping of man. This lies as yet far ahead, and will only become possible towards the end of this round; and these potent forces will not be fully utilized, nor fully known till the middle of the next round."

Cosmic Fire 492.

Radium, Radioactivity, the Radiant Quality, and the Energy Interplay Between Two Planes. There are certain substances and beings that are "radiant" due to the fact that they are in transition from one kingdom to the next higher. Radioactivity has to do with the "effect produced by the inner essence as it makes its presence felt through the form, when the form has been brought to a stage of such refinement that it becomes possible." (*Cosmic Fire* 1062). An example that is given for this "radioactivity" in the occult sense of that term in the vegetable kingdom is the eucalyptus tree. "There are forms of animal life equally at an analogous stage, and the human unit (as it approaches 'liberation') demonstrates a similar phenomenon"—the phenomenon of being "radioactive" or radiant. "Again, as a planetary scheme nears its consummation, it becomes 'radioactive,' and through radiation transfers its essence to another 'absorbent planet,' or planets, as is the case with a solar system also. Its essence, or true Life, is absorbed by a receiving constellation, and the outer 'case' returns to its original unorganized condition." (*Cosmic Fire*, p. 1062.

In the late 1800's it was discovered that uranium emitted particles and that this emission seemed to be a natural and unchangeable property of the element. The emission of particles was termed "radioactivity", from the Latin *radiare*, meaning to give off rays. In 1899 Ernest Rutherford discovered that uranium gave off different kinds of rays, which were termed alpha and beta rays. Later a third ray (gamma ray) was discovered.

Polish born Madame Curie discovered a new element—radium—that was 4 million times as radioactive as uranium. With the discovery of radioactivity, matter was no longer considered indestructible. Radioactivity forced a change in that theory.

Who is Keely of Philadelphia? In the passages above, H.P.B. made reference to Keely's motor that will "revolutionize the motor power of the world", and D.K. stated that Keely had gone far along the path of "the investigation of the nature of positive electricity." (As far as we were able to determine, Keely did not work with radium.)

In the *Secret Doctrine*, we find another reference to John Worrell Keely and his enigmatic discoveries.

> And if all this appears too *unscientific* to be even noticed, let Science explain "to what mechanical and physical laws known to it, is due the recently produced phenomena of the so-called "Keely motor?" What is it that acts as the formidable generator of invisible but tremendous force, of that power which is not only capable of driving an engine of 25 horse-power, but

has even been employed to lift the machinery bodily? Yet this is done simply by drawing a fiddle-bow across a tuning fork, as has been repeatedly proven. For the *etheric* Force, discovered by the well-known (in America and now in Europe) John Worrell Keely, of Philadelphia, is no *hallucination*. Notwithstanding his failure to utilize it, a failure prognosticated and maintained by some Occultists from the first, the phenomena exhibited by the discoverer during the last few years have been wonderful, almost miraculous, not in the sense of the *supernatural** but of the *superhuman*. Had Keely been permitted to succeed, he might have reduced a whole army to atoms in the space of a few seconds as easily as he reduced a dead ox to the same condition.   *Secret Doctrine*

Who is John Worrell Keely? Keely was born in Philadelphia on September 3, 1837. His mother died shortly after John was born; his father died when John was three years old. He was raised by an aunt (who died when John was sixteen), and his grandmother (who died when he was seventeen). He had some basic education in the public schools of Philadelphia, but dropped out of school at the age of twelve. He became a carpenter's apprentice and stayed with that activity until he was 35 years old (1872). He had mechanical ability, and he had a fascination with sound and with physics.

As a pure scientific thinker, he enjoyed making little experiments. As a boy of twelve walking the beaches of Cape May, New Jersey, he noticed, while holding various sea shells to his ear, that no two shells had exactly the same tone. His experiments with sound began with striking various chords on an organ and noticing the effect of the vibration on suspended glass dishes and other objects placed around the room. His first "intensifier" or "resonator" consisted of a steel bar with several pins in it, connected to hollow wooden tubes. His research reached a point in 1872 when he was able to start his own company and was able to find financial backers.

Disintegration of Stone and Other Demonstrations of the Etheric Force. In 1888 R. Harte, Secretary of the Theosophical Society, wrote an article highlighting some of Keely's accomplishments. Keely had devised a machine with which he was able to disintegrate rock in a matter of seconds. A group of twelve wealthy entrepreneurs visited Keely in his Philadelphia laboratory. Their mining interests led them to Keely. They were in search of an inexpensive method for extracting gold from granite rock. The group of millionaires watched Keely as he touched blocks of granite with his hand-held machine. The rock crumbled into small fragments before their eyes, leaving specks of gold standing out among sand particles.

The twelve men promised a large sum of money to Mr. Keely if he could succeed in demonstrating the power of his machine in a natural setting. He was taken to the Katskill Mountains, and a large section of quartz was pointed out to him. He asked the men to make note of the time. In eighteen minutes he had succeeded in carving a tunnel eighteen feet deep and four and a half feet in diameter. The entrepreneurs then went from New York to San Francisco, buying up old, abandoned, and apparently worthless goldmines.

In an interview with *Scientific Arena* in January, 1887, John Keely told the reporter that in order to disintegrate common quartz, the etheric force required was 42,800 vibrations per second. He also said that metal will successfully withstand the enormous force of 240,000 vibrations per second. Keely stated: "The first etheric chord on the first octave induces 42,800 vibrations per second."

Keely was frequently denounced as a "crank" in public print; his demonstrations were labeled "delusions of a fraud." The writer of the above article published in Scientific Arena describes Keely in the following way: "Tall, straight, broad-shouldered, and muscular. In manner he is courteous, frank and genial, cordial and generous with friends, keen and cautious with enemies, his presence is always magnetic, and so surely as his discoveries are the most stupendous ever given to man to accomplish, his memory will live while men cherish with pride the names of great benefactors."

Keely was somehow tapping into or harnessing etheric force. Another one of his demonstrations consisted of placing a thin wire around an iron cylinder weighing several hundred pounds. When the etheric force ran through the wire, he was able to lift the cylinder with his finger and move it to the other side of the shop.

Keely's Explanation; A Definition of Sound. According to Keely, his machine did not function like other machines, for it did not function on the principle of pressure. There was no pistons, no pressure-exhaust system. His machine functioned under the principle of what he called "sympathetic vibration." After many years of labor, innumerable experiments, and a "close study of the phenomenal properties that the substance 'ether' produced, I have been able to dispense with complicated mechanism and to obtain... mastery over the subtle and strange force with which I am dealing." He predicted that the power of the ether would be adapted to engines of all sizes, from the largest ship to a sewing machine, and that it would also be adapted to military weapons.

A key factor in liberating the etheric force, according to Keely, is *sound*. This goes back to his very first experiments as a boy. Sound is the primary element with which Keely worked and experimented. "In my estimation, sound truly defined is the disturbance of atomic equilibrium, rupturing actual atomic corpuscles; and the substance thus liberated must certainly be a certain order of etheric flow."

If everything, down to the atom, is in motion, then everything is vibrating, and it becomes necessary to discover the *laws of vibratory motion*. According to Keely, "There is no dividing of matter and force into two distinct terms, as they both are one. Force is liberated matter. Matter is force in bondage." The difference between matter and energy is simply rate and mode of vibration.

The Neutral Center. According to Keely, every rotary system is built around a neutral center. The neutral center itself is indivisible. Matter is the exterior manifestation of the neutral central. "Every aggregate mass consists of molecules, each of which has its neutral center where the three modes of vibration—dominant, harmonic, and enharmonic—meet in a center of sympathetic coincidence and are equated without cancellation of their energy." The neutral center is without weight. It is an "inter-etheric point in space", and it "communicates direct by means of its outflow of sympathy, with every planetary mass in the Universe. Through the inflow of sympathy, through the solar intermediate, the sun, it receives the life flow from the Supreme Neutral Center that enables it to perpetuate its existence." The Supreme Neutral Center is the pivotal point of the Universe—the indestructible and forever existing First Cause. It controls, through the "life flow", the existence and mass of every unit in the universe—from stellar, solar, and planetary mass down to each individual molecule.

The neutral center brings about a condition of "unstable equilibrium" between two forces—"the dispersing positive and the attractive negative." The neutral center stands as the deciding factor, the connective link, and the controlling tendency. Keely also calls this function or property the "Universal Will."

Keely endeavored to build a machine that draws upon the energy of this center—something that no other scientist had approached. The disturbance of equilibrium at the etheric level can be brought about through sound, which then releases a tremendous amount of energy. Keely experimented with the disintegration of the elements of water. This was accomplished in three stages, each as a result of different notes or chords. The first stage resulted in a gaseous compound of hydrogen and oxygen, the second stage produced a "low atomic ether", and the third stage "the low atomic ether resolved into a new element, which I denominate high or second atomic harmonic."

Foundations of a New Science: The Laws of Vibration. John Keely's work centers around the discovery of the laws of vibration. He discovered 40 laws that govern vibratory phenomena, and these have been published in the *Journal of Sympathetic Vibratory Physics*. Modern physics is based on laws governing mass and energy. Keely's laws of vibration deal with the inner nature of vibratory phenomena, which include amplitude, velocity, mode, sympathy, number and periodicity.

Keely's *Law of Harmonic Vibrations*: "All coherent aggregates are perpetually vibrating at a period-frequency corresponding to some harmonic ration of the fundamental pitch of the vibrating body; this pitch is a multiple of the pitch of the atomole." Atomole is defined as "elementary units of matter uniform in size and weight, and exist in solid, liquid, gaseous, and isolated forms." Atoms are multiple combinations of atomoles.
Law of Attraction: "Juxtaposed coherent aggregates vibrating in unison, or harmonic ration, are mutually attractive."
Law of Repulsion: "Juxtaposed coherent aggregates vibrating in discord are mutually repelled."

Gravity "is the mutual attraction of atomoles.... Gravity may be considered a negative force, for it tends to balance the positive forces. Gravitational forces are vibratory forces and might be defined as the centralization of vibratory forces ready to change into power by non-activity... Gravity is nothing more than an attractive, sympathetic stream, flowing towards the neutral center of the earth, emanating from molecular centers of neutrality; concordant with the earth's center of neutrality, and seeking its medium of affinity with a power corresponding to the character of the molecular mass."
Law of Variation of Atomic Pitch by Electricity and Magnetism: "Electricity and Magnetism produce internal vibrations in the atom, which are followed by proportional changes in volume and, therefore, pitch."
Law of Chemical Affinity: "Atoms whose atomic pitches are in either unison, harmonic or concordant ratios, unite to form molecules. When two atoms are indifferent, they may be made to unite by varying the pitch of either, or both."

Three Different Kinds of Electricity. According to Keely, there are three different kinds of electricity: The harmonic, the enharmonic, and the dominant.

The *dominant* is " electricity luminous, or propulsive positive.

The *harmonic* is the magnetic, "which is the attractive, with its wonderful sympathetic outreach."

The *enharmonic* is the "high neutral" and "acts as the assimilative towards the reinstatement of sympathetic disturbance."

The electricity that is generated by the velocity of our dynamos is of the harmonic or magnetic variety. "Electricity is but a certain condensed form of atomic vibration, a form showing only the introductory features which precede the etheric vibratory condition... We have to go far beyond this condition to reach the pure etheric one... The Vibratory Etheric tree has many branches, and electricity is but one of them. Though it is a medium by which the operations of vital forces are performed, it cannot in my opinion be considered the soul of matter."

John Keely's Rays. The depth of Mr. Keely's scientific work and the statements we have both from H.P. Blavatsky and D.K. would strongly suggest that Keely's soul is indeed on the 5th ray of science. The biographical information that we have about Mr. Keely is too sketchy and fragmented to make a ray analysis beyond the above statement. Due to the fact that we know he was born on September 3rd, however, some additional comment about certain psychological factors can be made. Mr. Keely's Sun sign was Virgo. One of Virgo's primary qualities has to do with the task of nurturing a seed for the future life. Expressed in other words, Virgo deals with the early, incubation stage of the Christ life. As such, Virgo is more interested in *getting the details right*, in *perfecting the delicate new spirit-filled form*, than it is in presenting the "new life" (the "new" truth or that truth that humanity is ready to hear and understand) to the public, to the market place or to the world at large. John Keely, it seems, was in no hurry to market his invention. Unlike Edison, if Keely's experiments did not prove immediately practical, that did not prevent him from continuing his experiments along the same line. What ray quality do we see here, along with the Virgo quality? We could probably eliminate the 3rd ray of intelligent activity. We would have to consider the possibility of the 6th ray of devotion and idealism. Keely apparently knew that he was touching God's Design. "God moves in a mysterious way his wonders to perform; and if he has chosen me as the tool to carve out certain positions, what credit have I? None; and, though it is an exalting thought that he has singled out me for specific work, I know that the finest tool is of no value without a manipulator." (Clara Jessup Bloomfield-Moore, "Mr Keely's New Philosophy." *Scientific Arena*, December, 1886.)

The Three Departments of the Spiritual Hierarchy; Where Science Fits In. From the East comes the teaching of the Spiritual Hierarchy with its three major departments:

1. The Department of the Manu.
2. The Department of the Bodhisattva or World Teacher.
3. The Department of the Mahachohan or Lord of Civilization.

"These three Departments represent in the Hierarchy the three aspects of the Logos as manifested in the solar system,—the Aspect of Will or Power, the Aspect of Love and Wisdom (which is the basic aspect for this system), and the Aspect of Activity or Intelligence."

Letters on Occult Meditation, 167.

The Manu manipulates matter and is occupied with the evolution of form, whether it is the dense physical form of animal, mineral, flower, human being or planet, or the form of races, nations, devas or the other evolutions.

The Bodhisattva or World Teacher works with the evolving life within the form, with the implanting of religious ideas and with the development of philosophical concepts both in individuals and races.

The Mahachohan, who synthesizes the four lower rays, deals with mind or intelligence, and, in collaboration with His Brothers, controls the evolution of mind whereby the Spirit or Self utilizes the form or the Not-Self.

Line of the Manu.................Force, Strength, Power to rule.
Line of the Bodhisattva........Magnetism, Attraction, Healing.
Line of the Mahachohan.....Electricity, Synthesis, Organization.

1. *The line of the Manu.*
This first line is specially the line of government, of racial development, of working in and with the matter of all forms on all the planes of human evolution.....

2. *The line of the Bodhisattva.*
This is the line of religion and of philosophy, and of the development of the indwelling life. It deals with consciousness within the form more than with the form itself. It is the line of

least resistance for the many. It embodies the wisdom aspect of the Logos, and is the line whereby His love is manifested in a predominant fashion. The solar system being in itself a direct expression of the Logos, and of His love aspect, all in manifestation is based upon it—love in rule, love abounding, love in activity—but in this second line the above manifestation is supreme, and will eventually absorb all the others....

3. *The line of the Mahachohan.*

This is the line of mind or intelligence, of knowledge and of science. It is the line of abstract mind, and of archetypal ideas. The man broods not so much upon the Law, not so much upon the Life, as upon the effects of both in manifestation, and upon the reason why. The man on this fivefold line ever asks why, and how, and whence, and seeks to synthesize, to comprehend and to make the archetypes and ideals facts in manifestation. He broods on the ideals as he senses them; he aims at contacting the Universal Mind, at wresting its secrets from it, and giving them expression. It is the line of business organization, the line also in which the artists, musicians, scientists and the workers of the world have their place. The Spirits of Love and Activity pass much time in each of its five departments before passing on to the lines of love and of power."

Letters on Occult Meditation 170, 171,172 .

Extrapolating from the above, we find the work of 5th ray souls falling primarily in the third department of the Lord of Civilization (Mahachohan). Their work is along the line of *mind or intelligence, of knowledge and of science.* Unlike the first ray man (who broods upon the Law, the task of government, the divine autocracy, and the work of the Lords of Karma) and unlike the second ray man (who broods upon the indwelling Life and consciousness), the line of the Mahachohan and the third ray man broods upon "the effects of both in manifestation." The third and fifth rays together would be working in a pronounced way (using intellect, science, and knowledge) to bring into manifestation the sensed scientific truths. The scientific type meditates upon the scientific problem, "and by brooding over it and by the employment of the lower mind, finds out all that can be known and sensed. Then, having done that, he seeks to raise the consciousness still higher till he taps the source of illumination, and gains the light and information required" (*Letters on Occult Meditation*, 172-3).

Alice Bailey Quote's Edison. Alice Bailey gave a series of lectures in New York in the 1920's and 30's. Some of these lectures have been brought out in book form. One series of her lectures comprise the book *Consciousness of the Atom* (1922) and have to do with the "testimony of science as to the relation of matter and consciousness." In the effort to bridge esoteric science (occultism) with the more advanced scientific theories and findings of the day, Alice quotes Edison at some length:

> When we speak of energy there must be that which energizes, that which is the source of energy and the origin of that force which demonstrates in matter. It is here that I seek to lay the emphasis. Whence comes this energy, and what is it?
>
> First of all, as we know, the atom is spoken of as possessing energy, and the power to change from one mode of activity to another. One writer has remarked that 'absolute intelligence thrills through every atom in the world.' In this connection I want to point out to you what Edison is reported by an interviewer as having said in Harper's Magazine for February 1890, and which is enlarged upon in the Scientific American for October 1920. In the earlier instance he is quoted as follows:
>
> 'I do not believe that matter is inert, acted upon by an outside force. To me it seems that every atom is possessed by a certain amount of primitive intelligence. Look at the thousands of ways in which atoms of hydrogen combine with those of other elements, forming the most diverse substances. Do you mean to say that they do this without intelligence? Atoms in harmonious and useful relation assume beautiful or interesting shapes and colors, or give forth a pleasant perfume, as if expressing their satisfaction...gathered together in certain forms, the atoms constitute animals of the lower order. Finally they combine in man, who represents the total intelligence of all the atoms.'
>
> 'But where does this intelligence come from originally?' asked the interviewer.
>
> 'From some power greater than ourselves,' Edison answered.
>
> 'Do you believe, then, in an intelligent Creator, a personal God?'
>
> 'Certainly. The existence of such a God can, to my mind, be proved from chemistry.'
>
> In the long interview quoted in the Scientific American, Edison laid down a number of most interesting surmises from which I have culled the following:

1. Life, like matter, is indestructible.
2. Our bodies are composed of myriads of infinitesimal entities, each in itself a unit of life; just as the atom is composed of myriads of electrons.
3. The human being acts as an assemblage rather than as a unit; the body and mind express the vote or voice of the life entities.
4. The life entities build according to a plan. If a part of the life organism be mutilated, they rebuild exactly as before....
5. Science admits the difficulty of drawing the line between the inanimate and the animate; perhaps the life entities extend their activities to crystals and chemicals....
6. The life entities live forever; so that to this extent at least the eternal life, which many of us hope for, is a reality."

Alice Bailey, *Consciousness of an Atom* 38-40.

Summary of Fifth Ray Indicators.

Early aptitude for science.
Developed his own chemistry lab.
Scientific experimentation with ever more refined observation.
Endless questions and curiosity about the working of things.
Aptitude for the invention of electrical and mechanical devices.
Love of accuracy.
Cautious approach to questions of conjecture.
Mastering a complete body of knowledge.
Major contribution to Science of Electricity.
No experiments are useless since all result in knowledge.
A grip of facts.
Strictly accurate statements.
A preference for understating results, rather than overstating
    or exaggerating results.
Brooding upon the effects of the Law and the Life in manifestation.
Deeply probing with the questions of why, and how, and whence, in
    order to comprehend and in order to make the archetypes facts
    in manifestation.

Summary of Third Ray Indicators.

Energetic and enterprising.
Aptitude for starting his own business at an early age.
Working long hours.
Turning his inventions into profitable business enterprises.
Adapt at reason.

Enjoying the activity of business.
Understanding the competitive race.
Understanding the need for the refinement of efficiency in order to have a successful business.

ALFRED LORD TENNYSON: SIXTH RAY SOUL

The sixth ray man will be the poet of the emotions (such as Tennyson) and the writer of religious books, either in poetry or prose. He is devoted to beauty and color and all things lovely, but his productive skill is not great unless under the influence of one of the practically artistic rays, the fourth or seventh. His music will always be of a melodious order, and he will often be the composer of oratories and of sacred music.

The method of healing for this ray would be by faith and prayer.

The way of approaching the Path would be by prayer and meditation, aiming at union with God.
Esoteric Psychology I, 209-210.

Alfred Tennyson's Childhood. Alfred Tennyson was born August 6, 1809, in Somersby, Lincolnshire, England. His father, Dr. George Tennyson, was a clergyman (vicar of Somersby), and his grandfather was a Member of Parliament. The grandfather, referred to as "the Old Man", brought four children into the world. George (Alfred's father) was the first male child, and Charles, his brother, was the youngest child in the family. Much of the grandfather's wealth came from an earlier inheritance. Charles was the Old Man's favorite. The different temperaments of the two sons became evident at an early age. George was more clumsy and ungainly. Evidently the Old Man could not see George following him in his footsteps; George was directed into taking priest's orders. Charles, on the other hand, did follow the Old Man's path and eventually became a Member of Parliament.

At some unclear point it became known that the youngest son, Charles, was to get the major portion of the Old Man's wealth. This had a very negative affect on George. As the eldest son, George felt that it was his right to acquire the significant portion of the father's inheritance. This would be in keeping with a very long and firm tradition. The favoritism shown Charles by the Old Man brought about a deep resentment in George. This became increasingly problematical in George's later years and was to have a damaging effect on his children.

George became the Rector of Somersby, married, and had 12 children (the first born died in infancy). Frederick was born in 1807, then came Charles in 1808, and Alfred was born (as mentioned above) on August 6, 1809. Altogether he had 6 brothers and 4 sisters.

The Somersby environment was rural. Alfred Tennyson was brought up in what might be called idyllic surroundings. The Rectory at Somersby lay between two ranges of low, rolling hills. A small brook meandered through the valley.

> On either side the river lie
> Long fields of barley and of rye,
> That clothe the wold and meet the sky;
> And through the field the road runs by....
>> From "Lady of Shallot."
> Lo! sweeten'd with the summer light,
> The full-juiced apple, waxing over-mellow,
> Drops in a silent autumn night.
> All its allotted length of days
> The flower ripens in its place,
> Ripens and fades, and falls, and hath no toil,
> Fast-rooted in the fruitful soil.
>> From "The Lotos-Eaters."

Alfred's father, George (also referred to as Dr. Tennyson), served two churches—one at Somersby where the family lived, and one a mile away at Bag Enderby. The Old Man provided funds to up-grade the churches. Additions were added to the Rectory at Somersby, in order to accommodate the growing family.

Alfred went to Louth Grammar School until 1820 (from 7 to 11 years of age). Little is known about this time other than he hated those years at the Grammar School. When Alfred was twelve, his father took him out of school and began to tutor both Alfred and his brother Charles on a full-time basis. The emphasis was on a classical, literary education. Central to this was a thorough knowledge of Greek and Latin. Homer and the *Odes* of Horace received a special focus. Also included was the *Arabian Nights*, Persian poetry, the Koran and many books on mythology and folklore. "The Doctor" (as his father was often called) had high academic standards.

First Book of Poetry. Alfred's first book of poetry was published in April, 1827 (he was 17 years old). It was entitled *Poems by Two Brothers*—a collection of verses composed by Alfred and his brother Charles. Alfred at this time was experimenting with several different styles of poetry. One very seldom finds one's own unique style, or one's own voice, at an early age.

Shelley and Bryon were the two poets that had the most influence on Alfred. When Bryon died (1824), Alfred felt that "everything was over and finished for everyone, that nothing else mattered." This almost adolescent response reveals something like an extreme religious devotion to a particular person. One might say that Tennyson's "religion" was poetry (the poetic literature of Greece, Rome, and Persia, as well as the Scottish, Irish, and English traditions) and that one of his "bibles" at an early age was the works of Lord Bryon.

When Dr Tennyson started tutoring Alfred at the age of twelve, the Doctor probably still had most of his wits about him. When Alfred was 15, however, the Doctor's health was deteriorating rapidly. The cause is not clear but it seems that there were several contributing factors. The diagnosis was "cholera morbus." The treatment included opium and calomel (mercurous chloride, Hg_2Cl_2). There was also a problem of a regular overuse of alcohol. This was accompanied by heightened emotionalism in the house and regular violent outbursts. The mother and the 12 children were often terrified. The psychological damage affected everyone in the household. Alfred's escape at first was to rush out of the house and spend recuperative time in nature. At 18 he was able to escape to college.

Trinity College at Cambridge. There were four significant events or developments during Tennyson's three years at Cambridge (1828-1831).

1) First of all, his *scholarly pursuits in the field of literature*, poetry, the classical Greek and Latin works continued and acquired more depth. He entered college already a serious poet. At Trinity he developed and refined his craft. His aspiration to become a major English poet was reinforced by his experience at Trinity.

2) A second factor or event of significance was the *winning of a poetry contest* (1829). Tennyson won the Chancellor's Gold Medal Award for his poem on the designated subject of Timbuctoo. His father had urged him to enter the contest. Alfred did so, but reluctantly and half-heartedly. He took a verse that he had begun five years earlier (when 15 years old) and made some alterations in it, so that it might fit the theme. Using a poem composed in blank verse, shows how little he cared about winning. The prize had never before been awarded to a poem written in blank verse. The winning of the prize established him as the superior poet among his group of literary friends, and the prize also brought him prominence throughout the College.

3) The third significant factor had to do with his society of friends. Tennyson developed over the years at Cambridge a *close association with a handful of like-minded young men*. His first year was solitary, but gradually he came into a group of philosophical and literary thinkers. The college organization known as the Conversazione Society elected him into the group after he won the Gold Medal Award for "Timbuctoo." This group referred to themselves as "the Apostles." It was an exclusive and somewhat secretive group. Their mission, as characterized by one of its members years later, was to "interpret the oracles of transcendental wisdom to the world of the Philistines" (Thorn 54). They were interested in the big metaphysical questions. They would discuss these questions at length and then vote on them, as if issuing some sort of a supreme court judgment. They were filled with lofty aspirations and were somewhat ego-centric, to be sure, but appropriately so for their age. Someday soon, they thought, they would be able to do very great things in society, in the nation, and in the world.

The friendships and associations of the group extended far beyond the college years. Tennyson was keenly interested in what his peers thought about his poetry. All of them were schooled in the classics; some had literary ambitions of their own. Some, in the years after college, were helpful in bringing Tennyson's work before the public eye. Some wrote reviews of his poetry in the important journals of the time.

Alfred's closest friend during this time was Arthur Hallam. He had been brought into the "Apostles" by virtue of his intelligence and debating skills. Hallam also developed a friendship with one of Alfred's sisters. It was a serious friendship that was moving slowly and cautiously towards marriage. It all ended tragically, however, in that Hallam died in his mid-twenties (1833) when on a vacation in Austria with his father. Alfred was deeply affected by the loss of his best friend. Alfred tried to resolve his grief by writing a long poem over several years—a poem that he eventually called *In Memoriam*. Death, the spirit world, the after life, religious faith, and related subjects were themes that emerged again and again in Tennyson's poetry.

Tennyson was often criticized for his lack of social graces. His clothes often appeared untidy. He was known to put his feet up on the furniture. There was an apparent tactlessness in his speech at times. In certain circles, such as a close-knit bunch of college friends, none of this is particularly offensive. Among artists, poets, and other bohemians, the dress code is often defined by the lack of having any code at all. It is not considered a particularly relevant issue. In other circles, social behavior—a delicate and refined etiquette, and a strict dress code—is considered extremely important.

Such was the case with Alfred's cousin. The cousin (son of the Old Man's favorite son) aspired to a career in politics. Both his father and the Old Man had been Members of Parliament. Interestingly, the cousin attended Trinity College at the same time that Tennyson did. The cousin was told politely but emphatically by his father to distance himself from the Tennyson brothers. "Your cousins," he was told, "are, I doubt not, very respectable and very clever, but their *habits* may be confined and their society limited."

Tennyson's moods were also a very visible factor during his college years as well as throughout his life. There was melancholy, to be sure. Sometimes he had dark moods. He frequently appeared pensively withdrawn and anti-social. Under the right conditions, however, he could be very positive, genial, and even entertaining.

During one of Tennyson's summer vacations back at Somersby, he noted that in the midst of the innocent gaiety of a dance, a "strange demon" would come over him and take away all the pleasure of the situation and turn him into something like a "churlish curmudgeon." He was twenty-one years old at the time.

As we mentioned in the Alice Bailey chapter, there are periods of crisis (crises of opportunity) in which the soul appropriates various aspects of the personality:

> A similar crisis *between the twenty-first and twenty-fifth years*, wherein the *mind vehicle is appropriated*. The man should then begin to respond to egoic influences, and in the case of the advanced man, he frequently does.
>
> A crisis *between the thirty-fifth and forty-second years*, wherein conscious *contact with the soul is established*; the threefold personality then begins to respond, as a unit, to soul impulse. (Italics added.) *Esoteric Psychology* II, 52-3.

As the soul appropriates the mind vehicle or mental body during the 21-25 year crisis, one of the responses has to do with a feeling similar to depression or despondency. At 35 there is, along with some depression, the sense that one has wasted one's life and the sense that now one must focus on the things that really matter. In the earlier crisis period at 21, there may be a despondency that could be characterized as a vast new realm of awareness that hovers over and descends upon the adolescent mind. One feels less protected, less sure of the ideas which nurtured it. A new level of responsibility descends upon the mind, and often it is not an easy one to carry and to assimilate. The following quote from *Esoteric Psychology* relates:

> We will confine our studies to the task of the aspirant as he reorients himself upon the probationary path, and becomes increasingly aware of the world of higher values, and of the existence of the kingdom of God. On this path he *senses his duality in an almost distressing manner,* and begins to aspire towards unity. This is the task today of the vast numbers of world aspirants. So widespread is the desire for this reorientation that it has produced the present world upheaval, and is the spiritual source of the specific cause of the ideological conflicts now going on in every country."
>
> *Esoteric Psychology* II, 344 (Italics added.)

> Exhilaration is also sometimes found as a result of the contact with a new world, and strong mental stimulation. Depression is as frequently a result, based upon a sensed incapacity to measure up to the realized opportunity. The man sees and knows too much. He can no longer be satisfied with the old measure of living, with the old satisfactions, and with the old idealisms. He has touched and now longs for the larger measures, for the new and vibrant ideas, and for the broader vision. The way of life of the soul has gripped and attracts him. But his nature, his environment, his equipment and his opportunities appear somehow to frustrate him consistently, and he feels he cannot march forward into this new and wonderful world. *Esoteric Psychology* II, 466.

During this time, Tennyson would frequently take long walks along the lanes, hills, and sand-dunes, absorbed in his own thoughts and encountering some fleeting impression that might re-emerge in a line of poetry. He was oblivious to the time of day. He would say good morning to people in late afternoon. Some thought him "crazed."

4) The fourth significant factor during his Cambridge years has to do with his *father's increasing inability to cope with circumstances.* Alfred and his brother Charles were spared many of the tumultuous scenes, since both were away at college. At one point the mother took the children to a nearby town, since she no longer felt safe. The father left for Paris and spent a year there, but his health and habits did not improve. In March 1831 Alfred Tennyson (21½ years old) was called home from Trinity; his father was in the final days of his illness. Alfred's time at Trinity was over.

After the death of Alfred's father, there was pressure from the grandfather (the Old Man) for Alfred to return to Cambridge to finish his studies, take a degree, and become a pastor. The other alternative presented was to study Physic (which was the term used for medical studies at the time). Alfred had it firmly in his mind not to follow his father's footsteps, but rather to make his way through life as a poet.

His Second Book of Poetry was Published. In 1830 Tennyson's second book of poetry—*Poems, Chiefly Lyrical*—was published. The book received mixed reviews. Several of his poems were poetic portraits of women ("Claribel", "Lilian", "Madeline", Adeline", "Mariana", "Isabel"). In the poem "Isabel" he extols the virtues of a "perfect wife."

> ...an accent very low
> in blandishment, but a most silver flow
> of subtle-paced counsel in distress,
> Right to the heart and brain, tho' undescried,
> Winning its way with extreme gentleness
> Thro' all the outworks of suspicious pride...
> From "Isabel."

Tennyson's sensitivity enabled him to identify with the female role and to portray that role effectively. There were also several poems addressing philosophical questions: "The How and the Why", All Things Will Die", "Nothing Will Die", "Love and Death", "The Dying Swan", "Supposed Confessions," among several others.

> Shall we not look into the laws
> Of life and death, and things that seem,
> And things that be, and analyse
> Our double nature, and compare
> All creeds till we have found the one,
> If one there be?
> From "Supposed Confessions of a second-rate sensitive mind not in unity with itself."

Alfred's friends urged him to collect his many other poems into another book, but a scathing review from the editor of *Blackwood's Magazine* stopped Alfred from rushing again into print too soon. One of the criticisms had to do with the opinion that other reviewers (his friends) were possibly spoiling a new talent with overly lavish praise.

Another Book of Poetry. Two years later another book of Tennyson's was published, entitled simply: *Poems of 1832*. In spite of illness (referred to as "hypochondriac depressions", and "extreme nervous irritation") and a short unproductive trip to the continent (France, Brussels), Tennyson continued to write and study and continued to take poetry in the spirit of a true and most serious calling. The reviews to his new book were similar to the ones from his *Chiefly Lyrical* book: Good reviews when his friends from Trinity had a hand in them, caustic reviews from some long established reviewers in the *Quarterly Review* and the *Literary Gazette*. The book included the well known "The Lady of Shalott" and "The Lotus-Eaters." There were some almost juvenile poems in the collection, but then Alfred was only twenty-three years old at the time.

John Croker's criticism in the *Quarterly Review* was unfair in that it over-emphasized the weakest poems, without giving due recognition to Tennyson's skill, developed craftsmanship, and great promise. Croker was drawing more attention to himself as critic than he was giving a serious appraisal. A couple of critical reviews must have had their effect on Tennyson, for it would be *ten years* before Tennyson published another book of poetry.

An Interim Decade. In the following decade Tennyson continued to write poems, re-write earlier poems, study, and make short trips to visit friends. He lived at home with his mother, he avoided any paid employment, and received a small annual amount of money from his Aunt Russel (£100). At this time he was also grieving over the death of his close friend Arthur Hallam—a death that deeply affected most of the family, since Arthur Hallam and Alfred's sister had planned on getting married.

During this period Alfred would write and re-write his long poem *In Memoriam*. How does one grieve over the loss of a loved one? Some psychological types would tend to put the matter behind them and to get on with new activity and new work. Tennyson did not choose that way of refusing to think about the matter and seeking diversion in other activities; rather he entered into and explored the emotion—a somewhat risky approach. He explored it over the years and from several different angles.

The immediate pain led eventually to philosophical rumination. Earlier questions of life, death, faith, immortality had now more of an immediacy about them. It was very important to resolve these questions. *Does life go on, or doesn't it?* This question was being asked in the context of profound social-psychological changes. Darwin was born in 1809, the same year as Tennyson. Napoleon had been defeated, the monarchy was restored in France, but the questions brought up by the French Revolution did not evaporate. Science, unquestionably, was receiving a new impulse of energy. The Industrial Revolution brought new economic opportunities along with urban squalor. Charles Dickens was the most popular prose writer of the 1830's and 40's. Unlike Tennyson's romantic and idyllic verse, Dickens' prose writings drew attention to the plight of the humble classes. The new science was in process of radically challenging accepted religious notions of the day. A simple, *unquestioning religious faith would no longer suffice*, at least, not for the intelligent leaders of the nation. What Tennyson brought was a *questioning spiritual faith*. Many people were not satisfied with the new scientific theories of evolution, neither were they satisfied with church platitudes. A leading poet—being a free thinker, unattached to any school of thought—was looked upon as one who might resolve some of the unsettling questions of *who we are* and be an interpreter for the spirit of the age.

> Words weaker than your grief would make
> Grief more. 'Twere better I should cease;
> Although myself could almost take
> The place of him that sleeps in peace....
>
> Sleep till the end, true soul and sweet.
> Nothing comes to thee new or strange.
> Sleep full of rest from head to feet;
> Lie still, dry dust, secure of change.
> From "To J. S."

Here, once again, we see Tennyson's poem filled with subtlety of feeling and emotion, as he remembers his friend's death and contemplates easing the pain of another through a letter of consolation.
Study and a Vague Search. Tennyson's systematic, self-imposed study during the decade included History, German, Chemistry, Botany, Electricity, Animal Psychology, Mechanics, Theology, Italian, and Greek.

Tennyson was also looking for someone to love. Financially, he was not in much of a position to propose to anyone. These more practical matters are often put aside by the romantic poet who has a vague sense that lofty aspirations in and of themselves will be able to sort out the intrusions of reality. He was enamored by a sixteen year old, Sophy Rawnsley, who considered his unconventional manners more interesting than "dapper young gentleman of the ordinary type." She noted that he loved music, was an excellent dancer, but that they both preferred talking to dancing. This friendship lasted for many years.

Tennyson also studied in considerable depth everything related to the Roundtable and King Arthur and wrote several poems highlighting various scenes in the epic legend.

> I think that we
> Shall never more, at any future time,
> Delight our souls with talk of knightly deeds,
> Walking about the gardens and the halls
> Of Camelot, as in the days that were.
> I perish by this people which I made,—
> Tho' Merlin sware that I should come again
> To rule once more....."
> From Tennyson's "Morte d'Arthur."

Tennyson developed a friendship with Edward Fitzgerald. "Fitz", as he was called, admired Tennyson for his noble images and thoughts that "direct us to our duty, purify and cleanse us from mean and vicious objects, and so prepare us for the reception of the higher philosophy" (Thorn, 142). Fitzgerald sensed a certain greatness in Tennyson.

Tennyson was also forming his political thought at this time which was conservatively English. That is to say, his trips abroad did not attract him to new and different ways, or to radical ideas, rather he preferred the even and reasonable way in which England moved cautiously forward. He was not a revolutionary in any sense of the word. "English good sense and moderation" were the keynotes. From the patriotic poem "Love Thou thy Land, with Love far Brought," we find his position well articulated:

> Not clinging to some ancient saw;
> Not mastered by some modern term;
> Not swift nor slow to change, but firm
> And in its season bring the law....

For most of this decade Tennyson was romantically attracted to some young women. His attraction to the sentiment of infatuation, along with the effect it had on his poetic creativity, was stronger than the more practical considerations of providing for a wife and family.

> In the Spring a livelier iris changes on the burnished dove;
> In the Spring a young man's fancy lightly turns to thoughts of love....
>
> Cursed be the social wants that sin against the strength of youth!
> Cursed be the social lies that warp us from the living truth!
> From "Locksley Hall."

When the Old Man died, some money came into the Tennyson family. The oldest brother, Frederich, lived in Italy, married an Italian woman, and developed a passion for music. He seemed much happier there than in England. The second oldest, Charles, married and settled in Caistor, which made Alfred—being the oldest male at home—the head of the household (which included his mother, four sisters and two younger brothers). His youngest brother, Edward, suffered from some form of mental illness and had been sent to an asylum in York where he spent the rest of his life. Edward had been sent there when Alfred was still at Trinity. This is very sad in that Edward, being the youngest, experienced the full impact of the father's psychological and physical disintegration, accompanied by many disruptive domestic scenes. The Tennysons thought they suffered from some "bad blood" in the family. The threat of or the presence of mental illness in the family was a concern over which Alfred would brood for some time.

In late 1836 Alfred became attracted to Emily Sellwood in a serious way. He was twenty-seven years old and did not yet see his way clear to settling down and getting married. Her family did not see a way either. Alfred's relationship with Emily was carried on primarily through correspondence at that time.

Tennyson met the British novelist William Thackery in 1838. Thackery was impressed with Tennyson: "He seems to me to have the cachet of a great man. His conversation is often delightful I think, full of breadth, manliness and humour: he reads all sorts of things, swallows them and digests them like a great boa-constrictor as he is." Tennyson was tall and slender with a strong jaw and deep voice. Thackery also mentioned Tennyson's "simplicity of manner"— something like a rustic simplicity. Others referred to Tennyson as lacking social decorum. Some friends tried to suggest to him that he needed more social graces. Tennyson preferred the manners that come readily and naturally, which probably meant that he really did not want to make any effort to adapt or change. The 1st ray personality of the British nation requires proper etiquette and correct social decorum. It is one of the factors that distinguishes the classes and is certainly related to the issue of power. It seems clear that Tennyson did not have any first ray in his psychological equipment and therefore found it difficult to resonate with this vibration.

A Financial Scheme. It was thought by the Tennyson family that Alfred's younger brother Septimus would some day become a Solicitor (lawyer). Septimus, however, as was the case with the youngest brother Edward, suffered from some mental instability. He placed himself under the care of Doctor Matthew Allen in an asylum at Fair Mead. Alfred went to visit Septimus there and got on very well with the patients, finding them very agreeable and reasonable. Alfred visited Septimus regularly and became well acquainted with Dr. Allen.

Allen disapproved of a machine called "the Tranquillizer" that was used in the asylum at York. The Tranquillizer was a quickly revolving chair that caused the strapped-in patients to vomit and to empty their bowels and bladders. The discharge of fluids was considered a cleansing process and one that brought about a right concentration of bodily fluids. Dr. Allen considered this method barbaric, left the institution at York, and started his own establishment. Alfred must have been impressed with Dr. Allen's less restrictive methods of working with patients.

Allen also appeared to have enterprising abilities. He was involved in a business venture that had to do with the "Patent Method of Carving Wood." This method utilized steam driven machines to make decorative wood-carvings, which were used primarily for ornamentation. Churches particularly were placing some orders and initially the prospects looked good. Alfred was pulled into the scheme and invested about £3000. This investment was supposed to yield £10,000 within a year. Initially Alfred was very enthusiastic about the venture and got his oldest brother Frederich and his sisters to invest. His friends were doubtful (as was Uncle Charles) and they advised him against it.

Machines broke down, Allen became increasingly evasive, and the whole venture quickly turned sour. It was a hard lesson for Tennyson, who was uncertain about his own financial status, about his prospects for getting married, and about his future as a poet.

The family lost altogether about £8000, which cut deeply into their finances. Alfred's married sister came to the rescue and took out an insurance policy on Dr. Allen, so that the family would recoup most of its losses at the time of Allen's death. This took place in 1845, five years after the beginning of the whole affair.

Poems of 1842. Ten years after *Poems* of 1832 was published, a two volume book of poems was brought out: *Poems* of 1842, the first volume consisting mainly of revised old poems, and the second volume being his new creations. The work was praised by the two leading writers of the time, Thomas Carlyle and Charles Dickens. Robert Browning had a problem with the revisions. According to him: "The alterations are insane....I have been with Moxon this morning [Tennyson's publisher], who tells me that Tennyson is miserably thin-skinned and sensitive to criticism" (Thorn 190).

One critic wrote that Tennyson's new collection of poems showed more maturity (less naively youthful) than the earlier collection, but they were representative of a poet who stood aloof from life and therefore a poet who was not fully engaged, not fully experiencing the human struggle.

> The rain had fallen, the Poet arose,
>   He passed by the town and out of the street,
> A light wind blew from the gates of the sun,
>   And waves of shadow went over the wheat,
> And he sat him down in a lonely place,
>   And chanted a melody loud and sweet,
> That made the wild-swan pause in her cloud,
>   And the lark drop down at his feet.
>   From "The Poet's Song."

The new collection sold relatively well. The critical reviews were definitely more positive than the reviews that followed the 1832 collection. Tennyson was apparently not hurt but somewhat disappointed, for he had hoped less for mild encouragement and more for downright praise.

The Thirty-Five Year Old Crisis. Once again we quote the following important passage from *Esoteric Psychology* (v.2, 52-3): "A crisis between the thirty-fifth and forty-second years, wherein conscious contact with the soul is established; the threefold personality then begins to respond, as a unit, to soul impulse."

Tennyson was right on schedule. As mentioned earlier, this crisis of soul contact cannot be likened to an angelic presence coming down and tapping one gently on the shoulder and saying pleasantly, "Well done! Now, follow me." It can more accurately be described with the statement that "the perfection of the soul brings imperfection to the surface." One may very well be shocked and depressed with the knowledge of one's own imperfections. The new, more expansive awareness may be particularly disturbing to the idealistic sixth ray type.

Aubrey de Vere was a young Irish poet who became acquainted with "the Apostles" circle at Trinity College. De Vere dropped in to visit Tennyson in July 1845. Tennyson was 35 years old and about to turn 36. De Vere made the following interesting notation in his diary:

> On my way in, paid a visit to Tennyson, who seemed much out of spirits, and said he could no longer bear to be knocked about the world, and that he must marry and find love and peace or die.... He complained much about growing old, and said he cared nothing for fame, and that his life was all thrown away for want of a competence and retirement. Said that no one had been so much harassed by anxiety and trouble as himself. I told him he wanted occupation, a wife, and orthodox principles, which he took well.
>
> *The Letters of Alfred Lord Tennyson*, v. i, 239.

✓ Everyone lives in a "bubble" of their own creation, which has to do with their glamours and illusions. We are all well-schooled in an illusory fantasy world of some sort. One's education is undertaken by people who have their own peculiar mixture of reality and unreality. The books and textbooks, even when they are so-called scientific, are filled with the inevitable distorted limitations of perspective and of the times. Today's textbooks are often sources of tomorrow's humor.

Yet the soul and spirit see to it that there is a thread of meaning and a thread of Reality that runs through humankind's struggle to gain consciousness.

✓ The soul is concerned with reality. The first "reality shock" or reality clarification one receives from the soul follows upon the stage of adolescence and occurs during the 21-25 cycle, as mentioned earlier. The second reality clarification occurs during the 35-42 cycle. The perfection of the soul—or the *reality* of the soul—reveals the unreality (the glamour and illusion) of the personality creations.

"Man only becomes aware of reality when he has destroyed that which he has himself created." (*Glamour: A World Problem* 200.)

Alfred Tennyson's reality clarification, coming from the depths of his soul, did not complement him on his devotion to Truth and Beauty. Rather the soul impulse revealed the next step ahead that was necessary in order to achieve a more balanced life—a life that would approach a greater wholeness. The basic sense of this impulse was translated into the very practical terms of *get a wife and get an occupational life.* In other words, be less dreamy, be less self-centered. Let the natural drive to mate and to raise a family pull you out of a preoccupation with yourself (a preoccupation with higher astral plane meanderings) and into a greater consciousness. The horizontal life of physical plane ✓ living needs tending to, in order to balance the vertical life of spiritual aspiration. The responsibility of an occupational life brings discipline and a connection with community. These disciplines can bring in the balancing work of the 1-3-5-7 line of ray energies.

Several important events and directions occurred during this critical cycle:

1) *A new reality was settling into the awareness.* This was accompanied by some unavoidable depression, but new motivations were taking hold.

2) *He received a pension.* His Apostle friends from Trinity had been petitioning the government for some years in the effort to secure some money for the poet. Prime Minister Peel granted Tennyson a Civil List pension of £200 per year. The quality of his poetry earned him the pension. One could argue that this is one of the indications of a civilized nation. The pension, along with the small annual income from his grandfather's wealth and his increasing royalties, enabled Tennyson to do more than romanticize about a relationship with a woman. He had sufficient security now to take some practical action.

Action included traveling around, seeing theatrical plays, visiting old friends, and meeting new ones. Mary Howitt noted in her *Autobiography*:

> The retiring and meditative young poet, Alfred Tennyson, visited us, and charmed our seclusion by the recitation of his exquisite poetry. He spent a Sunday night at our house, when we sat talking until three in the morning. All the next day he remained with us in constant converse. We seemed to have known him for years. So, in fact, we had, for his poetry was himself. He hailed all attempts at heralding a grand, more liberal state of public opinion, and consequently sweeter, more noble modes of living. He wished that we Englanders could dress up our affections in a little more poetical costume; real warmth of heart would lose nothing, rather gain by it; as it was, our manners were as cold as the walls of our churches.

3) His poem *The Princess* was published in 1847 (Tennyson was 38

years old). This was his first real financial success. The book sold steady for thirty years. The prologue includes:

> Quick answered Lilia "There are thousands now
> Such women, but convention bears them down:
> It is but bringing up; no more than that:
> You men have done it: how I hate you all!
> Ah, were I something great! I wish I were
> Some mighty poetess, I would shame you then,
> That love to keep us children! O I wish
> That I were some great Princess, I would build
> Far off from men a college like a man's,
> And I would teach them all that men are taught;
> We are twice as quick!" And here she shook aside
> The hand that played the patron with her curls.

Many friends had advised Tennyson that in order to establish himself as a major poet, it was necessary for him to write a long poem. *The Princess* was his first poem of length. This successful poem influenced many other poets, including T. S. Elliot and his poem *Waste Land*.

4) *He married Emily Sellwood.* The courtship had proceeded off-and-on for twenty years. The first uncertainty was Tennyson's financial position. This was now rapidly changing. They married in June, 1850 (Tennyson was 40 years old). There is no doubt that this marriage was very beneficial to Tennyson and also to Emily as well. Eventually they had two sons, to whom the parents were very devoted. Their first son had died in birth. The first son to survive was named Hallam in honor of Tennyson's close friend Arthur Hallam. Hallam Tennyson was close to his father and did much to look after him in his declining years. The second son was named Lionel. Much attention was given to procuring the right education for the two boys.

5) *His poem* In Memoriam *was published*—also in June of 1850. Tennyson started writing this collection of elegiac verses when his close friend Arthur Hallam died in 1833. The poem pondered the questions of death, faith, and immortality. People in England were struggling with these age old questions in a new way. The new science was forcing a new look at the old values. Tennyson's poems helped a great many people with the mental and emotional processing of some of the eternal questions. (Prior to mass media entertainment of the contemporary era, edifying works of literature were often read during the evening hours.)

This was Tennyson's second long, book-length poem. It sold well and was reprinted twice in the year of its publication with each reprint larger than the previous. It continued to sell well for many years.

In the early part of the poem Tennyson laments the loss of his friend:

> Dark house, by which once more I stand
> Here in the long unlovely street,
> Doors, where my heart was used to beat
> So quickly, waiting for a hand,
>
> A hand that can be clasped no more—
> Behold me, for I cannot sleep,
> And like a guilty thing I creep
> At earliest morning to the door.

Later in the poem he finds some connection with God:

> If e'er when faith had fallen asleep,
> I heard a voice 'believe no more'
> And heard an ever-breaking shore
> That tumbled in the Godless deep;
>
> A warmth within the breast would melt
> That freezing reason's colder part,
> And like a man in wrath the heart
> Stood up and answered 'I have felt.'

A reviewer in *Fraser's Magazine* considered it to be "The noblest Christian poem which England has produced for two centuries." The poem was both a commercial and a critical success.

6) *Tennyson became Poet Laureate of England*. This occurred also in the eventful year of 1850. The Laureateship had been vacant since Wordsworth's death on April 23, 1850. Tennyson's poem *In Memoriam* was critical in securing him the honor. Because of the public responsibilities the honor would bring, Tennyson was not sure if he should accept it. He decided in favor of accepting, over a bottle of port and a little help from his friends.

Tennyson and Whitman Compared. In *Esoteric Psychology* we find the following interesting statement: "The literary work of a first ray man will be strong and trenchant, but he will care little for style or finish in his writings. Perhaps examples of this type would be Luther, Carlyle, and Walt Whitman." (EP I, 202.) It must be remembered that all the rays can be found in all the professions, and that the sub-rays (particularly the personality ray and mental ray) also play a conditioning-influencing role.

Walt Whitman was born on May 31, 1819 in Long Island, New York. He attended public school for six years in Brooklyn, New York, and then became apprenticed to a printer. He worked in various printing shops in New York City, taught in country schools in Long Island (1835, sixteen years old), and edited a newspaper in Huntington, Long Island (1838-9, nineteen and twenty years old). He returned to New York City to work as a printer and journalist. He also made political speeches and became involved for a short time with the Tammany Hall Democrats. (Tammany was founded in New York City in 1789 as an anti-Federalists group. In 1800 they helped Thomas Jefferson get elected president. It was not until around 1868 that the Tammany Hall group become noted for their political corruption in the city administration. This was several years after Whitman's affiliation with the group.)

Whitman edited an influential newspaper, *The Brooklyn Eagle*, for two years. He took a trip, a relatively long journey in those days, to New Orleans, which had an expanding and profound effect upon him. The vastness of the country and the variety of the people inspired him—not to write his impressions into a journalistic article—but to put it all down in the form of poetry.

> I celebrate myself, and sing myself,
> And what I assume you shall assume,
> For every atom belonging to me as good belongs to you.
> I loaf and invite my soul,
> I lean and loaf at my ease observing a spear of summer grass....
>
> A child said *What is the grass?* fetching it to me with full
>   hands,
> How could I answer the child? I do not know what it is
>   any more than he.
> I guess it must be the flag of my disposition, out of
>   hopeful green stuff woven.
> Or I guess it is the handkerchief of the Lord,
> A scented gift and remembrancer designedly dropped, Bearing
>   the owner's name somewhere in the corners, that we may see
>   and remark, and say *Whose?*

> Or I guess the grass itself is a child, the produced babe of
> the vegetation.
> Or I guess it is a uniform hieroglyphic,
> And it means, Sprouting alike in broad zones and narrow
> zones,
> Growing among the black folks as among white,
> Canuck, Tuckahoe, Congressman, Cuff, I give them the
> same, I receive them the same....
> From Song of Myself.

In 1855 the volume of poetry entitled *Leaves of Grass* (which included "Song of Myself") was published at Whitman's own expense. He was 36 years old. The poetry was an enthusiastic celebration of life. The lack of rhyme and the loose structure broke the conventional rules of the day. The American poet Ezra Pound (1885-1972) had mixed thoughts about Whitman. Ezra Pound questioned Whitman's lack of scholarship but he loved Whitman's exuberance. In Pound's poem "A Pact" he refers to Whitman: "It was you that broke the new wood,/ Now it is time for the carving." Pound, like Tennyson, was a poet immersed in scholarship and tradition, while at the same time cautiously probing new directions. Their poems lacked Whitman's movement but, indeed, supplied the "carving" or the finish and the polish. Ralph Waldo Emerson commented that Whitman's book was the "most extraordinary piece of wit and wisdom yet contributed to American literature."

During the Civil War, Whitman went to Washington, D.C. to look for his wounded brother. His brother recovered. Walt got a job as a government clerk and also served as a hospital volunteer. He records his feelings and experiences in the poem "Drum Taps" (1865).

> Bearing the bandages, water and sponge,
> Straight and swift to my wounded I go,
> Where they lie on the ground after the battle brought in,
> Where their priceless blood reddens the grass, the ground,
> Or to the rows of the hospital tent, or under the roofed hospital,
> Or to the long rows of cots up and down each side I return,
> To each and all one after another I draw near, not one do I miss.
> An attendant follows holding a tray, he carries a refuse pail,
> Soon to be filled with clotted rags and blood, emptied, and
> filled again.

> I onward go, I stop,
> With hinged knees and steady hands to dress wounds,
> I am firm with each, the pangs are sharp yet unavoidable,
> One turns to me his appealing eyes—poor boy! I never knew you,
> Yet I think I could not refuse this moment to die for you, if that would save you. From "The Wound-Dresser."

Whitman's poems were full of action. He described what he did and what he observed. He pulled down from the clouds some arresting word phrases in order to startle the reader and charge the mind with new vistas. When seeing death, he did not brood about it; he confronted it. He extracted from the experience whatever could be extracted from it in an immediate and direct way, knowing that further mysteries would reveal themselves all in due time.

Tennyson's approach was far different. He took little action, and he brooded over matters a long time. He was self-absorbed in his own inner search for meaning. Whitman's approach was fearless and "grasping" in the positive sense of demanding and taking whatever could be seized in the fullness of the immediate moment. The softer Tennyson explored nuance of feeling and explored life and death from a safe distance. The fearless Whitman was also freer to break convention; criticism did not affect him in the same way it did Tennyson.

Both poets had some influence on each other. Tennyson was much admired on the other side of the Atlantic. Whitman wrote Tennyson, requesting a photograph and sending Tennyson a book of his poetry. Tennyson wrote back: "I had previously met with several of your works and read them with interest and had made up my mind that you had a large and lovable nature. I discovered great 'go' in your writings and am not surprised at the hold they have taken on your fellow countrymen." (*Letters*, iii, 9.) No reference is made to any lack of finish or polish. Everything is phrased in a polite and positive manner. Tennyson, however, probably felt quite superior to Whitman as a poet, the latter lacking scholarship and being somewhat untamed. Tennyson could easily see how Whitman's poetry had taken a hold on his fellow countrymen, for the whole country had a youthful, wilderness quality about it. Tennyson's poetry had a profound respect for tradition; Whitman's zest for living chose not be too encumbered by the time honored tradition. No seasoned poet could deny, however, that Whitman's spirited enthusiasm brought something of value to the traditional art.

Edward FitzGerald, one of Tennyson's closest friends, criticized Tennyson for his *lack* of go. FitzGerald suggested to Tennyson that had he (Tennyson) "led a more active life, in the manner of Scott or Shakespeare, or even, as Bryon, played the Devil a bit more, he might have *done more and talked about it less.*" (Thorn, 444, italics added.) **Tennyson is Devoted to His Family, His Pen is Never Still, His success Grows and Grows.** As Poet Laureate he was called upon or felt obligated to write a political poem from time to time, the first being "Ode on the Death of the Duke of Wellington," another being "The Charge of the Light Brigade."

> Forward, the Light Brigade!
> Was there a man dismayed?
> Not tho' the soldiers knew
>   Some one had blundered:
> Their's not to make reply,
> Their's not to reason why,
> Their's but to do and die:
> Into the valley of Death
>   Rode the six hundred.
>   From "Charge of the Light Brigade."

The Tennysons bought a house on the Isle of Wight, which provided, among other things, a sort of grounding for Alfred. The practical affairs dealing with maintaining a household helped greatly to balance Alfred's moods and musings. Once settled in the new house, a daily rhythm was established, which enabled Alfred to get much work done.

Benjamin Jowett visited Tennyson on a regular basis. Jowett made the following observations when Tennyson was fifty-one years old. Tennyson had been ill and somewhat depressed. "The more I see of him," noted Jowett, "the more I respect his character, notwithstanding a superficial irritability and uneasiness about all things.... No one is more honest, truthful, manly, or a warmer friend; but he is as open as the day, and like a child, tells any chance comer what is passing in his mind." His favorite topic of discussion has to do with "a future state," which he talks about with "a passionate conviction." Jowett concludes that "great mental troubles necessarily accompany such powers as he possesses." (*Letters*, ii, 271.)

A New Form of Dramatic Composition. Tennyson's poem *Maud* was at first highly criticized, but was later highly praised. Some say it is his most modern poem. It was criticized for being primarily a melodramatic account of murder, suicide, and madness. The *Asylum Journal of Mental Science* considered it an accurate portrayal of insanity. Tennyson was endeavoring to come to terms with the elusive phenomenon of mental illness. This was due partly because of its appearance in the family history (father and two brothers) and partly because of his own personal fears of some kind of mental disturbance. At forty-five, settled with wife and family, financially secure, professionally successful, he could now explore this difficult phenomenon with interest, experience, and also healthy detachment. Processing emotional-mental disturbance through the creative rendering of some art form is an approach often taken by the artistic temperament. This is one of several factors that suggest a mental body on the fourth ray of harmony through conflict.

> Dead, long dead,
> Long dead!
> And my heart is a handful of dust,
> And the wheels go over my head,
> And my bones are shaken with pain,
> For into a shallow grave they are thrust,
> Only a yard beneath the street,
> And the hoofs of the horses beat, beat,
> The hoofs of the horses beat,
> Beat into my scalp and brain,
> With never an end to the stream of passing feet,
> Driving, hurrying, marrying, burying,
> Clamour and rubble, and ringing and clatter,
> And here beneath it is all as bad,
> For I thought the dead had peace, but it is not so;
> To have no peace in the grave, is that not sad?
> But up and down and to and fro
> Ever about me the dead men go;
> And then to hear a dead man chatter
> Is enough to drive one mad..... From *Maud*.

In clarifying the work, Tennyson said that the narrator in the poem "feels that his father has been killed by the work of the lie, and that all through he fears the coming madness.... The whole was intended to be a new form of dramatic composition. I took a man constitutionally diseased and dipped him into the circumstances of the time and took him out on fire." (*Letter*, ii, 138.)

William Gladstone and Queen Victoria. The major work to follow *Maud* was *Idylls of the King*—a series of long narrative poems that used the King Arthur legends as theme and framework. William Gladstone (Chancellor of the Exchequer at this time and later Prime Minister) found *Idylls of the King* so moving—the work "has grasped me with a strong hand"—that he began to make a study of Tennyson's other poems. He also wrote a long article on Tennyson's poetry for the *Quarterly Review*.

Gladstone did not fully understand or appreciate the psychological poem *Maud*. He misread the poem's statements on war and peace, not realizing that the words were to be taken in the context of a man struggling with mental illness. He criticized the "heavy dreaminess" of the poem, and considered the poem the "least worthy of popularity."

Idylls of the King, however, received high praise from Gladstone. *Idylls of the King* is a medley of vignettes on the King Arthur theme rather than a full retelling of the legend. Gladstone considered it the "greatest poetical creation of the nineteenth century." He concluded his article with the words: "Of it [the *Idylls* as a whole] we will say without fear, what we would not dare to say of any recent work: that of itself it raises the character and the hopes of the age and the country which have produced it, and that its author, by his own single strength, has made a sensible addition to the permanent wealth of mankind." (*Gladstone*, Roy Jenkins, 211.)

Gladstone, as a highly accomplished statesman, had a developed 1st ray energy of will and power somewhere in his psychological constitution—the mental ray in all probability and also either the personality or soul ray. Tennyson's poem of the legendary King Arthur resonated well with Gladstone's own concerns and enormous responsibilities of political leadership. It is not surprising that his own bias singled out that poem as being the "greatest poetical creation of the nineteenth century." The more 4th and 6th ray *Maud* poem of deep psychological introspection found little if any resonance in the political minded Gladstone. It speaks very well of Tennyson, however, that he was able to write on King Arthur in such a way as to grasp the 1st ray Gladstone in a strong way.

On one occasion Tennyson read his play *Harold* (1876) to Gladstone and family. The next day a discussion developed on such subject matter as prayer, eternal punishment, and immortality of the soul. Gladstone's daughter Mary noted in her diary: "Tennyson does not appear to be much of a Christian, and I suspect is no theologian, but is very religious." (Thorn 445.) On another occasion Tennyson mentioned to his friend Sir James Knowles: "If I ceased to believe in any chance of another life, and of a great personality somewhere in the Universe, I should not care a pin about anything. People must have some religion." (Thorn 421).

Queen Victoria reigned from 1837 to 1901. Her reign was the longest of any monarch in British history. She admired Tennyson's poem *In Memoriam* and sent a command for him to come to her official residence, the Osborne House, on the Isle of Wight (March, 1862). Tennyson was extremely nervous, but the meeting went well. The second visit with the Queen was arranged a year later with Tennyson's whole family and several princes and princesses. Later, there were a couple of other visits with the Queen. The Queen wanted to know the poet's thoughts on the subject of death and immortality. She also requested his services from time to time. On one occasion she had a bronze statue made of one of her most faithful servants who had recently passed over to the other side, and she wanted Tennyson to choose one or two appropriate lines to be inscribed on the pedestal:

> Friend more than servant, loyal, truthful, brave!
> Self less than duty, even to the grave.

These succinct commemorative lines written by Tennyson strike a profoundly simple sixth ray note. The Queen chose the right person to find the right words to commemorate a loyal and devoted servant.

The Metaphysical Society. Tennyson's work was the writing of poetry. It was a creative process that required an alignment with the Muse, with soul. A great deal of academic study prepared the ground, so that there were fertile conditions over and upon which the spirit-like Muse could move and play. The poetry had erudition and sophistication. It was ennobling and edifying. It wrestled with (more than explored) metaphysical questions.

His work was one thing—the writing of poetry in the solitude of his undisturbed chamber or creating verse during his stroll in a pastoral setting—and his recreation was another. His "recreation", or his balancing activity, was primarily traveling around to have literary, political, and philosophical discussions with his friends. In his mature years, when he enjoyed considerable fame, his friends, admirers, and other literary people made the journey to see him. The literary, political, philosophical, even scientific discussions provided a sort of sounding board for incubating ideas. Out of one of these discussions with his good friend Sir James Knowles there grew a plan to form a

Metaphysical Society. Tennyson made the remark that it would be good if speculative metaphysical subjects could be argued within a learned society. The more practical Knowles immediately offered to get it started.

There was popular interest in spiritualism (communicating with those on the other side of the veil), interest in the occult (due to the work of the Theosophical Society), and interest in theories of evolution (Darwin's Origin of the Species had been published in 1859). The fundamental polarity was between scientific materialism on the one hand and religious mysticism on the other. The Society provided an opportunity for a free exchange of ideas between "those of faith" and "those who were ranged on the side of unfaith."

Scientific Materialism and Religious Mysticism. There are many ways of looking at this extremely important polarity. If we can understand something of the energy that stand behind these two attitudes, then we can see that the names change during different eras, in different places, and in different disciplines, but the energy is the same or very similar.

"Those of faith and those who were ranged on the side of unfaith" is one way of identifying the polarity. One could also designate it as "those of scientific knowledge and those without scientific knowledge." Either way, of course, is unfair, because either way loads the argument in a prejudicial way.

We have the familiar softer, more abstract line (the 2-4-6 line) favoring faith or religious mysticism during the Victorian Age, generally speaking. We also have the more concrete line of ray energies (1-3-5-7 line) favoring government, business, organization, and science during the budding industrial age. Industry was given an enormous boost by the new scientific attitudes and the new scientific inventions of that time.

These two mainstream energies pull one in opposite directions. The softer, abstract line pulls one mystically inward-upward, into the world of consciousness—the contemplation of things spiritual. The more dynamic concrete line pushes one out into the world of form. The concrete line is more extroverting, more willful, more controlling than its counterpart. Tennyson was clearly on the softer line. *Faith* was at the heart and soul of his existence.

The design and dynamic in this archetypal polarity generates conflict and guarantees a perpetual unrest. This is perhaps related to the fact that one of the rays governing humanity as a whole is the 4th ray of harmony through conflict. ("The ray which governs the sum total of the human kingdom is the fourth Ray of Harmony through Conflict", *Esoteric Psychology* I, 343.) Humanity is thrust outward into the world of form and forced to struggle for its survival. At the same time humanity is called upon to recall its Source, to align with Source, and to bring the inspirations from Source down into outer manifestation.

This archetypal polarity or "stretch" is very similar to the polarity existing between what Rudolf Steiner called the Ahrimanic and the Luciferic forces. The Ahrimanic impulse "is clearly evident in the spread of the belief that the mechanistic, mathematical conceptions inaugurated by Galileo, Copernicus, and others, explain what is happening in the cosmos." Cosmos is actually "permeated with soul and spirit." The Lucifer tendency, on the other hand, awakens mystical experience and the brooding over experiences of one's inner life. "The Ahrimanic tendencies in people today live themselves out in science, the luciferic tendencies in religion, while in art they swing between the one extreme and the other." Both tendencies or impulses lead to very problematical conditions. Luciferic tendencies lead eventually to illusion, to "wallowing in abstractions", and to a dreamy, impractical nature. The Ahrimanic impulse leads to an intelligence that does not touch spirit ("you cannot truly experience spirit if you get no further than mere intelligence"), to an overemphasis upon the political and economic needs devoid of spiritual considerations ("the soulless devouring of material food leads to the side-tracking of the spirit"), and to an intellectual life that fails to penetrate to deeper layers of truth. (Steiner 17, 18, 31.)

What is the resolution of these opposite impulses? The resolution has to do with being able to use the energy of one in the work of the other. This brings about a balance. In other words, one uses the cold, intellectual clarity of the Ahrimanic impulse when exploring the abstraction of consciousness. "The essential is that people should approach their own inner nature with ahrimanic cold-bloodedness and dispassion." One should avoid all illusions about one's own inner life by means of the ahrimanic nature. One should observe oneself as one would observe the outer world. On the other side of the equation, one should endeavor to understand the material world, not with cold intellect, but with the warmth of the luciferic quest for spirit. One should approach knowledge of the material world with "fiery enthusiasm and interest,... which is itself luciferic." (Steiner 34, 35.)

These are extremely profound and important matters. In terms of working towards the balancing of these apparently opposing forces,

Tennyson was right on track in the effort to form a Metaphysical Society in which the questions relating to the scientific and mystical polarity, were to be brought forth and discussed.

Reaching Into Heaven. In May of 1890 a representative of Thomas Edison's enterprises visited Tennyson and brought along the latest phonograph. Tennyson's deep voice was recorded on a cylinder as he recited part of his well-known poem "Charge of the Light Brigade." Tennyson enjoyed the invention. Later a formal recording session was arranged.

Close to the end of his years on earth, Tennyson remarked to a friend: "The only tolerable view of this life is as a vestibule to a better."

He had a dream in which he was "the Pope bearing all the sins and miseries of the world on his shoulders." He had another dream in which he was "building a tower of brightly colored pagodas reaching up into heaven" (Thorn 505).

He died October 6, 1892, at the age of 83. He was buried in the Poets' Corner of Westminster Abbey.

The Rays of Tennyson. The 6th ray soul radiated through the personality. Speculatively, we suggest that his rays might have been the following:

        Soul.................. VI
        Personality......... 2
            mind............ 4
            astral............ 6
            physical....... 7

The clearest of these, other than the given 6th ray soul, is the 4th ray mind. His mind was attracted to literature, creative writing, alignment with the Muse, attunement to beauty, and to the abstractions of the inner planes. Considering the other two rays that commonly condition the mental body, he did not have a 5th ray mind—he read some science, but did not enter it deeply or seriously. He certainly did not have a 1st ray mind. He preferred to leave most of the administrative details of the household to his wife. When Tennyson expressed his opinions on politics and government, he spoke as one who really was not familiar, not knowledgeable, about life in that realm. People like Gladstone and Queen Victoria had great respect for Tennyson as a poet, but his political opinions were tolerated in the manner that one would tolerate the opinions of a child. John Adington Symonds made the following observations of Gladstone and Tennyson, comparing the two as they debated informally:

Gladstone with his rich flexible voice, Tennyson with his deep drawl rising into impatient falsetto when put out: Gladstone arguing, Tennyson putting in prejudice; Gladstone asserting rashly, Tennyson denying with a bald negative; Gladstone full of facts, Tennyson relying on impressions; both of them humorous, but the one polished and delicate in repartee, the other broad and coarse and grotesque.... Gladstone is some sort of man of the world; Tennyson a child, and treated by him like a child.   (*Letters*, v.11, 415.)

In the political domain (where one finds "men of the world" or men-of-affairs, or people-of-action) Tennyson was clearly outside of his element, which again strongly suggests a lack of the more controlling 1-3-7 line of ray energies. Gladstone was awed by Tennyson's poetry. Perhaps Tennyson should have been less opinionated and should have tried to listen more to Gladstone when discussing the world of government and rule of law.

One of the remarkable qualities about the sign of Leo, however, has to do with *self-confidence*, which is related to the important Leo quality of being *uninfluenced* by others. (As mentioned, Tennyson was born on August 6th, 1809.) The development of the quality of *Self* should not be confused with selfishness or self-centeredness.   Leo makes a tremendous contribution to its eleven brothers with its kingly or regal quality of self-identity, self-containment, which enables one to emerge, often dramatically, out of mass consciousness.   There is generally a fundamental *graciousness* with this self-contained move or stance, due probably to the second ray of love-wisdom (the ray which conditions the Sun, which is Leo's ruling planet).

Another related quality of Leo is that of *creative self-expression*. This also requires confidence and being uninfluenced by others, since the significant others around one invariably advise against this fundamental Leo urge. The creative self-expression of Leo often brings one into the field of the arts. And here Tennyson chose a difficult road and he accomplished much. Along with the 6th ray soul, which was devoted to the spiritual questions of the day, we find the soul energy creatively expressing itself in the field of poetry, of literature, with much help from the Leo personality and the 4th ray mind.

The 6th of August would place Tennyson's Sun in the 12th degree of Leo, which places it in the 2nd decanate—the decanate which some say is ruled by Jupiter. Jupiter is a 2nd ray (love-wisdom) planet and is also ruler of the 2nd fire sign Sagittarius. At one level of manifestation this influence would augment the religious-philosophical probing that seeks to explore the big questions.

The 2-4-6 line of ray energies clearly predominates in Tennyson's psychological equipment. This was both an asset and a debit, since developed and focused energy enables one to accomplish much in the chosen field, but also results in certain deficiencies or imbalances.

Great Britain has a second ray soul and a first ray personality. (See *Destiny of Nations*.) One might say that (related to Britain's 1st ray personality) the Queen and other prominent political leaders found Tennyson's 6th ray patriotism acceptable and, above all, non-threatening. Tennyson was a patriot—there was no doubt about that. When Tennyson was selected as the Poet Laureate, skill as a poet was the primary concern, to be sure, but his political inclinations were not ignored. More important, however, was Tennyson's ability to *touch the soul of the nation in some way*. The difficulties during the Victorian Age, as mentioned earlier, were many. The new sciences brought the old religion into question. The new industry brought both benefit and squalor. The political upheavals and social unrest on the continent, which began with the French Revolution, were far from being settled or resolved. Nineteenth century Britain began with a long period of reaction against political and social change. In the later half of the century the ruling powers developed a policy of controlled and gradual change, rather than endless resistance to reform. Change brings stress, and a lot of dynamic and fundamental changes bring a lot of stress. Tennyson was not a beacon of light that illuminated the way into the next century. But he did provide another kind of light. He gave eloquent voice to basic tenets and values that were sometimes especially British and always fundamentally human—values upon which one could rest one's soul during a very troubling time. His voice was never a complex one that served only the elite; his voice reached across the entire nation, all social classes, and then to other continents, and it became a sort of shared intimate voice of the people.

It is not easy in this day and age for the contemporary man to put oneself back into another era. We live in a time when the mass media and the entertainment of television tend to dominant the evening scene. In Tennyson's day, however, after the evening repast and during the heart-sharing hour, people reached for the *Bible*, or for a Dickens' novel, or for Tennyson. The title Poet Laureate encouraged many to reach, and most were not disappointed. Every new set of poems was eagerly purchased by more and more people. It was as if they were all struggling with the same questions, the same suffering and pain, the same hopes. Tennyson gave the struggles a most eloquent voice; the pain was alleviated through beauty of word and thought. One could momentarily relax and rest into soul. So could the Queen, so could such great political leaders as Gladstone, and, collectively, so could the whole nation.

Summary of Sixth Ray Indicators.

• *Loyalty to friends.* This is a very strong 6th ray indicator. It follows upon the tendency to put people into good-or-bad, with-me-or-against-me, categories. Perhaps the highest expression of this quality is the willingness to lay down one's life for one's brother, or leading a life of self-sacrifice that enables others to survive. Surrounding oneself with a few very close friends is something that the 6th ray person tends to do or wants to do. *Strong affections and strong attachments* result. Once again, Tennyson's words on the pedestal of a bronze statue of the Queen's servant characterize perfectly the attitude of loyalty: "Friend more than servant, loyal, truthful, brave!/ Self less than duty, even to the grave!"

• *High ideals.* Idealism tends to bring one to the higher levels of the emotional or astral plane. The *ideal* is something that is somewhat "fuzzy" or not altogether clear, something that is *sensed or felt.* There is also a strong transcendent quality about the ideal. The ideal aspires to something that is higher and loftier than self and higher than intellect. The 6th ray rules the astral plane and seeks an alignment with the Cosmic Waters, Neptune, and the intuitive 4th plane of Buddhi. Tennyson often talked passionately about a "future state" as he explored vaguely a spiritual ideal.

• *Impracticality.* When idealism is over-emphasized and unbalanced, there can be the appearance, metaphorically speaking, of a person walking around with his head in the clouds. If such types are not careful, they will stumble. Their feet do not seem to be well-planted on the ground. They may walk in a gingerly fashion. They may appear to be floating through space. There attention is vaguely elsewhere. They are troubled by what they see. They may seek to float free of the many troubles around them.

The American publisher James Fields wrote of Tennyson: "He stumbles about in a kind of Tennysonian fix which he does not seem to be trying to move away from."

The American writer Nathaniel Hawthorne said of Tennyson: "He seemed as if he did not see the crowd nor think of them, but as if he defended himself from them by ignoring them altogether; nor did anybody but myself cast a glance at him."

• *Zealousness.* Mars and Neptune are 6th ray planets. We have the gentle 6th ray that would not hurt a flea, but we also have the 6th ray that is strong by the virtue of its youth and its onepointedness. If there is also a 1st ray influence, we might find the person who fights tenaciously for one particular principle, in the manner of a crusader. "The sixth Ray is either militant and active, or mystical, pacific and futile." (*Destiny of Nations* 98.)

• *Faith.* "Death, the spirit world, the after life, religious faith, and related subjects were themes that emerged again and again in Tennyson's poetry." Faith is closely related to idealism and devotion. Faith often is an especially key attitude of the 6th ray type. "One's faith can be renewed as an immutable force. Faith that does not guide one's entire life is worthless....Faith is the realization of Truth, ✓ tempered in the fire of the heart."   *Fiery World I*, para. 340, 433.

• *Feeling Higher Than Reason.* The 6th ray type knows well that feeling transcends reason—"I have felt" reaches higher than "freezing reason's colder part." Feeling touches something higher than human mind and something that cannot be expressed in words. The 6th ray type may prefer to navigate with the help of feeling rather than with the help of detailed knowledge, planning, or reason. At one level this appears something like superstition. On another level, however, answers and directions often do come on the wings of faith.

• *Other Worldly.* Tennyson remarked to a friend: "The only tolerable view of this life is as a vestibule to a better." An "other worldly" attitude can lead to lack of responsibility when dealing with concrete issues. On the other hand, seeing this world as a "vestibule to a better" can lead to *archetypal perception.* It opens one up to the realization that there are other worlds that stand behind the world of appearances and that bring the world of appearances into manifestation.

• *Lack of a Dress Code.* When the 6th ray type is other worldly oriented (spiritually or artistically), there is sometimes little concern for personal appearance or a socially correct dress code. This type may, however, be very willing to accept a dress code of a religious order or something similar, since such a code is one of simplicity. It also relegates dress to a point below the threshold of consciousness, which is to say, one does not have to give it any thought.

• *The Female Role.* One of Tennyson's special skills as a poet was his ability to "imagine himself so effectively in the female role." The 2-4-6 line of ray energies is the "softer" line.

• *Duty, Noble Images, Purification, and the Higher Philosophy.* Tennyson's friend Edward Fitzgerald admired Tennyson for his noble images and thoughts that "direct us to our duty, purify and cleanse us from mean and vicious objects, and so prepare us for the reception of the higher philosophy." All the rays are at work in this ennobling and edifying process. We see here, however, something that might be called the reaching for and the sounding forth of the high ideals.

- *Employment Difficulties.* The matter of employment may be problematical for the 6th ray type. The busy physical activity and the mental cleverness of the market place (the business world) may provide something like a puzzling irritant to the 6th ray type. The 6th ray type would tend to prefer the quiet of the monastic setting and the simplicity of the pastoral landscape. There are often too many conflicting ideals or lack of ideals in the employment world for the 6th ray type to find there its peace and repose. (This will be modified, of course, when influenced by the 1-3-7 line of ray energies.) Tennyson succeeded in avoiding the world of employment altogether. It would have interfered with his contemplative scholarship. Employment can serve, however, as an important balance for the 6th ray type. It can help to connect the feet with the earth, metaphorically speaking.

- *Thin-Skinned and Sensitive to Criticism.* Tennyson took criticism very seriously. According to his publisher, Tennyson could be miserably thin-skinned at times. In *Discipleship in the New Age* I, 407, we find the observation: "Your sixth ray has also given you a sensitive emotional nature which means a solar plexus too active in its functioning. This you know well. Upon this, the heart quality must supervene." This was written to a person who had a 6th ray personality and a 6th ray astral body.

- *Aloof, Not Fully Engaged.* Some criticized Tennyson's poems, saying "they were representative of a poet who stood aloof from life and therefore a poet who was not fully engaged, not fully experiencing the human struggle." There are various forms of aloofness. There is the aloofness of the 1st ray type, which relates to the quality of *impersonality*. This type of aloofness enables the 1st ray type to stand free of emotion and penetrate straight to action. The 1st ray type tends to be fully engaged. There is also the aloofness of the 5th ray scientific type. Here the aloofness is *detached observation*. Sometimes this attitude of mind leads to engagement in the human struggle and sometimes it leads to a kind of "ivory tower" existence. The aloofness of the 6th ray type has to do with the aloofness of the *sensitive*, and the personal sensitivity of the *solar plexus center*. It also has to do with having exceedingly *high ideals*. Personal sensitivity is often mixed with fear. There is the fear of failure, which makes action and engagement much more difficult. With sensitivity and high ideals, one tends to avoid engagement. One tends to place blame on others and on situations as not being good enough for one's labors. It is necessary to remember, however, that the 6th ray energy can impel one into action (similar to the thrust of 6th ray Mars energy), or it can turn one towards the effort to intuit direction from above (with a little help from 6th ray Neptune). Tennyson was clearly in the latter category. Also, one may sometimes shift from one attitude to another. When the sensitive builds up within himself a certain amount of frustration (due to inaction), then there may occur a sudden burst of engagement and action. It is similar to the melancholic suddenly becoming the choleric.

• *Religious.* Gladstone's daughter Mary noted in her diary: "Tennyson does not appear to be much of a Christian, and I suspect is no theologian, but is very religious." "Pure religion, undefiled and spiritually focused, is the higher expression of the sixth ray (working as is ever the case under the influence and potency of the second ray) and for us Christianity in its earlier days was the great and inspiring symbol. In the same connection, among the lower aspects of the sixth ray are to be found all forms of dogmatic, authoritative religion as expressed by the organized and orthodox churches." (*Nations* 39)

• *Not a Good Executive.* Unless modified by the 1st ray, the 6th ray type generally does not make a good executive. Tennyson was not a particularly good manager of his domestic help. He would tend to be too lax with them, and on occasion react too strongly to a particular incident, or he would simply avoid the responsibility by letting his wife tend to the work of supervision. A neighbor observed: "Every trifle of life disturbs him. The buildings getting up are a nightmare to him, the workmen not getting on are a daily vexation to him."

• *Difficulty in Seeing the Group Life.* "It is so difficult for a person who has sixth ray qualities predominantly present (either as the result of this life's direction, or as carried over as predisposing influences from another life, as is your case), to realize the one-pointed intention ... of a group. One's own point of view, one's own dharma, one's own problems and one's own unfoldment are followed so one-pointedly and—complicating the difficulty—with such truly right and high motives." (*Discipleship in the New Age* I, 298-9)

• *Reaching up into Heaven.* He had a dream in which he was "building a tower of brightly colored pagodas reaching up into heaven." "Six being the number of the sixth ray, it is therefore the number of idealism and of that driving force which makes mankind move forward upon the path and in response to the vision and press upward towards the light. It is in reality devotion to an unseen goal, ever on ahead, and an unswerving recognition of the objective." (*Rays and Initiation* 79.)

"THE SIXTH RAY OF DEVOTION
Special Virtues:
Devotion, single-mindedness, love, tenderness, intuition, loyalty, reverence.
Vices of Ray:
Selfish and jealous love, over-leaning on others, partiality, self-deception, sectarianism, superstition, prejudice, over-rapid conclusions, fiery anger.
Virtues to be acquired:
Strength, self-sacrifice, purity, truth, tolerance, serenity, balance and common sense." *Esoteric Psychology* I, 209.

Dream of Tennyson. We conclude with a dream impression of Alfred Lord Tennyson.

              Dream of Tennyson

      Tennyson knew someone approached.
         Neither his face nor long stride altered
     as he moved so slightly to the right,
         flanked by four of like-dress, all black
     with broad rimmed black hats, shielding
         the Master Poet in their perfect unison.

     I approached without yet any
         formulated word.
     No cause here for pointless words,
         the Poet might have thought,
     and moved on just enough to the right
         to avoid any needless pleasantries—

     Not somber, not morbid, as some have claimed,
         but with a quietly tense intent—
     Not melancholic, but with a
         slightly darkened mood
     that comes from living poetically
         and painfully outside of heaven—

     The line to heaven being on the
         sweetest song and on the phrase
     that settles within the magic
         mixture of light, breeze, and gesture—

so rare, so painfully and exquisitely rare,
>   the right mix of breath, sound, and shadow.

The black clad group moved in unison,
>   slightly to the right, discerning
quite correctly that the tenuous
>   line to heaven could not well
be served in an unformulated approach,
>   no matter how pleasant the pleasantries.

And thus another line
>   in the ever shifting sands of water-time
>   was firmly drawn.

Brief Summary of Sixth Ray Indicators.
The need for some sort of "bible" or major book that evokes utter reverence and devotion.
Sensitivity to the emotional plane.
Devotion to beauty and color and all things lovely.
Attracted to melodious and sacred music.
Deep and intense emotional responses.
Deep devotion and loyalty to a particular person.
Belonging to an "exclusive and somewhat secretive group" fits in with the 6th ray preference for strong loyalties.
Interest in the big metaphysical questions—questions of abstraction rather than immediate concretion.
Lofty aspirations.
The theme of death often intrigues the 6th ray type. From one angle it is essentially a religious theme.
A propensity towards moodiness, a susceptibility to the dark moods (the dark mood occurs when one suffers from falling short of the ideal).
With one's head in the clouds, there is often a tendency to neglect the more mundane practical matters.
Verse filled with "noble images that direct us to our duty, purify and cleanse us from mean and vicious objects, and so prepare us for the reception of the higher philosophy."
A deep desire to have "sweeter, more noble modes of living."
Desire to replace cold manners with "real warmth of heart."
Sometimes there is a "lack of go" or a lack of practical action.
Brooding about an idealistic future state.
A deep religious sense, whether belonging to a particular church or not.

"People must have some religion."

A 6th ray epitaph: "Friend more than servant, loyal, truthful, brave! Self less than duty, even to the grave."

Faith in things unseen—an essential component for the 6th ray.

It might be said that the 6th ray endeavors to "build a tower of brightly colored pagodas reaching up into heaven."

The 6th ray draws the line in the sand.

MARIE CURIE
SEVENTH RAY SOUL

At these times there is an increased radiatory activity. This can be noted at this time in the discovery of radio-active substance, as the incoming ray increases its potency, decade by decade. A certain amount of radiation is basic and fundamental in any world cycle. But when the seventh ray comes in there is an intensification of that radiation, and new substances appear to come into new activity. This intensification leaves the entire mineral kingdom, as a whole, more radioactive than before, until this increased radiation becomes in its turn basic and fundamental. As the seventh ray passes cyclically out of manifestation a certain measure of inertia settles down on the kingdom, though that which is radiatory continues its activity. In this way the radiation of the mineral world steadily increases as the cycles come and go, and there is necessarily a paralleling effect upon the higher three kingdoms. People today have no idea what effect this radiation (due to the incoming ray) will have, not only upon the surrounding mineral world but on the vegetable kingdom (which has its roots in the mineral kingdom), and upon men and animals in lesser degree. The power of the incoming cosmic rays has called forth the more easily recognized radio-activity with which modern science is now concerned. It was three seventh ray disciples who "interpreted" these rays to man. I refer to the Curies and to Millikan. Being themselves on the seventh ray, they had the necessary psychic equipment and responsiveness to enable them intuitively to recognize their own ray vibration in the mineral kingdom.   *Esoteric Psychology,* v.1, 225-6.

Marie Curie was born in Warsaw, Poland, on November 7, 1867. Approximately 3½ months later Robert Andrews Millikan was born on March 22, 1868, in the small town of Morrison, Illinois (U.S.A.). Both rose to the top of their professions. Both received the Noble Prize for Physics. Madam Curie received the prestigious prize in 1903, which was jointly awarded to her husband, Pierre Curie, and to Henri Becquerel. Robert Millikan received the Noble Prize for Physics in 1923. Madam Curie won an unprecedented second Nobel Prize—this time in Chemistry—in 1911. She was the first woman to receive a Noble Prize, and she was the first person to receive two Nobel Prizes.

Marie Curie Early Years. Her maiden name was Sklodowska and her first name was Maria, later changed to the French form Marie. She was born, as mentioned above, in Warsaw, Poland. Many, but certainly not all, great souls seem to have been blessed with having a loving and understanding mother. In Maria's case it was her father who brought an extraordinarily beneficial care and influence not only to her but to her three sisters and brother as well.

When Maria was nine years old, her mother and oldest sister, Zosia, went to Nice, France, for a year. The mother had tuberculosis, but the family was optimistic and prayerful. Upon their return from Nice, however, the mother knew that her strength was waning. The situation became increasingly more difficult. Along with the problem of illness, the father's professional status began to suffer. He was a schoolteacher, specializing in physics and math. His salary was reduced when he was suspected of promoting the Polish culture in the classroom. In order to survive economically, the family was forced to take in boarders. One of the boarders suffered from typhus. The two oldest daughters, Zosia and Bronya, became ill with typhus. Bronya survived, but Zosia did not. It was a beautiful family. All were lovable, intelligent, cultured, and very kind. Zosia died, and then the mother, unable to hold on any longer, also passed over to the other side. Maria, ten years old, had been praying. She would pray that, if somehow it would save her mother, could the Lord please arrange to take her instead.

Maria, the Scorpio child, became acquainted with death at an early age. Her oldest sister, very dear to her, and then her mother, were both no longer there. There was an emptiness, a vacancy, in the household. Two precious and loving beings left an unfathomable void for the little girl, Maria. At this point, with prayers unanswered, she began to drift away from the Church. Maria replaced Church and mother with a self-disciplined study. There was an intensity about the little girl. She wanted very much to excel academically and so that through her achievement she might one day be of great service to her country, Poland.

Poland—A Country Desperate to Maintain Body and Soul. Poland's climb to Renaissance greatness began with an alliance between Poland and Lithuania in 1384. This alliance was bought about in order to secure Poland and Lithuania from their common enemies or threats—the Russians to the East and the Teutonic Knights to the West. Secure borders were particularly difficult for Poland to maintain, due to that fact that there were no natural borders—no large rivers, no mountains. Poland's Golden Age occurred under Sigismund I (1506-1548) and his son Sigismund II (1548-1572). In 1523, during Sigismund II's rule, Erasmus (one of the great secular scholars of the humanistic movement during the Renaissance) wrote of Poland: "I congratulate this nation which now, in sciences, jurisprudence, morals, and religion, and in all that separates us from barbarism, is so flourishing that it can rival the first and most glorious of nations" (*Life and Culture of Poland*, Lednicki).

Sigismund I married the daughter of the Duke of Milan. She brought a variety of Italian scholars, artists, and musicians with her, and they were welcomed by the King. Both Sigismund I and Sigismund II were men of intelligence and culture, patrons of the arts, and rulers who strongly favored religious tolerance. The University of Cracow was a flourishing university. At one point it enrolled over 15,300 students at one time. Under Ladislas IV in the early 1600's religious debate was encouraged, art and music was supported, Rubens paintings were purchased, the Polish theatre was brought in existence, and Italian operas were performed.

The difficulty of establishing and then maintaining relative religious and cultural freedom was enormous. Every sect and every faction conspired to increase their own power and influence within the nation. When this was impossible, they often invited foreign governments to intervene, giving the foreign government an excuse to invade Poland. The Greek Orthodox Church in the Eastern section appealed to Russia; the Protestant Western section appealed to Prussia.

The governing and legislative body—the Sejm—was comprised of relatively wealthy and powerful nobles. They were the large landowners of the feudal type system. Each nobleman in the legislative body had the power to veto the majority. *The result was that a consistent national policy and a strong centralized government were impossible.* The failure of Poland to establish a strong centralized government led to a condition that foreign governments found relatively easy to exploit. Russia came from the East, Prussia came from the West, and Austria came from the South. They were satisfied with a partitioning of Poland.

Nicolaus Copernicus. Nicolaus Copernicus was born on February 19, 1473, in Thorn (now Toruń), Poland. When 18 years old he studied at the University of Cracow. He later went to the University of Bologna, studied medicine and canon law, taught mathematics and astronomy in the University of Rome, before returning to Poland. Through his uncle he obtained a position as a church administrator in Frauenberg (now

Frombork). The position had primarily financial responsibilities. He had been born into a family of merchants and this fact probably provided the connection. For King Sigismund I, Copericus wrote a treatise on money, which discussed the problems of issuing debased coinage. Good coins become horded or sent abroad, while the king, through taxes, is paid back in his own "bad coin." He translated and published Theophylactus's book on morals—it was a Greek to Latin translation. Copernicus also practiced medicine, treating the poor without charge.

During this time he continued his research and mathematical calculations in astronomy and wrote a *"Little Commentary"* which laid down the principles of the heliocentric system. This *Little Commentary* was for the most part ignored. An enthusiastic young Wittenberg professor, Rheticus, came across it and became an avid supporters of Copernicus's heliocentric system. Due to the efforts of Rheticus and Osiander (a Lutheran minister at Nuremberg), Copernicus's major work, *On the Revolutions of the Celestial Orbs*, was printed. On May 24, 1543, a copy was brought to him on his deathbed. He appeared well pleased and died within the hour. His mathematical proof of the heliocentric solar system replaced the confusion of Ptolemy's machinery of spheres, epicycles, and eccentricities. The Church tolerated the Copernican view as long as it was put forward as an hypothesis. Many rejected it as being contrary to the *Bible*, to God, and to observation.

Copernicus had *interests and accomplishments in several fields*. They included law, mathematics, moral treatises, medicine, the world of finance, and astronomy. The world of finance interested him not as a businessman but as a vital aspect of *social order*. The astronomy of Ptolemy was not compact enough to satisfy Copernicus. Early on during his studies in Italy he sensed that it was wrong. Nature had a more *elegant kind of order* to it.

We are told that "the seventh Ray of Ceremonial Order began to come into manifestation in 1675." (*Destiny of Nations* 29.) We are wondering if Copernicus was a forerunner of this ray energy? It can be noted that the 3rd ray in one particular cycle came into manifestation in 1425 A.D., which has much to do with the whole Renaissance expansion of learning. The 5th ray of science began its cycle in 1775. (*Eso. Psych.* v.1, p. 26.) These cycles refer to the incarnating of souls on a particular ray. Copernicus appears to be a forerunner in many ways.

Newton, Copernicus, Galileo, Harvey, and the Curies are, on their own line of force, lightbringers of equal rank with H. P. B. All revolutionized the thought of their time; all gave a great impulse to the ability of man to interpret the laws of nature, and to understand the cosmic process, and only those of circumscribed vision will fail to recognize the unity of the many force impulses emanating from the one Lodge. *Treatise on Cosmic Fire*, 1038.

Jan Sobieski—King John III. In the later half of the 1600's the military and diplomatic genius of Jan Sobieski temporarily secured the Polish borders. Jan Sobieski married Maria Kazimiera, of French royal blood and became King John III. He was described as a king of body and soul as well as in name. As a ruler, one might say, *he did what he could*. As a military leader, he did more than any other European general at the time in expelling the Ottoman power from Europe. He defeated them in the Ukraine and in Vienna. Culturally, he fostered religious freedom, supported all cultural endeavors, and brought in French and Italian artists, painters, and architects. Poland produced its own writers and poets. Sobieski, himself, was a learned man, reading Descartes, Galileo, Pascal, Molière, and many others. He was particularly fond of everything French, having spent a year in Paris as a young man.

The things he *could not do,* however, were the following. He could not improve the lot of the peasant, he could not continue to maintain a strong army (earlier he had on several occasions paid for soldiers and arms out of his own pocket), and he could not make the rich pay taxes. The noblemen who made up the Sejm had veto power (*liberum veto*) over the king. The wealthy noblemen controlled the peasants, they did not want to pay for an army, they did not want to have themselves taxed. They themselves selected who would be king, and often they sold the position of king to the highest bidder. Therefore, there were many things that Sobieski wanted to do, but he was unable to do them. He died in 1696.

The Partitioning of Poland. The strong Polish families—the powerful landlords and noble—perpetuated a property based feudal system that depended on serfs. This economic system was rapidly becoming obsolete, but the strong regional noblemen refused to see it. Many of them negotiated with foreign powers as if they were a country unto themselves. Some sided with Russia, and some preferred Prussia. Catherine of Russia and Frederick of Prussia liked the Polish system of government, because it virtually guaranteed a weak Poland. Poland missed every opportunity to unite around a strong leader and draft a new constitution. At one point (1772) Jean Jacque Rousseau submitted his *Constitution of Poland* at the request of a group who was trying to save the integrity of the country. By the time Rousseau's *Constitution* was finished, however, it was too late. Poland was already being partitioned. Kosciusko, the great Polish general who helped the American Colonies gain their independence from Britain, sought to expel the Russians in 1794. He had some initial success—the effort was truly heroic—but he was soon defeated by an army twice the size of his own. When the Third Partition Treaty was signed on January 26, 1797, about half of Poland went to Russia, and a quarter each to Prussia and Austria. Poland was no longer a state, that is to say, no longer a government, but *she was still very much a people, a culture, a language, and a civilization.* There was a strong concerted effort to keep all that alive and vibrant in the hearts of the people.

Another opportunity came when Napoleon's army was sweeping through Europe. Napoleon had gained substantial victories over Austria and Prussia, and he entered Warsaw on December 19, 1806. Prussia surrendered claims to central Poland, and the grand duchy of Warsaw was established as an independent state. Many Poles eagerly joined Napoleon's army on its march to Moscow. After 1814, however, Napoleon could no longer protect the duchy. In 1815 the Kingdom of Poland was created, along with a liberal constitution, with Czar Alexander I of Russia as king. Polish nationalists, however, wanted a complete break with Russia. They organized an insurrection in 1830 but were defeated after a few months.

After 1831 things got worse. There was no longer a constitution, they had no voice in the government (no Sejm), and few civil liberties. Russia took their literary and art treasures and made every effort to "Russianize" Poland, culturally, economically, and politically.

The Poland of Maria Sklodowska. Maria's parents grew up in the Poland that Russia was trying to assimilate. The Russians, for the most part, were Greek Orthodox. The Poles became more tenacious in their adherence to the Catholic Church, for this became an important part of their distinction and identity. Not to be Catholic was close to treason in the eyes of a Pole. The Russian language, not Polish, was taught in the schools. The children learned Polish at home, and the teachers also, whenever possible, spoke Polish in the classroom and taught Polish history. The torch of national identity burned not openly but very brightly in the hearts of the Polish people.

In the 1800's the Poles learned that armed insurrection was fruitless, at least at that time. The movement for independence and identity had to go underground. The new heroes were the artists, the intellectuals, the writers, the priests, and the schoolteachers. Such a hero was Maria's father. He knew Greek, Latin, and Russian, learned French, English, and German. He kept up on the latest developments in physics and chemistry. As a school teacher he did much surreptitiously to keep the Polish culture alive both in the home and in school. It was necessary to present an agreeable and condescending face to the school principal and others in authority, while at the same time to work in contrary ways. Even little Maria was forced to live this duplicity. Whenever an inspector entered her classroom, the teacher almost always called on Maria to respond to questions on Russian history. Her excellent Russian and her knowledge of facts were very impressive. She was the first in every subject—Russian, French, German, writing, history, and literature. Her memory was phenomenal. She could recite a poem faultlessly after hearing it only twice. Her classmates could not believe it. They thought she was learning the poems secretly. In spite of the duplicity of the underground culture and the official culture, she liked school. She liked learning. She was an avid reader in a family where everyone was a student and where learning was not only the key to individual success but also the key to their national and group identity.

On June 12, 1883, she graduated from her secondary studies with a gold medal, as did two of her siblings earlier. After graduation she took a year off from serious study and relaxed in the country with relatives. She tutored a child in French and did all sorts of enjoyable things—picked wild strawberries, learned how to ride a horse, took walks in the woods, rolled hoops, played games with the other children, gathered mushrooms, etc. It was one of the few extended times of fun and relaxation that she had in her life.

The Floating University. Upon her return to Warsaw, she tutored students for a small fee. Some of her friends talked about plots and assassinations, while others talked about educating as many of the poor people as possible. She chose the later alternative. A movement in education and learning across Europe at that time had to do with a shift from literature to the sciences.

She was introduced to the underground "Floating University" through a 26 year old high school teacher, Miss Piasecka. There was no education beyond high school for women in Poland at that time. That was one of the societal problems that the Floating University sought to rectify. Lessons were given in a variety of subjects, including anatomy, natural history, and sociology. These were new subjects or old subjects receiving a new impulse. These studies were held in private homes in small groups of eight or ten. These meetings were illegal. Had they been caught, they would have been imprisoned.

As a "student" of the "Floating University," it was also required that Maria teach others. She began by reading aloud to a group of poor, uneducated women who were working as dressmakers. She also got together, book by book, a small library for these women to use. Several qualities were beginning to emerge in Maria's being:

1. She loved learning. She loved the world of ideas. Each year new vistas of knowledge opened up before her.
2. She was gifted. She had a good memory and a keen intellect. She was always the top learner among peers.
3. She was patriotic. Patriotism had a very special meaning to many Poles at this time. Patriotism meant something like the survival of the group life. Patriotism kindled a fiery aspiration in her. This youthful aspiration led either towards action and the sword, or towards learning and education. She chose the latter and evidently saw no intelligent reason, under the circumstances, to chose the former.
4. She felt a social responsibility, an humanitarian impulse. Her gifts were to be used to benefit the community, which, she felt at this time, was Poland. She would achieve for the sake of others.

Her demeanor at this time was described in the following way: "There was a cool and moderate dignity in her nature, an innate gravity that accompanied her enthusiasm—not to say her passion. We shall never see her affect any snobbishness of revolt or bad manners. She will never even have the wish to light an innocent cigarette." (*Madam Curie* 54.)

Poland's Astrological Signs. In the book *Destiny of Nations*, Poland's rays are not given. The ruling signs, however, *are given* and this might help us understand something of the life of that struggling country. The ruling sign of Poland's soul is Taurus, and the ruling sign of the personality is Gemini. Fourth ray Mercury is the exoteric ruler of Gemini, and this often brings one into literary fields and into various forms of communication. A key quality of this important sign has to do with *fluidity*. As D.K. phrases it in *Esoteric Astrology*:

> "Mercury increases in the Gemini subject the latent sense of duality in its various stages and also the sense of distinction, leading to that mental agility and that fluidity of mind which is one of the major assets as well as one of the major difficulties of this sign." (EA 354.)

Gemini would tend to open the Polish mind to cultural influences from other countries, and this most certainly seems to be the case. She was quick to accept renaissance ideas from Italy and France. She imported paintings and architects from Italy and France, but under the Gemini influence she was quick to develop her own Polish poets, writers, and men of letters. She has a very rich literary tradition. There has been much positive "fluidity" in terms of religion in Poland, particularly among those who were advancing the cultural frontier. It would be very difficult, if not impossible for another country, such as Russia, to impose a single language (replace Polish with Russian) and a narrow culture upon the Polish people. The duality of Gemini could present one face to those in authority and quite another to the underground movement. An oppressive authority could never rest secure in its organization, for the word of Gemini at the personality level is: "Let instability do its work." The "instability" in Gemini has to do with the fact that there is always an opposite, and Gemini will find it and will bring it fourth in Air—in the realm of thought, ideas, and some form of communication.

Taurus is the ruling sign of the soul of Poland. This might account in part for Poland's will to find and maintain the integrity of her own borders. Property has always been equated with one of the most fundamental values held strong by the Bull of Desire. At the soul level, however, desire becomes aspiration and the goal becomes light and illumination. "The two horns (duality) protect the 'eye of light' in the centre of the Bull's forehead; this is 'the single eye' of the New Testament which makes the 'whole body to be full of light.'" (EA 154). The word for Taurus at the soul level is: "I see, and when the eye is opened, all is illuminated." The ruling aristocracy of Poland was blinded by their own personal power and property, and they failed to see the way into the new developing order. The feudal order was passing, but they refused to let go, which resulted in the suffering of their nation and the people. But the nation continued to look for light, and this seeking after the light of truth seemed to be a very vibrant quality in the whole Sklodowska family.

Working as a Governess. Maria's oldest sister, Bronya, wanted to go to Paris to study medicine at the Sorbonne. She had saved enough money to last a year in Paris, but the study required five years. Maria, after talking it over with the father, made the suggestion that Bronya go to Paris and that she, Maria, and the father send Bronya money on a regular basis. The plan was that Bronya could then later help Maria go to the Sorbonne, after Bronya had become a doctor. Bronya was overjoyed and very grateful.

Maria got a job as a governess (January, 1886) for the Zorawski family that administered some of the lands of the powerful Prince Czartoryski. The job paid room and board and 500 rubles a year. Her pupil was a ten year old girl, described as "disorderly and spoiled." Maria got along particularly well with the older daughter, Bronka, in the family. Maria described her as "a rare pearl both in her good sense and her understanding of life." Conversation in the country living centered around "the neighbors, dances, and parties." For Maria this required quite an adjustment. The spirit of learning, the probe into new frontiers of knowledge, social responsibility, and patriotic zeal all seemed to be absent. Maria learned to go to church every Sunday without pretending that she had a headache. She learned to participate in the life of the country estate without revealing a critical attitude. After all, she had a purpose for being there, and things were never perfect.

The peasant children were illiterate. With the help of Bronka, she found a way to give lessons to a peasant's child. Soon there were ten children, then eighteen. She wrote to a friend: "Great joys and great consolations come to me from these children." (*Madame Curie* 68.) She also continued to read and study on her own. Literature, science, and sociology all interested her, but eventually she narrowed down her interests to physics, chemistry, and mathematics.

The eldest son in the family (a mathematics student at the University of Warsaw) fell in love with Maria. He told his parents he wanted to marry her. His father became extremely angry and the mother almost fainted. He was told that a person of his standing *does not marry a governess!* One marries in order to enhance one's own economic and political standing. Maria was very hurt but kept her composure.

Maria stayed with the Zorawski family for three years. When the children were old enough she was no longer needed. She was also beginning to feel certain constrictions of provincial life. She was in need of a change. One tends to get "very dull, in spite of the best intentions," she wrote in a letter to her brother Joseph. She also wrote that she was losing her ambition to become somebody. Her ambition was transferred to her sister Bronya and to her brother Joseph.

She found another position as governess. This time in Warsaw with a rich industrialist's family. Her sister Bronya wrote from Paris to tell her that she, Bronya, was going to get married to a medical student and that Maria should come to live with them. Maria was no longer certain that she wanted to go to Paris and the Sorbonne. Money was still a major question and some of her earlier enthusiasm had left her. She worked as a governess in Warsaw for a year, and then stayed an additional year in Warsaw, tutoring, going to the Floating University, becoming reabsorbed in the cultural life, and trying to add to her savings. Her cousin was director of a small museum. The museum was actually more of a front to carry on the work of the Floating University than anything else. It was here that Maria tried to develop some skill in laboratory work. She tried to reproduce some experiments described in physics and chemistry texts. "From time to time a little unhoped-for success would come to encourage me, and at other times I sank into despair because of the accidents or failures due to my inexperience." (*Madame Curie* 86.)

At last the time was right. In the fall of 1891, about to turn twenty-four years old, Maria Sklodowska left for Paris.

Paris and the Sorbonne. There was a feeling of liberation. In Warsaw one had to be careful about speaking the outlawed language of Polish. In Paris one could speak any language one wished. The bookstores could carry any books in any language. She changed her name "Maria" to the French spelling "Marie."

Maria enrolled in the Faculté de Sciences, University of Paris. There were 1,800 students enrolled and only 23 of them were woman. It was not that it was difficult for a woman to enroll, rather higher education at that time was generally not something that women pursued. It was interesting, however, that more than two thirds of the women were not French. These women were all truly pioneers in breaking through the limitations of the cultural norms. She arrived in the lecture halls early and sat in the front row. She devoted almost all of her time to study. She had tried to keep up on the latest science in Poland, but she was discovering some basic deficiencies in her education. It was also difficult for her to understand all the subtleties of the French language. She simply studied with more resolve and long into the night. Whereas most students sought one degree, she planned to obtain two masters degrees, one in mathematics and one in physics.

She lived with her sister and her husband for a while, then moved into a garret room closer to the University. Bronya had married a medical student also from Poland. Marie did not seek out any kind of social life, but her sister managed to bring Marie into their little society of Polish friends from time to time. For three years Marie's life was one of "monastic simplicity." She lived on three francs a day, which paid for room, food, clothes, paper, books, and university fees. There was no heat in her room, so she often studied till late at night in one of the libraries. At times she suffered from malnourishment.

To study science with some of the best teachers in the world—this was a dream come true. The academic world was changing. The Renaissance brought Greek and Latin scholarship, philosophy, rhetoric, history, and literature to the forefront. Now in nineteenth century Europe the new science—chemistry, physics, botany, biology, zoology, geology, along with their many new specialized sub-divisions—was pushing forward the frontiers of knowledge. Marie's biological chemistry professor was Emile Duclaux—one of the earliest supporters of Pasteur's theory that diseases were spread by microbes. Her physics professor was Gabriel Lippmann—he was in the process of inventing color photography. Her mathematics professor was Henri Poincaré—the greatest mathematician of the period.

Marie pushed herself beyond reasonable limits in order to absorb and to learn as much as possible. In 1893 she passed first in the class in the master's examination in Physics. As a woman, and as a foreign woman, and as a student at one of the most prestigious universities in the world, this accomplishment was astonishing to many. In 1894 she obtained her masters in mathematics. This time she came in second.

In 1893 her financial situation became desperate. There was not enough money for her to attend the Sorbonne year. Mlle Dydynska, who had met Marie in Paris, "moved heaven and earth" in Warsaw to get Marie the Alexandrovich Scholarship—a scholarship for Polish students studying abroad. A few years later Marie saved money from her first earnings and returned the 600 ruble scholarship money. The administrators of the fund did not know quite how to handle this; no one had ever done this before. Marie considered the scholarship more of a loan. She did not want to deprive another needy student of a similar "life buoy" that could keep someone "afloat" for yet another year.

In the fall of 1893 Lippmann, her physics professor, offered her a job as a research assistant in his laboratory. The work entailed doing experimental research into the properties of various metals. This work gave her valuable laboratory experience.

Marie's Goals. At 26 years of age Marie's goals were taking definite outline. There were three or four primary goals:
1. Her first goal was to further herself educationally. This she had known for a long time, but now, in the university study of physics and mathematics, there was more focus and concentration.
2. Related to the above, a somewhat new goal was emerging that had to do with the dynamic energy of science itself. Something electrifyingly new—in the sense of the vivification of consciousness—

was happening in the field of science. The professors for the most part were filled with the enthusiastic drama of opening up new vistas of knowledge. There was developing in Marie Sklodowska the hope of being able to add something significant to this wonderful new world of knowledge.

3. Never once did Marie forget her fundamental purpose. She did not come to France in order to forget Poland and to become French. She came to Paris because of the great educational opportunities it offered. Her intention was always to return to Poland in order to serve her birth nation through elevating the people in an educational way.

4. Related to the above was an emerging and general goal of simply *helping humankind.* This went beyond the borders of Poland and beyond the scientific disciplines, although Poland and science might well be the particulars and the specifics of the soul impulse.

She had no plan and no goal to get married and have children. What she had felt in this regard, while a governess with the Zorawski family, led only to disappointment. One could almost take this as a sign that marriage was not to be. In Paris there was no time at all to explore such possibilities. There was only time to catch up, to learn as much as possible, and then to excel. Also in the background of her mind was her father. Her father had raised four children. He brought them up in a culturally rich environment. He made endless sacrifices, so that his children might grow up and make a difference in Poland and the world. He would need someone in his reclining years. She would live with him and look after him in his old age. All his children loved him dearly. But then she met Pierre Curie.

Meeting Pierre Curie. Pierre Curie was born in Paris on May 15, 1859. His father was a medical doctor. Similar to Marie, he was raised in a cultured family with a strong scientific inclination. He was devoted to science and had no time for romance. Pierre at the age of 35 was already an accomplished scientist. Pierre and his brother Jacques discovered that quartz and other non-conducting crystals developed an electric charge under pressure. This was known as the *piezoelectric* effect, *piezo* meaning "to press." They made use of the phenomenon to construct an electrometer that could register minute charges of electricity. At the age of 32 Pierre was head of the laboratory at the Paris School of Industrial Physics and Chemistry. At 35, when he met Marie, he was busy on his doctorate, which had to do with the effect of heat on magnetic properties. At a certain critical temperature a ferromagnetic substance—such as nickel or iron—will lose its ferromagnetic properties. This temperature became known as the Curie Point.

It just so happens that Marie was working on a related matter in Professor Lippmann's laboratory. The laboratory space and equipment, however, was inadequate. She enquired of a visiting Polish professor, Joseph Kovalski, if he could help in any way with the laboratory problem. Kovalski arranged a meeting between her and "a scientist of great merit," Pierre Curie. Marie was different from any other woman he had met. She was extremely knowledgeable about scientific matters. He could discuss subtle details about his work and she would follow along with keen interest. She lived science and had no time for anything else. She was also young, attractive, and unattached to any man.

Pierre was very interested and he pursued her. A friendship quickly developed. She encouraged him to write out his experiments on magnetism and submit his doctoral thesis. He invited her to meet his father. Many scientific projects and problems were discussed on a regular basis. He asked her to marry him, but she said that she had to return to Poland. It was impossible for her to abandon her country. His argument was that if she returned to Poland, she would be abandoning science.

This was 1894. She returned to Poland for the summer. Pierre wrote to her regularly.

We have promised each other—haven't we?—to be at least great friends. If you will only not change your mind.... It would be a fine thing, just the same, in which I hardly dare believe, to pass our lives near each other, hypnotized by our dreams: *your* patriotic dream, *our* humanitarian dream, and *our* scientific dream. Of all those dreams the last is, I believe, the only legitimate one. I mean by that that we are powerless to change the social order and, even if we were not, we should not know what to do; in taking action, no matter in what direction, we should never be sure of not doing more harm than good, by retarding some inevitable evolution. From the scientific point of view, on the contrary, we may hope to do something; the good is more solid here, and any discovery that we may make, however small, will remain acquired knowledge.

The reasoning mind, of course, will always find good reasons. But the man's heart was aflame and destiny was bringing these two soul mates together. It was only a matter of time—time and persistence. Marie returned to Paris in the fall. Pierre rented a large apartment that could be divided into two independent units. The understanding was that this would be a friendly arrangement; the accommodations were far better than the garret rooms Marie had been living in in Paris. She agreed. Another proposal was the following: If he went to Poland, taught French and somehow carried on with his scientific research, would she marry him? Pierre went to Bronya, Marie's sister, and discussed the matter with her. Pierre's mother also talked to Bronya. Bronya was completely won over to their side. Pierre was deeply attracted to Marie's great intelligence, her courage, her nobility, her idealism. And, evidently, in this situation he was the Taurus Bull (Pierre's sun sign) that was not going to take "no" for an answer. On July 26, 1895, they got married at the city hall in Sceaux, followed by a small gathering of friends at the home of Pierre's parents. There was Bronya and her husband, some university people, and also Marie's father, Professor Sklodovski, who had come from Warsaw for the wonderful occasion.

Their marriage was a true union on several levels. In some ways, being eight years older than Marie, Pierre was her mentor. But Marie was brilliant, so before long he was learning from her, which is to say, they were a perfect team, each learning from the other. Marie was probably more relaxed and less intense during these years. She still had very high goals and ideals, to be sure, but she and Pierre would also take excursions on their bicycles out into the countryside on weekends. They would leave their bicycles by a country road and tramp into the woods, explore the flora and fauna of a hidden pond, discuss their current scientific experiments, breathe the fresh country air, and find an out of the way country inn to spend the night. Marie's academic study and scientific work were balanced by the beauty of nature, exercise, good food, relaxation, and the love of a soul mate. On September 12, 1897, Marie gave birth to a her daughter, Irène, who was to follow in her parent's footsteps and become an outstanding scientist.

Discovering Radium. In 1895 (the same year that Marie and Pierre got married) the German scientist Wilhelm Röntgen discovered what he called the "x-ray." He began by investigating luminescence, which led to the discovery of an unknown radiation emanating from a cathode ray tube. This unknown radiation could pass through certain materials (paper, wood, thin sheets of metal) and it could also affect photographic paper. His discovery was sensational and it traveled rapidly through the scientific community, leading to the development of its practical application. Röntgen received a Nobel Prize for physics in 1901.

The French chemist Henri Becquerel had been investigating fluorescence and phosphorescence for some time. Becquerel experimented with a double salt of uranium (potassium uranyl sulphate) which produced high fluorescence. He discovered accidentally that sunlight was *not needed* to induce the "fluorescence" or radiation, and that it was not the same as x-rays. How could the potassium uranyl sulphate crystal give off a stream of radiation, continuously and in all directions? Science at that time said that this was impossible.

The Curies had followed the discoveries of Röntgen and Becquerel with great interest. Marie was finished with her work with Professor Lippmann's research team and was looking for a subject for her doctorial thesis. She also needed a laboratory. It was Pierre's dream to someday have a spacious laboratory with all the right equipment. He managed to find an old storage space at the School for Industrial Physics and Chemistry for Marie, which they fashioned into a lab. It lacked many essentials, but nevertheless it was enough and it did serve. It was a happy time of hard work on their labors of love.

Marie began her new work by repeating some of Becquerel's experiments. She measured the power of ionization of the uranium rays and determined that it depended not on sunlight or temperature but simply on the amount of uranium in the samples. She hypothesized that the "radioactivity" (a word she coined) was an *atomic property of uranium*. She also asked the question, Why not other elements? Perhaps uranium was not the only element to have this mysterious property. Testing every known element, she soon discovered that thorium also emitted a ray, or is radioactive. She determined also that certain uranium ores were more radioactive than uranium itself. This led her to believe that there was at least one *unknown element* in the uranium ore obtained from pitchblende. Other scientists suggested to her that perhaps her measurements were inaccurate. She had run her various tests several times. She was sure that there was *a new, undiscovered radioactive element in the uranium ore*. At this point Pierre began to realize that Marie's work was potentially of greater significance than his own research work. He temporarily put aside his own work and joined forces with Marie.

The unknown substances turned out to be high in radioactivity but low in amount. This made the work of separating them out long and tedious. There was less than even one millionth per cent of new radioactive elements in pitchblende. "We soon recognized," wrote Marie in her book *Pierre Curie*, "that the radioactivity was concentrated principally in two different chemical fractions, and we became able to recognize in pitchblende the presence of at least two new radioactive elements: polonium and radium. We announced the existence of polonium in July, 1898, and of radium in December of the same year." (Marie was 31 years old.) They only had small traces of the new elements in the pitchblende samples on hand. In order to provide sufficient evidence to satisfy the scientific community, much larger quantities of pitchblende were required. They were able to obtained several tons of pitchblende from the Austrian government at a low price.

It was in this miserable old shed that we passed the best and happiest years of our life, devoting our entire days to our work. Often I had to prepare our lunch in the shed, so as not to interrupt some particularly important operation. Sometimes I had to spend a whole day mixing a boiling mass with a heavy iron rod nearly as large as myself. I would be broken with fatigue at the day's end. Other days, on the contrary, the work would be a most minute and delicate fractional crystallization, in the effort to concentrate the radium. I was then annoyed by the floating dust of iron and coal from which I could not protect my precious products. But I shall never be able to express the joy of the untroubled quietness of this atmosphere of research and the excitement of actual progress with the confident hope of still better results. The feeling of discouragement that sometimes came after some unsuccessful toil did not last long and gave way to renewed activity. We had happy moments devoted to a quiet discussion of our work, walking around our shed.... Thus the months passed, and our efforts, hardly interrupted by short vacations, brought more and more complete evidence. Our faith grew stronger, and our work being more and more known... It had taken me almost four years to produce the kind of evidence which chemical science demands, that radium is truly a new element. One year would probably have been enough for the same purpose, if reasonable means had been at my disposal. The demonstration that cost so much effort was the basis of the new science of radioactivity.

Pierre Curie, by Marie Curie.

Fundamental Changes in Physics. The science of physics underwent fundamental change during Marie's life, and her development of the new science of radioactivity contributed significantly to the changes. Physics is defined as a science that deals with matter and energy and their interactions in the fields of mechanics, acoustics, optics, heat, electricity, magnetism, radiation, atomic structure, and nuclear phenomena. The word "atom" comes from the Greek *atomos*, and from *a + temnein*, to cut, meaning "no cut" or indivisible. The atom as the smallest particle of matter was postulated by Democritus in the fifth century BC.   Aristotle's view, however, that the earthly realm is composed of a blend of four elements—fire, earth, air, and water—became the dominant view and prevailed throughout the middle ages. Galileo (1564-1642) disagreed with it, as did Pierre Gassendi (1592-1655)—a French philosopher and mathematician, who attacked the theories of Aristotle and revived Democritus's notion that matter was made up of tiny indivisible and invisible parts. The atomic theory continued to gain momentum— particularly through the work of British chemist John Dalton, the Italian physicist Amedeo Avogadro, and the Russian chemist Dimitry Mendeleyev in the early 19th century—but with Marie Curie's discovery of radium, the theory began to move from a hard, indivisible particle to "a positive nucleus of energy."

Alice Bailey was very much interested in this subject matter. She gave a series of lectures on the subject, which were later published as the book *The Consciousness of the Atom*.

> About twenty years ago...(in 1898), a new element was discovered which was called Radium, and this discovery entirely revolutionised the world's thought about matter and substance. If you will go to the textbooks of the last century, or search the old dictionaries, seeking for the definition of the atom, for instance, you will usually find Newton quoted. He defined the atom as 'a hard, indivisible, ultimate particle,' a something which was incapable of further subdivision. This was considered to be the ultimate atom in the universe, and was called by the scientist of the Victorian era 'the foundation stone of the universe'; they considered they had gone as far back as it was possible to go, and that they had discovered what lay back of all manifestation and of objectivity itself. But when radium, and the other radio-active substances, had been discovered, an entirely new aspect of the situation had to be faced. It became apparent that what was considered the ultimate particle was not so at all.   *Consciousness of the Atom* 33-34.

Sir Isaac Newton. We include here a brief note about the English physicist Sir Isaac Newton, due to his possible affiliation with the 7th ray energy. Again, we recall the earlier quoted statement that the *seventh ray began a cycle of manifestation in the year 1675.* (The fifth ray of science began its cycle in 1775.) We are dealing here with subcycles of the Sixth Ray, since the Sixth Ray was the major ray during the Piscean Age. The Sixth Ray of Idealism and Devotion "colored" the energies of the other rays during that approximately 2000 year cycle. This is the reason why the religious life, the religious questions and themes, played such a dominant role throughout that age. As we emerge from the Piscean Age and enter the Aquarian Age this fact— the prominence of the religious note— is becoming increasingly more difficult to appreciate. Unfortunately, instead of being able to enter into the psyche of that earlier age and being able to appreciate its note and labor, there is a tendency to judge it from the vantage point of the present age and psyche. In this transition period, the tendency is to *repulse* the earlier note, and rightly so as we move on to other labors, but there results also a tendency to judge the earlier era in a superficial, non-applicable way.

Isaac Newton was born on Christmas Day in 1643 and lived a long 84 years. Most of his adult life was spent at Trinity College, University of Cambridge—first as a student (18 to 26 years of age) and then as a professor of mathematics (26 to 58). He was an avid student, reader, learner, experimenter, thinker. His style of learning was to *pour all his energy into completely mastering the particular subject matter.* He would read and often acquire every available book on the subject; he would take extensive notes and make dictionaries or glossaries of terms with as many as 7000 terms. He would read, study, and experiment late into the night, usually until 2 or 3AM and sleep 4 or 5 hours. He would take no recreation or pastime; he did not ride a horse, walk about town, or socialize. He considered time spent away from his studies was time lost. He often was so engrossed in his studies and experiments that he forgot to eat. His physical exercise at that time was walking about his room, usually deep in thought.

His areas of study were primarily three: Science (physics, mathematics), Alchemy, and Theology (the *Bible*). He pursued these studies comprehensively and indefatigably. "Science" is the contemporary term for what was then called *natural philosophy.* His studies and accomplishments were in the field of physics (he established the study of optics or the behavior of light, formulated laws of universal gravitation and motion, built the first reflecting telescope), and mathematics (invented calculus). His two major scientific works were *Principia Mathematica* (1687, written in Latin) and *Opticks* (1704, written in English). Principia Mathematica was "probably the greatest single work of science ever written." He intentionally made the book difficult to read in order "to avoid being bated by little smatterers in mathematics" (White 190, 217).

With the *Principia*, Newton not only unified the disparate theories of Galileo and Kepler into a single, coherent, mathematically and experimentally supported whole: he also opened the door to the Industrial Revolution. Along with solutions to age-old puzzles such as how the tides are produced and how comets travel through the heavens, Newton addressed more exotic ideas—for example he explained the Earth's 'wobbling' as being due to the varying strength of gravity at different points on the globe. The Principia laid the cornerstone for the understanding of dynamics and mechanics which would, within a space of a century, generate a real and lasting change to human civilization. (White 221.)

Science has to do with knowledge, or more precisely with exact knowledge—the kind of knowledge that is based on measurable and objectively observable data—knowledge of form. Alchemy is considered by many as a Medieval attempt to transform base metals into gold, and also as a forerunner to modern chemistry. Alchemy actually had to do primarily with the occult science of *transmutation*, which was *symbolized* with the lead-to-gold metaphor. Again, in order to appreciate this, we must endeavor to see this within the "backdrop" of the dominant 6th ray energy of the Piscean Age. If science, or knowledge, was not in some way related to the divine quest, it was considered utterly useless. The goal of all worthy endeavor was to unite with the Divine. *There could be no phenomenon that was devoid of noumenon.* Interestingly, the word "phenomenon" has to do with appearance, or what is visible to the senses, and is etymologically related to the word "fantasy" (and therefore to "enchantment" or *maya*). "Noumenon" is related to the word "mind" and is defined as "a ground of phenomena that is unknowable by the senses but is conceivable by reason." The "pure" 6th ray quest for the Divine and for the *mystical union* uses primarily a Bahkti Yoga approach, which uses the higher aspirational energy of the emotional plane to connect with the intuitive buddhic plane. The occult science of alchemy brought in another factor, an additional factor. Along with the dominant mystic aspiration of the Age, there was added the more difficult scientific note brought in either by means of the 5th ray qualitative energy or the 7th ray energy. Here we find a path of greater resistance accessible only to the more advanced people of the Age.

As a young lad attending King's School in Grantham, Isaac boarded with Eduard Clark and family, the local apothecary. Mr. Clark's library was extensive, and it served to ignite many sparks in young Isaac's mind. This was Isaac's first real acquaintance with the vast world of learning. He had his first introduction to chemistry while observing Mr. Clark's preparation of various medicines. Later at Cambridge, Newton explored other areas: "First he absorbed the limited arena of conventional chemistry, then he moved on the what he considered to be the more exciting realm of alchemy—a subject which must, to his eye, have held almost limitless potential" (White 133). Newton had in his library 138 volumes of pure alchemy and 31 other books that came under the category of chemistry, although the line between the two disciplines was definitely blurred (John Harrison's *The Library of Isaac Newton*).

"Alchemy," according to Newton, "does not trade with metals as ignorant vulgars think, which error has made them distress that noble science; but she has also material veins of whose nature God created handmaidens to conceive and bring forth its creatures.... This philosophy both speculative and active is not only to be found in the volume of nature but also in the sacred scriptures, as in Genesis, Job, Psalms, Isaiah and others. In the knowledge of this philosophy God made Solomon the greatest philosopher in the world." (King's College Library, Cambridge. Keynes MS 33, fol.5v.)

Carl Jung studied alchemy from a psychological perspective and wrote two books on the subject. He found within the quest of alchemy an abundance of archetypes that are extremely helpful in understanding the depths and dynamics of the human psyche:

> Alchemy, with its wealth of symbols, gives us an insight into an endeavor of the human mind which could be compared with a religious rite, an *opus divinum*. The difference between them is that the alchemical opus as not a collective activity rigorously defined as to its form and content, but rather, despite the similarity of their fundamental principles, an individual undertaking on which the adept staked his whole soul for the transcendental purpose of producing a *unity*. It was a work of reconciliation between apparently incompatible opposites, which, characteristically were understood not merely as the natural hostility of the physical elements but at the same time as a moral conflict Since the object of this endeavor was seen outside as well as inside, as both physical and psychic, the work extended as it

were through the whole of nature, and its goal consisted in a symbol which had an empirical and at the same time a transcendental aspect.
Carl Jung. *Mysterium Coniunctionis*, 554.

Alchemy related to Newton's purpose of trying to discover an all-embracing model of the universe. Alchemy, for Newton, reached beyond mathematics and physics. He studied the subject for about 30 years and left unpublished notes and writings on alchemy totaling over 100,000 words. A book entitled "Praxis" was never completed.

A third area of major interest to Newton was theology. He was raised a Puritan. While at Cambridge, in order to receive his BA and MA degrees he had to sign an agreement, attesting to the acceptance of the Thirty Nine Articles of the Anglican Church. As a professor, he was required to take holy orders. This he managed to avoid through an appeal to the right people that eventually led to King Charles II, who granted Newton a special dispensation. Newton took religious questions and theological argument very seriously. He found it impossible to accept the doctrine that God and Christ were the same entity. He carefully researched the *Bible* and also traced the matter historically, which led to the uncovering of the original dispute. During the First Council of Nicaea in 325 there was a dispute between Arius, an Alexandrian priest, and Anthanasius, the Bishop of Alexandria. Arius, who believed that God and Christ were separate, lost the argument—the Council sided with Anthanasius, and the Roman Catholic Church sided with the Council. Arius was exiled to Illyria, but the debate spread throughout the Christian world. The heretical doctrine became known as Arianism, named after its founder Arius. Arianism became Newton's faith, but he was extremely careful about mentioning this fact. Many knew, however, that he was very well-versed in the *Bible.* An archbishop observed, "You know more divinity than all of us put together." John Locke said of Newton's knowledge of the Bible: "I know few his equal." (Durant, *Louis IX*, 543.)

"The first religion," wrote Newton, "was the most rational of all the others till the nations corrupted it. For there is no way without revelation to come to the knowledge of a deity but by the frame of nature." (White 154.) The Book of Revelations was of particular interest to Newton, as was the esoteric science of numerology. He called King Solomon the greatest philosopher in the world. Newton was fascinated with the Temple of Solomon, studied the Book of

Ezekiel in three different languages, and drew a floor plan of the Temple from the dimensions given in the *Bible*. All this had to do with the effort to gain knowledge of deity through the "frame of nature." "Newton perceived himself as the new Solomon and believed that it was his God-given duty to unlock the secrets of Nature, whether they were scientific, alchemical or theological." (White 162.)

Newton's life changed considerably when he was 54 years old. The Whigs came into power in the election of 1694, and Newton's friend Charles Montagu was appointed Chancellor of the Exchequer. In 1696 Montagu appointed Newton Master of the Royal Mint in London. This opportunity and dramatic change came at a good time in Newton's life. He had spent 35 years in Cambridge, and he was experiencing some difficult depressions. Although he had made advances in the fields of mathematics and physics that could only have been made by a genius, he felt that his dream of finding a unifying explanation of all the forces of nature was eluding him. He needed a change.

His position as Warden of the Mint is one that he could have managed with a minimum of time, assigning most of the responsibility and labor to others. Surprising to many, however, he took the job very seriously, applied himself with energy and intelligence, and turned out to be a very able administrator. The work of the mint was of critical importance at that time due to the fact that extensive counterfeiting over the years was threatening to bankrupt the nation. By using cheaper metals, and also by chipping the edges off coins and reshaping them, counterfeiting was relatively easy and lucrative. It was also a capital crime. Trust in the currency had eroded, and mass recoinage was necessary in order to avoid a sever economic depression. He learned every aspect of the work, improved the efficiency of the operation, and worked what amounted to a double shift. Government contractors responsible for the melting and refining processes were overcharging the government. Newton, with his alchemical background, knew a great deal about this process, and he forced the contractors to lower their prices. He researched charters to determine exactly what power the Mint had. Then he sought to increase his own power and responsibility by re-claiming certain rights. He also studied economics extensively, reading every book available on the subject. He made it a point to become acquainted with several experts in the field so that he could discuss theory and get their opinions. He began to write a history of economics, a theory of commerce, and principles of the monetary system—none of which was every published. He pursued counterfeiters, reluctantly at first, but, when the Solicitor-General would not do the job, Newton assumed the responsibility with zeal. He became a private investigator and prosecutor. As an investigator, he had to use a network of agents in eleven countries, arrange secret meetings with informants and bounty hunters in sordid public houses and brothels, become justice of the peace in neighboring counties in order to gain information on known criminals. As a prosecutor, he had to send several men to the gallows.

As Newton settled into his new life, he had the opportunity to acquire more influence in the Royal Society—the prestigious, London based, society of scientists. He was voted its President in 1703. The administrative skill that he developed so rapidly at the Mint he now applied to the Royal Society. The Society was on the edge of bankruptcy, and its membership was becoming an exclusive medical fraternity. Newton quickly changed all that. The Society published Newton's second major scientific work, *Opticks*. "To avoid being engaged in disputes about these matters," Newton delayed the printing of this book for 30 years. This book discussed and explained refraction and reflection of light, mirrors and prisms, the phenomenon of rainbows, how the eye functions, the phenomenon of gravitation, metabolism, sensation, and also discussed the Great Flood and Creation.

Newton's Rays. It is not at all an easy matter to determine Newton's rays, due in part to his genius—he was gifted in so many areas. It seems that the sixth ray of idealism and of the Piscean Age was present; Newton was a deeply religious man. Newton's profound interest in alchemy (an occult or spiritual science) and his *life long quest to find an "all-embracing synthesis of the microcosm and the macrocosm"* strongly suggest the possible presence of the seventh ray of organization and ceremonial magic. (As mentioned, this ray was coming in on a sub-cycle beginning in the year 1675.) As Newton mentioned, "There was no way (without revelation) to come to the knowledge of a deity but by *the frame of nature*." Number, as well as having great mathematical and scientific significance, also has great occult significance. Associated with his interest in alchemy, Newton also had much interest in biblical chronology, numerology, and mythology. Newton pursued many of the esoteric fields in his effort to find the keys to the universe, or to unlock some of nature's greatest secrets. He had the unquestioning faith, belief, and idealism of the 6th ray, but he also had a great will-to-know the divine-physical order and the laws of manifestation. The seventh ray quality of synthesizing Spirit and Matter seems to have been present in Newton's equipment.

As we see in the case of the Curies, Millikan, and Newton, it is very difficult to distinguish the 5th ray of science from the 7th ray of organization. These two rays are so compatible with each other that it is difficult to determine which one is in the more prominent position and where one ray leaves off and the other begins.

As a mature man, Newton proved himself to be a very capable administrator. His earlier years as an intense scholar at the University of Cambridge suggests the presence of the 6th, 7th, and 5th rays. His later work at the Mint and at the Royal Society suggests the addition of the 1st ray, with an emphasis on one and seven. Also, one could also not rule out the possibility of the presence of the 3rd ray.

There are several references to Sir Isaac Newton in the Secret Doctrine. We include two:

"But do the men of Science understand the innermost thought of Newton, one of the most spiritual-minded and religious men of his day, any better now than they did then? It is certainly to be doubted." (*Secret Doctrine* I 492.)

"The innermost thoughts and ideas of Newton were perverted [by the scientific materialism that followed], and of his great mathematical learning only the mere physical husk was turned to account. Had poor Sir Isaac foreseen to what use his successors and followers would apply his 'gravity,' that pious and religious man would surely have quietly eaten his apple, and never breathed a word about any mechanical ideas connected with its fall.
(*Secret Doctrine* I, 484.)

Once again, we quote D.K.'s statement regarding some most outstanding people of science:

Newton, Copernicus, Galileo, Harvey, and the Curies are, on their own line of force, lightbringers of equal rank with H. P. B. All revolutionized the thought of their time; all gave a great impulse to the ability of man to interpret the laws of nature, and to understand the cosmic process, and only those of circumscribed vision will fail to recognize the unity of the many force impulses emanating from the one Lodge. *Treatise on Cosmic Fire* 1038.

The Noble Prize. During the early years of their happy marriage, the labors of Pierre and Marie Curie were focused in three areas:
1) Teaching. Marie became a professor at the Higher Normal School for Girls at Sèvres near Versailles (even though an all girl school, Marie was the first woman on the faculty). 2) Experimental research. The primary focus here was on the rapidly growing science of radioactivity. Several articles by Marie and Pierre were published in the scientific journals on the subject of radium and radioactivity.

3) Their daughter Irène. Their home life and raising their daughter Irène were of major importance. They had little time to enter into much of a social life outside of Pierre's family and Marie's Polish friends. They had to play the political games that are helpful for career advancement. As a result, recognition for their work came more quickly from outside of France than within. In 1900 the University of Geneva offered Pierre a chair in physics with a handsome salary, laboratory, and two assistants. A position was also offered to Marie. They turned it down, for the work with radium was not yet complete.

Finally, at 45 years of age, one of Pierre's dreams came true. He obtained the position of professor at the Sorbonne in 1904. This came after the whole world had recognized his achievement. A year earlier Pierre and Marie Curie, along with the French chemist Henri Becquerel, won the Noble Prize for physics for their discoveries in radioactivity. In the same year of 1903 Marie submitted her doctorial thesis. *This was the first advance research degree awarded to a woman in France.* Receiving the Noble Prize and the first woman to do so, Marie Curie was suddenly world famous. This celebrity status brought a pestering wave of people who wanted to meet her, write her, receive money from her, or interview her. This was an extremely unwelcome intrusion into the life of the hard working, quiet, and not very social family. There was really too much work to do for them to spend time with anyone beyond a few family friends and relatives. They were not interested in developing a social network, no matter how much it might improve their status in University circles.

Tragedy Occurs. In December of 1905 their second daughter Eve was born. Early the next year, April 1906, tragedy occurred. Pierre was accidentally struck by a horse drawn wagon, while hurrying home in the rain from the Sorbonne. Marie was devastated. She went into an emotional shock-withdrawal for several weeks. They had spent so much time together everyday in the laboratory; she had hardly a life separate from Pierre. It was extremely difficult for her to accept his sudden absence—an absence that came without any warning, allowing for no period of transition or adjustment. After his death, she would address him in her diary: "My Pierre, I think of you without end, my head is

burning with it and my reason is troubled. I do not understand that I am to live henceforth without seeing you, without smiling at the sweet companion of my life." (Eve Curie 254)

What remained was her children and the work—the most excellent reasons for carrying on. The council of the Faculty of Science at the

Sorbonne puzzled over who would take Pierre's position as professor of physics. They soon came to the conclusion that the only teacher worthy of succeeding Pierre was Marie Curie herself. Marie accepted the offer with the words: "I will try." At times she thought that this would be the easiest way to live, and at other times she thought that she was "mad to accept it." A woman professor at the Sorbonne was unprecedented. On November 6, 1906, Marie delivered her lecture in a hall filled with students and reporters. *It was the first lecture given by a woman in the 600 years of Sorbonne history.* Marie was 39 years old. Not particularly ambitious in a personal way but very hardworking and highly gifted, Marie continued to achieve in an unprecedented manner.

After two years as professor of physics, she compiled her lectures and had them published in a 970 page volume entitled *Treatise on Radioactivity.* Marie's research work continued to expand with a growing team of student-assistants. She taught others to develop such skills that they would never make a mistake. The secret, she suggested, "is in not going too fast." In 1911 the Swedish Academy of Sciences awarded Marie Curie the Nobel Prize in Chemistry—the first time that the prestigious prize was awarded to the same person on two different occasions. She was a great inspiration to scientists and to women all over the world. Her daughter Eve remembers Albert Einstein coming to visit Marie. Eve and her older sister Irène were walking along when suddenly Einstein seized Marie's arm and said, "You understand, what I need to know is exactly what happens to the passengers in an elevator when it falls into emptiness." The two children roared with laughter. (Eve Curie 284.)

Her Work During the War. In July, 1914, a great dream of Marie's came true: The Institute of Radium in Paris, with a well-equipped modern laboratory, was complete and ready to carry on with the research work that Marie had begun. Unfortunately, however, in the following month of August Germany invaded France. Almost all of Marie's laboratory workers joined the army. She herself volunteered to help organize the medical service and soon discovered an urgent need. The hospitals both near the front and well behind the lines lacked X-ray equipment. For the next four years, 1914-1918, she worked very hard to fill this need.

X-rays were needed in order to locate bullets and shell fragments in the wounded. Marie developed small mobile units that were able to follow the army. She obtained funds from the Union of Women of France and X-ray materials from manufacturers. Her mobile unit consisted of an ordinary car or small truck, a Roentgen apparatus, and a dynamo that supplied the necessary electrical energy. The dynamo was driven by the automobile engine. Her radiology cars were nicknamed "little Curies." She pressured several wealthy ladies into loaning their limousines for the duration of the war. She had to learn how to operate the Roentgen apparatus, perfect her technique, and then train others. She also learned how to change a tire, clean a dirty carburetor, and also how to drive a car, for she could not always depend upon having an assistant. At that time men drivers out numbered women 500 to 1.

The fact that she was a civilian (not part of the military personnel) made it very difficult to get passes into certain areas and to get needed supplies. She had to explain, persuade, demand, and will her way through many bureaucratic obstacles in order to meet the particular need. She managed to equip 20 vehicles, install 200 radiology rooms in various emergency hospitals, which altogether served over a million injured.

She traveled in all kinds of weather, ate what was available, and sleep wherever she could—in a hospital, a tent, in the car, or in the open air. In her scientific mind, one might say, she tended to be clear, detached, and almost cold. When tending to the needs of the wounded, she was very patient and loving in a motherly way. When the soldiers were frightened by the x-ray apparatus, she would assure them that it was the same as taking a photograph. Toward the end of the war she was asked to write about her experience, which she did in the book *Radiology in War.*

After the war, Marie resumed her work of setting up and developing the Institute of Radium in Paris. The Institute became a world-renowned center for nuclear physics and chemistry. Marie was the director of the Institute and her daughter Irène was her major assistant. (Irène won the Noble Prize for chemistry in 1935.) Marie was living proof of the fact that women could do as well as or better than men in science. This inspired many women all over the world to enter the scientific professions.

"Very naturally, this idealist was bound to be attracted by the Wilsonian doctrines and to have faith in the League of Nations. She obstinately sought remedies for the barbarity of the peoples and dreamed of a treaty which would truly efface rancor and hatred." (Eve Curie 308.) She felt that during times of trouble, the leading intellectuals should truly lead. They should be defenders of civilization and defenders of freedom of thought; they should not allow themselves to become accomplices in wrongful programs of a lawless regime. On May 15, 1922, by unanimous vote, the Council of the League of

Nations named Marie Curie-Sklodovska a member of the International Committee on Intellectual Co-operation. This Committee included Albert Einstein, Bergson, Gilbert Murray, Jules Destrée, and many others.

In 1921 Marie Curie visited the United States. President Harding presented Marie with one gram of precious radium, worth $100,000. (America thirsted after publicity more than any other country. An "enormous mob" waited to greet her at the landing pier in New York. This terrified her, but she managed to see the journey's purpose as a great official act. The Americans were surprised to find this larger-than-life woman "timid, tired, and plain dressed.") A major part of her life now included scientific conferences, lectures, university ceremonies, visits to laboratories, and the receiving of many honorary degrees and other awards and recognitions. She gave lectures in Brazil, Italy, Holland, England, Belgium, and Spain. In 1932 she traveled to Warsaw, Poland, where a Radium Institute was being established. Her sister Bronya was appointed director.

On July 4, 1934, near Sallanches, France, Maria Sklodowska-Curie died of leukemia, caused by her exposure to the radium that made her famous. She was 66 years old. After her death the Radium Institute was renamed the Curie Institute in her honor.

Marie Curie's Rays. Marie Curie had a seventh ray soul—that is the given factor and the most important factor. We could also say with almost absolute certainty that Marie had a 5th ray scientific mind. After that, matters pass quickly into the realm of conjecture.

Marie's Sun Sign was Scorpio. I have found over the years that people who have a Scorpio Sun are often the most difficult to estimate in terms of their possible rays. One of the reasons for this has to do with the "magic" of Scorpio. Scorpio is the most "magical" sign of the 12 signs of the zodiac. This has to do with the following factors:

> a) The "M" of Scorpio indicates a triple influence or spirit-soul-form, whereas most of the other signs proceed from a duality of soul-form, or soul-personality. What the touch of spirit is able to do appears magical from the personality perspective.
>
> b) At one level the "magic" touch manifests as a veil of deception. Scorpio often has the uncanny ability to appear to be anything it wants to be. At a higher level—the level of the triumphant warrior—the magic touch is actually a

dispersing of the veil, a penetration to what stands behind the veil. The word "secretive" is often associated with

Scorpio. The Scorpio person can become involved in the intrigue and the secrets of life, or the person can uncover and reveal that which is hidden. Scorpio has the gift of penetrating to and revealing some of Nature's well-kept secrets. At the personality level Scorpio says: *Let maya flourish and let deception rule.* At the soul level the Word says: *Warrior am I and from the battle I emerge triumphant.*

Marie's persona appears to be seldom one of deception—although deception and intrigue might have played a necessary role in the illegal work of the "Floating University"—and it appears far more often to be one of the truly triumphant warrior emerging from some very difficult battles. Also, Marie quickly found the work and the research directions that led to phenomenal new discoveries. It must be remembered that, although Pierre was 8 years older than Marie and a far more experienced scientist, *he followed her lead* into the work of uncovering the important new element radium. When he saw the significance of her direction, he dropped his own work in order to assist her.

So, what ray do we see as a possible personality ray? In my opinion, there could be either a 6th ray personality or a 1st ray personality. The will and determination of the 1st can often be confused with or mistaken for the one-pointed determination of the 6th ray. My guess is that she had a 6th ray personality, exemplified by her high ideals, her devotion to science and family, her initial deep devotion to her country Poland.

It also seems to me that at the astral and/or physical level she was an exception to the rule. Generally, at the astral level, the emotional body is conditioned by either the 2nd ray or 6th ray, and the physical-etheric body is conditioned by either the 3rd ray or the 7th ray. It seems to me that the 1st ray was present at one of these two levels, *or possibly at both of them.* Marie was a highly self-disciplined person, which is strongly suggestive of the 1st ray. There was time for work, and little time for anything else, throughout her whole life.

TABLE of 21-YEAR CYCLES, and 7 YEAR SUB-CYCLES

1867...............born Nov. 7. Maria Sklodowska, Warsaw, Poland.
    1883... age 16..completes secondary education and wins gold medal from Russian Lycee in Warsaw.
1888.......... **age 21**..outstanding student, interest in science, devoted to Poland
        24..goes to Paris to study at the Sorbonne. Intensely conscientious and isolated student.
        26..first in physical sciences, Sorbonne.
    1895.... **age 28**..marries Pierre Curie.
        30-31..discovers polonium and radium. has first child.
        33...taught physics at girl's college.
1902..... **age 35**...doctorate of science degree.
        36...Nobel Prize for physics, also Davy Medal of the Royal Society.
        37...Second daughter is born.
        38...Pierre dies.
        39...first female lecturer at the Sorbonne.
1909........... **age 42**.
        43. Her treatise on radioactivity was published.
        44...Nobel Prize for chemistry.
        47...Radium Institute completed.
    1916..... **age 49**..War work with mobile radiography units, 1914-1917.
        51...Resumes work at Radium Institute.
        54...U.S. President Harding presents Marie with a gram of radium.
    1923..... **age 56**..Lectures, works on Committee of League of Nations , and becomes something like an international ambassador of science.
1930........... **age 63**. continues to direct research and give lectures.
        66...dies of cancer due to radiation exposure.

If we consider the three major life cycles of 21 years each, we find that:
1) *During the first major 21 year life cycle*—the formative years—*Maria belonged to her birth family and Poland*. Significant intellectual and scientific aptitude is evidenced, along with the intent to be of service to others.

2) *The second major 21 year life cycle* moves from the development of form-through-activity to the work of the *deepening of consciousness.* During this stage *Marie belonged to Science and to France.* Her birth family, although very important, is superceded by her new family and France. Her scientific knowledge deepens. The activity gradually shifts from one of acquiring knowledge from the work of others (although that never ends) to one of *sharing one's own knowledge* through writing and through teaching, and to one of *doing original research.* Anybody who has ever done any original research knows that there is a very subtle sensing of right direction that is required here. Without that *sensing of right direction,* research becomes simply minor variations of old and over-worked themes. The sensing of right direction requires soul alignment and the intuitive spark. The possibility for this alignment to occur is the great opportunity during this developmental phase. The pivotal choice at 35 years has to do with the choice between a continued pursuit of the intuited direction or a settling into a more conservative life-style based on societal norms and already achieved successes. Marie considered herself something of a "dreamer" in this regard; she continued to pursue the greater vision—even through the difficult time of the devastating loss of her highly accomplished husband.

3) *The third major 21 year cycle begins at 42.* During this stage one could say that *Marie belonged to the world.* Her years of long labor are crowned with international recognition and influence. She has become what is technically called *a world disciple.* Her personal life had long been secondary to the furthering of science and also to a non-religious caring for the human condition.

Some Seventh Ray Indicators in the Works of Alice Bailey.
"It is for this reason that the seventh ray is spoken of as governing the mineral kingdom and also as manifesting through its mediumship that significant soul characteristic and quality which we call radiation. That word effectively describes the result of soul stimulation upon and within every form. The life of the soul eventually radiates beyond the form and this radiation produces definite and calculated effects."

Destiny of Nations 123.

"One of the major characteristics of the seventh ray disciple is his *intense practicality.* He works upon the physical plane with a constant and steady objective in order to bring about results which will be effective in determining the forms of the coming culture and civilisation"   *Destiny of Nations*   126.

The seventh ray worker "wields force in order to build the forms which will meet his requirements and does this more scientifically than do disciples on other rays." *Destiny of Nations* 126.

"The seventh ray disciple works consciously by means of certain laws, which are the laws governing form and its relation to spirit or life." *Destiny of Nations* 130.

"The keynote of the seventh ray disciple is 'Radiatory Activity.' Hence the emergence in world thought of certain new ideas—mental radiation or telepathy, the radiatory use of heat, the discovery of radium. All this connotes seventh ray activity."
Destiny of Nations 133.

"On this ray are to be found: Masons. Financiers. Great businessmen and organisers of all kinds. Executives are found with these energies in their equipment" *Discipleship in the New Age* I, xiv.

"Under the influence of disciples on the seventh Ray of Organisation or of Ceremonial Order, that powerful physical concretisation of energy which we call 'money' is proving a topic of the most definite concentration; it is being most carefully considered, and the minds of thinking financiers and of wealthy humanitarian persons and philanthropists will be gradually led forward from a strictly philanthropic activity to an activity which is impulsed and brought into expression by spiritual insight, and by a recognition of the claims of Christ (no matter by what name He may be called in the East or in the West) upon the financial reservoir of the world. This is a hard thing to bring about, for the subtle energies of the inner worlds take much time in producing their effects upon the objective, tangible plane of divine manifestation. Money is not yet used divinely, but it will be. Nevertheless, the task is well in hand and is engaging the attention of disciples upon all the rays, under the guidance and the impression of the powerful seventh ray Ashram—now already in process of externalisation." *Discipleship in the New Age* II 221-2.

"The bringing of spiritual energy into contact with substance, and consequently with matter, is the unique work of the seventh ray."
Externalization of the Hierarchy 693.

"The seventh ray person is faced with the difficulty of being able to create exceedingly clear-cut thoughtforms." *Glamour* 222.

"The spiritualising of forms might be regarded as the main work of the seventh ray, and it is this principle of fusion, of coordination and of blending which is active on etheric levels every time a soul comes into incarnation and a child is born on earth." *Esoteric Psychology* I, 53

"The sixth ray fostered the vision. The seventh ray will materialise that which was visioned." *Esoteric Psychology* I, 359.

"The seventh ray will foster the group spirit, and the rhythm of the group, the objectives of the group, and the ritual-working of the group will be the basic phenomena." *Esoteric Psychology* I, 361.

"The seventh ray will convey to man the power to recognise the cosmic Christ, and to produce that future scientific religion of Light which will enable man to fulfill the command of the historical Christ to permit his light to shine forth." *Esoteric Psychology* I, 362.

"He [the 7th ray disciple] must speak those Words of Power which are a group word, and embody the group aspiration in an organised movement, which, it will be noted is quite distinct from an organisation. A striking instance of the use of such a Word of Power being enunciated by a group has lately been given in the Great Invocation which has been used with marked effect. It should continue to be used, for it is the inaugurating mantram of the incoming seventh ray. This is the first time such a mantram has been brought to the attention of humanity." *Esoteric Psychology* II 145.

"It is harder to differentiate between the higher and the lower expressions of the seventh Ray of Ceremonial Order, for this ray is only in the process of manifestation and we know not as yet what its major expressions will be, either higher or lower. Human reactions have their place and—as I have earlier pointed out—even the Masters Themselves do not and cannot foretell what the results of the impacts of force may be nor what may eventuate as a result, though They can frequently determine the probable happenings. If I say to you that the higher expression of the seventh ray is white magic, do you really understand what I mean? I question it. Have you any true idea of what is intended by these two words? I doubt it. White magic is realistically the power of the trained worker and executive to bring together into a constructive synthesis the "within and the without" so that that which is below may be recognisably patterned upon that which is above. It is the supreme task of bringing together in accordance with the immediate intent and plan and for the benefit of the evolving life in any particular world cycle:

1. Spirit and matter.
2. Life and form.
3. The ego and the personality.
4. The soul and its outer expression.
5. The higher worlds of atma-buddhi-manas and the lower reflection of mind—emotion and the physical nature.
6. The head and the heart, through the sublimation of the sacral and the solar plexus energies.

7. The etheric-astral planes and the dense physical plane.
8. The intangible subjective levels of existence and the outer tangible worlds.

"Such is the task of the white magician and as evolution proceeds and becomes more complicated and complex it will nevertheless be more rapid and more accurately defined in the mind of the magician. All, therefore, that is conducive to human sensitivity and to increased awareness is the work of the white magician; all that tends to produce better forms through which the living principle of deity can express itself is the work of the white magician; all that serves to thin or tear away the veil between the worlds wherein those who have no physical bodies live and move and work and the worlds of outer form is the work of the white magician." *Destiny of Nations* 41-42.

Summary of Seventh Ray Indicators.
Social sense. Good manners.
Sense of right relationship.
A deep sense of the socially correct way of doing things.
Leading to humanitarian concerns. Social responsibility.
Organized in study. Studying systematically and thoroughly.
Wanting to know in a comprehensive, whole way, leading to skill in several fields.
Interest in and special abilities in the occult sciences, such as alchemy and numerology.
In combination with all the other rays:
> Seven and One: Interest and work in the political and social order.
> Seven and Two: Skill in the healing professions.
> Seven and Three: Work in finance and economics.
> Seven and Four: Artistic ability, three-dimensional arts, sculpture.
> Seven and Five: Scientific fields. Mathematics. Mineral kingdom.
> Seven and Six: Religious ceremony.
> Seven and Seven: Profound occult science of number. Ceremonial magic. Pyramid power—union of Spirit and geometric form.

Effort to find *"all-embracing synthesis of the microcosm and the macrocosm."*
Effort to *"come to the knowledge of a deity but by the frame of nature."*
Synthesizing Spirit and Matter.
Seventh ray is spoken of as manifesting through the mediumship of the mineral kingdom and is related to the soul characteristic and quality which we call radiation.
Intense practicality.

Steady objective in order to bring about results.
Wields force scientifically in order to build the required forms.
Works consciously with the laws governing form.
Radiatory activity.
Seventh ray often found among skilled executives.
Seventh ray related to the divine use of money, which is related to the synthesizing of spirit and matter.
Bringing spiritual energy into contact with substance.
Creating of clear-cut thoughtforms.
Work of blending, coordination, fusion.
Materializes the vision.
Fosters the group spirit—the rhythm of the group, objectives of the group, and the ritual-working of the group.
The seventh ray is related to the cosmic Christ, and the future scientific religion of Light.
Ability to understand and use words of power.
Higher expression of the seventh ray is white magic.
Power to bring into a constructive synthesis the within and the without.
Patterning that which is below upon that which is above, relating:
1. Spirit and matter.
2. Life and form.
3. The ego and the personality.
4. The soul and its outer expression.
5. The higher worlds of atma-buddhi-manas and the lower reflection of mind—emotion and the physical nature.
6. The head and the heart, through the sublimation of the sacral and the solar plexus energies.
7. The etheric-astral planes and the dense physical plane.
8. The intangible subjective levels of existence and the outer tangible worlds.

Producing forms through which deity can express itself.

FURTHER READING AND STUDY

THE ALICE BAILEY BOOKS. The great teaching on the Seven Rays has been given forth in the Alice Bailey books. The books of special importance on this subject are the five volume series known as the *Treatise on the Seven Rays*. The five volumes are:
  Vol. I—Esoteric Psychology
  Vol. II—Esoteric Psychology
  Vol. III—Esoteric Astrology
  Vol. IV—Esoteric Healing
  Vol. V— Rays and Initiations.
Other Bailey books that deal with additional seven ray related subject matter include the following: *The Destiny of Nations* discusses the rays of nations. *Discipleship in the New Age*, vol. I and II, includes a series of letters written to several of D.K.'s disciples or students. These letters go into specific detail in regard to a person's psychological ray make-up. These are the main monumental books that focus on the far-reaching and important subject matter of the seven rays.

Other Bailey books of special interest and importance on the rays are *The Externalization of the Hierarchy, Treatise on White Magic, Letters on Occult Meditation, Glamour: A World Problem, Telepathy and the Etheric Vehicle,* and *Treatise on Cosmic Fire.*

THE ARCANE SCHOOL. The following paragraphs are quoted from the web site of the Lucis Trust—www.lucistrust.org.

"The Arcane School was established by Alice A. Bailey in 1923 to help meet an obvious and growing demand for further teaching and training in the science of the soul.

"The Arcane School was created as a training school for adult men and women in meditation techniques and the development of spiritual potentiality. The School provides sequential courses of study and meditation, and practical training in group service.

"The Arcane School is nonsectarian, and respects the right of each student to hold his/her own view and beliefs. It does not rely upon an authoritarian presentation of any one line of thought or code of ethics. Material used in the lesson courses is drawn from a variety of sources.

The knowledge, insight and wisdom, and capacity to wield spiritual energy resulting from work and training with the Arcane School should be expressed and applied in daily living service in helping to materialise the Plan of God and to aid in solving the problems of humanity.

"The Arcane School is conducted by correspondence through headquarters in New York, London, and Geneva.

The Arcane School is nonpolitical and nonsectarian. All are served. Since 1923 tens of thousands of students have taken advantage of the training.

"No charges are made by the School for its services. The work is financed through the Lucis Trust by the voluntary contributions of students and those interested in the work of the School and in the teaching. Each gives according to personal circumstances.

"The purpose of the esoteric training given in the Arcane School is to help the student grow spiritually toward acceptance of discipleship responsibility and to serve the Plan by serving humanity. Esotericism is a practical way of life."

Their address in the United States is: Lucis Trust,
120 Wall Street,
24th floor,
New York, NY 10005

In Great Britain: Lucis Trust
suite 54
3 Whitehall Court
London, SW1A 2EF
UK

And in Geneva: Lucis Trust
1 rue de Varembe (3e)
Case Postale 31
1211 Geneva 20
Switzerland

BOOKS on the SEVEN RAYS by KURT ABRAHAM
PUBLISHED BY LAMPUS PRESS

Psychological Types and the Seven Rays. This book explores primarily the three rays that generally condition the lower mental body—rays one, four, and five. This is done through a close look at how some prominent world figures thought.

The first ray mind we call the *administrative mind*. The examples we explore are Jane Addams and Mahatma Gandhi.

The fourth ray mind we call the *artistic-intuitive mind*. Examples discussed are Henry David Thoreau and Vincent van Gogh.

The fifth ray mind is the *scientific mind*. The examples we use to illustrate this mode of thought are Charles Darwin and Thomas Henry Huxley.

"By presenting a detailed evaluation of the personality, work, and life of real people, these distinct mental types come alive and support the use of ray analysis as a means to understand the whys and wherefores of human endeavors." E. James Faubel, in *Transformation Times*.

"Your book should be really useful to many. It establishes a precedent. I am honored to have the book dedicated to me." Mary Bailey, former President of the Lucis Trust.

Threefold Method for Understanding the Seven Rays and Other Essays in Esoteric Psychology. The lead essay in this book discusses three sequential approaches to understanding the seven rays. The firststage has to do with the academic familiarization with the ray energies. This method employs primarily the intellect. At the same time, however, there is a gradual assimilation of ray knowledge that speaks to deeper levels of one's being.

The second stage has to do with a recognition of the group interplay of ray energies. The love of one's own type and ray is replaced by love of the which completes the whole. This moves more directly into the soul perspective. Several examples are given in order that one might see the livingness and the practicality of the ray energies.

The third stage has to be with becoming another ray. Sometimes circumstances forces developed people to move out of specialization and into "energies" and fields of work that are foreign to their own psychological ray make-up. Knowledge of this fascinating stage can help prepare one to recognize special opportunity. This third stage goes beyond soul and brings in a touch of spirit.

Other essays in the book include: "The Use of the Seven Rays in Dream Interpretation." "The Three Rays of Aspect and Stages of Development." This essay discusses the 3-2-1 sequence of first activity (growth through doing), then the deepening of conscious-ness, followed by maturity, power, and control. Seven year cycles and 21 year cycles are considered in this sequence.

"The Third Ray of Intelligent Activity Contrasted with Rays Four and Five." Subtle psychological differences between the approaches of these three rays are considered in some depth.

"First Ray: 'For You, There Must Be Not a Circle, But a Line.'" This essay considered the different approaches of the first ray and the second ray. The second ray type moves in a circle, looking at a broad base and comprehensive knowledge. The 1st ray type moves directly to the point of power in a straight line.

"Mr. Abraham's approach is pragmatic, using biographical information concerning prominent individuals to correlate an understanding of their life crises with an analysis of the Seven Ray make-up. His work will encourage further investigation into the nature and practical application of this most interesting field of study." *The Beacon*, published by the Lucis Trust.

"The Tibetan, throughout the Bailey books, exhorts us to study carefully the rays which are currently lacking in our equipment. To this end Abraham discusses several well-known personalities and how they coped, successfully or otherwise, with ray energies and qualities lacking in their makeup. These are brilliantly done and add much to our understanding of the rays and how they function in our lives.... This book helps loosen the girders of our concrete mind and widens the field of consciousness without neglecting to emphasize the important areas of work in the ray-fields." Rusi J. Daruwalla, in *Mandala, Esoteric Knowledge for the New Age*, published in Mumbai, India.

Techniques of Soul Alignment: The Rays, the Subtle Bodies, and the Use of KEYWORDS. This book discusses an important psychological technique which has to do with "avoiding the trap of many words"— a trap into which intellect and personality invariably fall—and using the *soul-to-soul single keyword technique*. This technique was used by D.K. in his work with his western students. It deals with a psychology of profound simplicity that leads to the revelation of one's higher spiritual possibilities.

There is always a subtle esoteric science behind the selection of a keyword. The keyword identifies and embodies a particular quality that is needed for balance and for soul unfoldment. This generally relates to the development or enhancement of a particular ray energy.

There is also a chapter dealing with four methods whereby one may discover one's own keywords.

Balancing the Pairs of Opposites; The Seven Rays and Education; and Other Essays in Esoteric Psychology.

From the text: "What does it mean to 'balance the pairs of opposites' and to 'walk the middle path'? How important a concept is this? Is it peripheral to the practicalities of daily life, or does it touch all aspects of our physical and psychological lives? Are there specific and practical techniques that can be used in the process of balancing the pairs of opposites?....

"It is important, it seems to me, to try to discuss this matter as concretely as possible, for the subject matter itself is primarily a psychological process or relative abstraction. Also it seems to me that if the interplay of opposites is 'at once the most individual fact and the most universal,' then there is also a most practical application of this 'union' or relationship in nearly every human situation and at most every developmental level. Alice Bailey attests to the comprehensiveness of this process in the following statements: 'The interplay of the opposites . . . is the underlying theme of the entire creative and evolutionary process.' 'Through the interplay of the poles, and through the friction of the pairs of opposites light flashes forth. The goal of evolution is found to be a gradual series of light demonstrations." (*Esoteric Astrology, Treatise on White Magic* 9.)"

"A reading of Mr. Abraham's book *Balancing the Pairs of Opposites* makes one whisper 'Here's richness.'...This book is to be read several times; only then can one gain from the immense insights so casually granted by Kurt Abraham in paragraph after paragraph." Rusi J. Daruwalla, in *Mandala, Esoteric Knowledge for the New Age*, published in Mumbai, India.

The essay on the "Seven Rays and Education" includes:
Determining the Child's Note and Quality.
The Rays and Stages of Development.
Feeling Beauty, Strength, and Wisdom—Differences in Learning
    Approaches Between Children and Adults.
The Feeling Approach.
The Rays and the Emotional Plane.

The Mental Approach. The Ray of Mind.
The Higher Self or Soul. Meaning, Quality, Value.
Love, Patience, Understanding, and Ordered Activity.
The Science of Service. Future Schools.
A Transition Period. The Time Factor.

Other essays in the book include:
"The Seven Rays in Literature:" King Arthur—First Ray Type. King Lear and a second ray Glamour. A Character Drawing in Legend of Sleepy Hollow.
"Carl Rogers and His Most Prominent Rays."
"The Ray of the Elephant."

The Moon Veils Vulcan and the Sun Veils Neptune. This book explores the enigmatic statement in Esoteric Astrology: "The Moon is usually regarded as 'veiling' or 'hiding' some planet and of these there are three which the Moon may be veiling. Here the intuition of the astrologer and of the esoteric student must be called out. These planets are Vulcan, Neptune or Uranus.... Instead of working with the Moon, let astrologers work with Vulcan when dealing with the undeveloped or average man and with Uranus when considering the highly developed man.... If the investigating astrologer will study the 'fluid area' where the planets, veiled by the Sun and Moon, come into play and will realize that he must decide what is the point in evolution reached and which of the three veiled planets is the ruler, he will get much intuitive understanding."

The Seven Rays and Nations: France and the United States Compared. Sub-headings of the essay on France and the US are:
The Intellectual Plays a Prominent Role in France.
Rhetorical Tricks of Staggering Ingenuity.
Lack of Practicality.
A 'Bogus Politeness' Resulting in 'Suspiciousness.'
The 2nd and the 6th Rays in American Companies.
An Experience in France.
Attraction or Repulsion to a Foreign Culture
    due to One's Own Individual Rays.
The Leo Influence and the French Personality.
The Leo Personality and the Third Ray.
The U.S.'s Noninterference by Government compared
    to France's Complex Bureaucracies.

The Soul of France.
French and American Films Contrasted as they
    Present Characteristics of the National Rays.
The French and American People Contrasted.
The Difficulty of Seeing Oneself or the Rays of
    One's Own Nation.

"I was extremely impressed by your book on the Rays and Nations. Your comparisons of France and the united States was especially insightful. I also thought that your applications to business were extremely practical. This is an area that I have been working in for a number of years. I have incorporated many of your ideas in the workshops that I give for business people."

John Cullen, President of International Association for Managerial and Organizational Psychosynthesis.

BOOK ORDERING INFORMATION. We welcome orders direct to the publisher. For ordering information, including prices, our latest books, and books from other publishes, please write to our email address: <lampus@wizzards.net> or our mailing address:

    LAMPUS PRESS
    19611 ANTIOCH ROAD
    WHITE CITY, OREGON 97503

SCHOOL FOR THE STUDY OF THE SEVEN RAYS.
The School for the Study of the Seven Rays (SS7R) offers a Home Study Course that is approximately 2 years in length with additional material for advanced studies. No fees are charged. The School is supported entirely by contributions from the students.
Extensive individual attention is given to the work of each student.
Sample Newsletters are available on request.

"Pioneers" are sorely needed in this slow but steady work of bringing in a more meaningful psychology—a psychology that addresses the spiritual/soul aspects of being (as well as the threefold personality), and also a psychology that greatly enhances one's ability to be of service to others.

The Psychology of Nations. "All of the great nations are controlled by a personality ray, which is the dominant potent and main controlling factor at this time, and by a soul ray," which is sensed only by the more developed in every nation.   *Destiny of Nations.*
We have students and co-workers from several countries around the globe, including Russia, India, Poland, France, Great Britain, Brazil,

and Switzerland. The rays of one's own nation are becoming a topic of increasing interest as global relationships are being developed at a more rapid rate.

"**The Psychology of the Future** will direct attention to the discovery of the two rays which govern soul and the personality. Having done this through a study of the physical type, emotional reactions and mental tendencies, attention will then be directed to the discovery of the rays governing the specialized vehicles."   *Glamour: A World Problem*

The Seven Rays and Education.

"One of the major functions of those who train the infant minds of the race will be to determine, as early as possible in life, which of the seven determining energies are controlling in each case....*A child's note and quality will be determined and his whole planned training will grow out of this basic recognition.*"   *Education in the New Age.*

"When the ideas contained in the teaching on the seven rays are of general recognition, we shall find the growth of psychological understanding, and the nations and the world religions will arrive at mutual understanding."   *Education in the New Age* 125

We also have Supplementary Study Sets on Education, with a focus on the early years. This study material is based on Steiner's Waldorf education as well as the esoteric soul psychology of Alice Bailey.

For further information please write:

SS7R
19611 ANTIOCH ROAD
WHITE CITY, OR 97503
U.S.A.

Selected Bibliography

Abraham, Kurt. *Threefold Method for Understanding the Seven Rays.* White City, Oregon: Lampus Press, 1984.
——— *The Seven Rays and Nations: France and the United States Compared.* White City, Oregon: Lampus Press, 1987.
Bailey, Alice. *Consciousness of an Atom.* New York: Lucis Publishing Co., 1922.
——— *Destiny of Nations.* New York: Lucis Publishing Co., 1949.
——— *Discipleship in the New Age,* 1 & 2. New York: Lucis Publishing Co.
——— *Education in the New Age.* New York: Lucis Publishing Co
——— *Esoteric Psychology,* v. 1&2. New York: Lucis Publishing, 1936, 1970.
——— *Externalization of the Hierarchy.* New York: Lucis Pub. 1957.
——— *Glamour: A World Problem.* New York: Lucis Publishing Co., 1950.
——— *Letters on Occult Meditation.* New York: Lucis Publishing Co.
——— *Problems of Humanity.* New York: Lucis Publishing Co.
——— *Rays and Initiation.* New York: Lucis Publishing Co., 1960.
——— *The Unfinished Autobiography.* New York: Lucis Publishing Co., 1951.
——— *Treatise on Cosmic Fire.* New York: Lucis Publishing Co.
——— *Treatise on White Magic.* New York: Lucis Publishing Co.
Bailey, Mary. *A Learning Experience.* New York: Lucis Publishing Co., 1990.
Baldwin, Neil. *Edison—Inventing the Century.* New York: Hyperion, 1995
Blake, Robert. *Disraeli.* New York: St Martin's Press, 1967.
Blavatsky, Helena Petrovna. *Isis Unveiled.* Theosophical University Press. in Pasadena, California.
——— *The Secret Doctrine.* Adyar: Theosophical Publishing House.
Bolles, Edmund Blair, ed. *Galileo's Commandment: An Anthology of Great Science Writing.* New York: W.H. Freeman, 1997.
Bonadio, Felice. *A.P. Giannini.* University of California Press, 1994.
Bramly, Serge. *Discovering the Life of Leonardo da Vinci.* New York: HarperCollins, 1991
Callow, Philip. *From Noon to Starry Night: A Life of Walt Whitman.* Chicago: Ivan R. Dee, Publisher. 1996.

Canby, Henry Seidel. *Walt Whitman, An American.* Boston: Houghton Miffflin, 1943.
Coulton, G. G., *Life in the Middle Ages.* Cambridge University Press, 1930.
Curie, Eve. *Madame Curie, A Biography.* New York: Da Capo Press, 1937.
Curie, Marie. *Pierre Curie.* Translated by Charlotte and Vernon Kellogg, 1923.
Davies, Norman. *Europe, A History.* Oxford: Oxford University Press. 1996.
Durant, Will and Ariel. *The Renaissance.* New York: Simon and Schuster, 1953.
———*Rousseau and Revolution.* New York: Simon and Schuster,1967.
———*The Age of Louis XIV.* New York: Simon and Schuster, 1963.
English Poetry. P.F. Collier & Son Corporation, 1938.
Fiery World, I. New York: Agni Yoga Society.
Fölsing, Albrecht. *Albert Einstein, A Biography.* New York: Penguin Books, 1997.
Harpur, James, *Revelations: The Medieval World.* New York: Henry Holt, 1995.
Holmes, George, ed., *The Oxford History of Italy.* Oxford University Press, 1997.
Hunter, Archie. *Kitchener's Sword Arm: The Life and Campaigns of General Sir Archibald Hunter.* New York: Sarpedon, 1996.
Israel, Paul. *Edison: A Life of Invention.* New York: John Wiley & Sons, 1998.
Jenkins, Roy. *Gladstone, A Biography.* New York: Random House, 1995.
Jung, Carl. *Mysterium Coniunctionis.* Princton University Press, 1963.
Letters of Alfred Lord Tennyson. London: Clarendon, 1982.
Manchester, William, *A World Lit Only by Fire: The Medieval Mind and the Renaissance.* New York: Little, Brown and Co., 1992.
Marius, Richard. *Martin Luther, the Christian Between God and Death.* Harvard University Press, 1999.
Millikan, Robert A. *Autobiography.* New York: Prentice-Hall, 1950
Notebooks of Leonardo da Vinci. Compiled and Edited by Jean Paul Richter.

Olcott, Henry Steel. *Old Diary Leaves: The History of the Theosophical Society.* Adyar, India: The Theosophical Publishing House, 1895.

Pollock, John. *Kitchener: Architect of Victory, Artisan of Peace.* New York: Carroll & Graf Publishers, Inc., 1998.

Pond, Dale, John Keely, Nikola Tesla, Edgar Cayce, and others. *Universal Laws Never Before Revealed: Keely's Secrets. Understanding and Using the Science of Sympathetic Vibration.* Santa Fe, New Mexico: The Message Co, 1994.

Steiner, Rudolf. *The Influences of Lucifer and Ahriman.* New York: Anthroposophic Press, 1919 Lectures.

Strathern, Paul. *Curie and Radioactivity.* London, Arrow Books, 1998.

A Synthesis of Alchemy. Ashland, Oregon: Pentarba Publications, 1994.

Tennyson, Alfred Lord. *The Works of Alfred Lord Tennyson.* Wordsworth Poetry Library, Ware, England, 1994.

Thorn, Michael. *Tennyson.* New York: St Martin's Press, 1992.

Valentiner, W. R., "Leonardo as Verrocchio's Coworker" New York: *Art Bulletin,* 1930.

White, Michael. *Isaac Newton, The Last Sorcerer.* Reading, Massachusetts: Addison-Wesley, 1997.

INDEX

A

Abdullahi, Khalifa, 10
Alchemy, 199-202
Allen, Dr. Matthew, 156-7
Arcane School, 51-2
Arianism, 202
Aristocracy, 38
Asquith, Herbert, 28-9
Atlantis, 86-7

B

Bailey, Alice, 3, 31-55, 142, 198; Arcane School, 51-2; childhood, 31-4; evangelist, 40; marriage, 45-6; rays of, 51-4; work at soldiers home, 39-40, work in a sardine factory, 48
Bailey, Foster, 49-54
Bailey, Mary, 3, 53
Balfour, Arthur, 25, 28
Batchelor, Charles, 124
Becquerel, Henri, 181, 196
Besant, Annie, 53
Blavatsky, 49, 53, 127, 133
Boer War, 18-21
Bodhisattva, 140
Borgias, Caesar, 95, 101
Botha, Gen Louis, 19
Browning, Robert, 157
Buddha, 81
Byron, Lord, 147

C

Calvin, Jean, 93
Cancer, 6, 8, 10, 19
Carlyle, Thomas, 157, 163
Center (etheric), see chakra.
Chakra (etheric center), 2, 176
Church of England,
Churchill, Winston, 14
Christ, 34, 39, 47, 72, 81, 82, 87, 89, 93, 139, 202
Colonialism, 17
Copernicus, 183-5
Crisis, five points, 44-5, 157
Cromer, Lord, 17, 18
Curie, Marie, 134, 181-216; born, 181; childhood, 182-4; cycles, 211; Floating University, 187-8, 191; goals, 192; governess, 189; marriage, 195; Noble Prize, 205; radium discovered, 195; rays of, 209-10; Sorbonne, 191; war work, 207-8
Curie, Pierre, 181, 193-6; death, 206-7
Curzon, George, 22-26, 28
Cycles, 7 year, 41-3
Cyprus, 8, 22

D

da Vinci, (see Vinci).
Davy, Sir Humphry, 118-119, 128
Darwin, Charles, 35, 38, 169
Depression, 69, 79
Dickens, Charles, 35-6, 153, 157, 173
Disraeli, 17, 35, 38
D.K., 3, 53, 188

E

Edison, Thomas, 11-144; battery, 130; destiny, 115; education, 112,115; job, first, 112;

Menlo Park, 126; patent, first, 121; phonograph 130; rays of, 113, 118-119, 121, 129; telegraph business, 122; Western Union, 113-114; youth, 111
Egypt, 8-9, 11, 15, 26
Einstein, Albert, 207
Electricity 120, 125, 128, 130, 132, 139
Emotional body, ray of, 2, 70
England 34-8
Envy, 100
Eritrea, 11
Ethiopia, 11

F

Faith, 169, 175
Faraday, Michael, 117-121, 124, 128
Fitzgerald, Edward, 154, 175
Florence, 82-4, 91, 95, 101
France, 28, 34, 116, 119, 129, 189 (see also Curie)
Franklin, Benjamin, 124
Freemasonry, 7, 19, 30
French Revolution, 34-5, 153, 173
Francois I, 108

G

Gemini, 36-8, 47, 53, 188-9
George, Lloyd, 28-29
Germany, 28-9, 36, 90
Giannini, A.P., 57-80; Ameritalia, 68; Bank of America, 66; Bank of Italy, 62-63; born, 57; branch banking, 63-4; brother, Attilio, 68; death, 75; depression, 69; education, 58; Liberty Bank, 66; marriage, 60; movie industry, 66; Naples, 65; New York bankers, 68-9; parents, 57, politics, 60-1; produce business, 58-60; rays of, 70-3, 75-8, 80; social services, 65-6
Girouard, Percy, 13
Gladstone, William, 17, 119, 167, 171-2, 177
Gordon, Gen. Charles, 9-10, 12, 15; Memorial College, 15
Great Britain, 34-8, 173
Greek, 90-1, 93-4, 187

H

Hallam, Arthur, 148
Hierarchy, Spiritual, 86-7, 96
History, 4, 88
Howitt, Mary, 159
Humanists, 90-1
Hunter, Archibald, 11, 13-14

I

India, 17, 22-25, 40-1
Ireland, 6, 39, 158
Italians, Italy, 11, 81-100, 129, 189

J

Johannesburg, 18
Jung, Carl, 202
Jupiter, 172

K

Keely, John Worrell, 133-140; rays of, 139
K.H., 34
Khartoum, 9-10, 12-15
King Arthur, 5
Kitchener, Herbert, 5-30; in Cyprus, 8; death of, 29;

education of, 6; in Egypt, 8; father, 6; Gordon Memorial College, 15; governor general of the Sudan 15-17; High Commissioner South Africa, 20; in India, 22-5; mother, 6; in Palestine, 5-7, rays of, 6, 12; Secretary of War, 27-29; in South Africa, 18-21; in the Sudan 9
Knowles, Sir James, 168-9

L

Laws of Vibration, 138 (see Keely)
Leo, 8, 172
Luther, Martin, 85, 93, 162

M

Mahachohan, 140-1
Mahdism, 10
Manu, 140
Mars, 174, 177
Masters, 51, 53
Medici, 83-5, 92, 95
Mental body, ray of, 2, 70
Mercury, 188
Michelangelo, 85, 107
Milan, 95-7, 107, 129, 182 (see also Sforza)
Military Member, 23-25
Millikan, Robert, 181, 205
Milner, Sir Alfred, 18-21
Minto, Scottish Earl, 26

N

Napoleon, 5, 8, 14, 34, 153, 186
Neptune, 174, 177
Newton, Sir Isaac, 198-205, rays of, 204
Neutral Center, 137 (see Keely)

Nicholas, Czar, 29

O

Olcott, Col, 127

P

Paine, Thomas, 116
Palestine, 5-7, 22
Papal Schism, 90
Paracelsus, 94
Peace, 5, 19, 21
Peel, Prime Minister, 159
Personality, ray of, 2, 70-1, 75, 107, 120-1, 167, 171
Physical body, ray of, 3
Piscean Age, 91
Plague, 88-9
Plato, 85
Poland, 182-7, 191, 194; 188-9
Pretoria, 18
Principle, 74-5

R

Ray(s), of Buddhas, 55; fifth, 2, 71, 106-7, 111, 113, 119, 123, 128-9, 139, 141, 143, 175; first, 2, 5-7, 12, 30, 52-4, 70-3, 75-8, 80, 92-4, 167, 176; fourth, 2, 33, 70, 77-8, 81-2, 97, 106-7, 167, 170-1; of mind, 2, 33; of physical, 171; second, 2, 52-4, 78, 120, 171; seventh, 3, 6, 7, 12, 22, 30, 78, 93, 171, 181, 184, 210, 212-217; sixth, 2, 53, 70, 77-8, 91-3, 139, 145, 167, 171, 174-180, 199, 210, 213; third, 2, 3, 59, 70-3, 78, 80, 87, 91-4, 97, 113, 119, 121, 129, 139, 141, 143, 210
Reformation, 92

Religion, 5
Renaissance, 82, 86-93, 96, 108, 184
Roberts, Gen. Frederick, 18, 23
Roman Catholic Church, 89-90, 92-3, 95, 202
Roosevelt, F., 73
Root Races, 86
Rousseau, J.J., 186
Russia, 17, 28, 182, 185-9

S

Salisbury, Prime Minister, 11, 17, 20, 25
Secret Doctrine, 51, 53, 86, 125, 131-3
Sellwood, Emily, 160
Scorpio, 209-210
Sforza, Ludovico, 95-8, 100-1
Sinai Desert, 9
Slatin, Rudolf, 13
Sobieski, Jan, King John III of Poland, 185
Solomon, King, 202
Steiner, Rudolf, 42, 53, 170
Sudan, 9-11, 15-16
Soul, 43; progress, 4; ray of, 2, 70, 74, 80, 82, 107
Suez canal, 17

T

Taurus, 36-8, 58, 188-9, 195
Tennyson, Alfred, 129; 145-180; childhood, 145; father, 146-7, 155; *Harold*, 167; *Idylls of the King*, 167; marriage, 160; *Maud*, 165-7; *In Memoriam*, 152; Metaphysical Society, 168-171; *Morte d'Arthur*; pension, 159; Poet Laureate, 161; *The Princess*, 159-160;

rays of, 171-2, 174-7; Septimus (brother), 156; Trinity College, 147-151, 155
Thackery, William, 155
Theosophical Society, 49-50, 53, 127, 135, 169
Transvaal, 18
Turkey, 17, 26

U

Universal Will, 137
Uranium, 134, 196

V

Vasari, Giorgio, 82, 107
Vere, Aubrey de, 158
Verrochio, 82-3
Vinci, da, Leonardo, 81-110, 129; anatomy studies, 83, 102-4; childhood, 81-2; engineering skills, 97-106; with King of France, 108; in Milan, 96-7; Notebooks, 98-106; parents 81-2; Verrochio's studio, 82-3
Victoria, Queen, 167-8, 171
Virgo, 139
Virtue, 100

W

Whitman, Walt, 161-4
Will, 137
Wingate, Reginald, 13, 18
World War I, 27-29

Y

Youssoupoff, Prince, 29

Z

Zwingli, Huldrych, 93